*The French Peasantry
in the Seventeenth Century*

The French Peasantry
in the Seventeenth Century

PIERRE GOUBERT

translated by
IAN PATTERSON

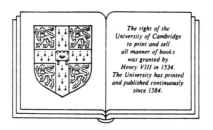

The right of the
University of Cambridge
to print and sell
all manner of books
was granted by
Henry VIII in 1534.
The University has printed
and published continuously
since 1584.

CAMBRIDGE UNIVERSITY PRESS
Cambridge
New York   New Rochelle   Melbourne   Sydney

Published by the Press Syndicate of the University of Cambridge
The Pitt Building, Trumpington Street, Cambridge CB2 IRP
32 East 57th Street, New York, NY 10022, USA
10 Stamford Road, Oakleigh, Melbourne 3166, Australia
and Editions de la Maison des Sciences de l'Homme
54 Boulevard Raspail, 75270 Paris Cedex 06

Originally published in French as *La vie quotidienne des paysans français au XVIIe siècle* by
Hachette Littérature, 75 Boulevard Saint Germain, 75288, Paris, 1982
and © Hachette, 1982

First published in English by Editions de la Maison des Sciences de l'Homme and
Cambridge University Press 1986 as *The French Peasantry in the Seventeenth Century*

Reprinted 1987

English translation © Maison des Sciences de l'Homme and
Cambridge University Press 1986

Printed in Great Britain at the University Press, Cambridge

British Library cataloguing in publication data

Goubert, Pierre
The French peasantry in the seventeenth century.
1. Peasantry – France – History – 17th century
2. France – Rural conditions
I. Title   II. La vie quotidienne des paysans
français au XVIIe siècle
305.5′63   HD1339.F/

Library of Congress cataloguing in publication data

Goubert, Pierre.
The French peasantry in the seventeenth century.
Translation of: La vie quotidienne des paysans
français au XVIIe siècle.
Bibliography: p.
Includes index.
1. Peasantry – France – History – 17th century.
2. France – Rural conditions.   I. Title.
HD1536.F8G6813 1986   305.5′63   85–22348

ISBN 0 521 26007 8 hard covers
ISBN 0 521 31269 8 paperback
ISBN 2 7351 0133 9 hard covers (France only)
ISBN 2 7351 0134 7 paperback (France only)

To Nicholas, Claire, Emmanuel, Isabelle, and Eric, who may if they so choose one day find in it a reflection of the lives of their own distant ancestors, all of whom were probably peasants, in Anjou, Berry, Languedoc, Normandy, Brittany, Burgundy, Limousin, and elsewhere.

Contents

Contents

Preface

For years peasants were misrepresented – as pastoral shepherds, shrewd farmers, and country bumpkins – or more often ignored or despised, but recently their image has been refurbished and they have been enthusiastically adopted by the slightly absurd colour-supplement world of urban fashion, although that does not amount to much more than a few exposed beams, country-style stews, Paris-made clogs, restored thatch roofs, some approximate folk-lore, and a certain amount of disarming ecology. As a result, though, swarms of ethnologists and sociologists, specially equipped and weighed down with instruments and questionnaires, have descended on what still remains of the countryside and put solemn questions to the last surviving village patriarchs, who more often than not make fun of them, apparently without the pseudo-scientists noticing. They talk at length about attitudes, sign language, or traditions, sexuality, inversions and introversions, festivities, carnivals, witches and magicians, deviancies and wanderings, all determinedly rural, and all eagerly 'written down' or 'told' by people who are as enthusiastic as they are incapable of telling wheat from barley.

It will be clear that this small book was not suggested or undertaken in an attempt to be fashionable. For almost fifty years French historians (and some historians in other countries too), following in the footsteps of Henri Sée, Georges Lefebvre, and Marc Bloch, and their predecessors, have tried to reconstruct the actual fabric of peasant life from the Middle Ages to the first years of this century, which has not been an easy task, and has involved sifting through quantities of dusty, semi-legible, and often sybilline archives. Having myself spent over thirty years in the study of this absorbing world, and having done what I could to help or to follow a few small groups of researchers pursuing similar or related work, I hope I have succeeded in recreating this fabric both precisely and accurately. The chapters that follow, which are neither erudite nor complacent (although I am not sure that they give a true picture of everyday life), are limited in scope to the seventeenth century, that is – so far as is practically possible – to the period between the re-establishment of peace in 1598 and the death of Louis XIV. This brings with it the difficulty that the documentation is much less plentiful than it is for the eighteenth century, particularly for the years before the Revolution. And even here, though the Revolution was clearly not unexpected, it is the peasant side which is least documented.

As I was pondering and writing this book it became very clear to me that this series of pictures or snapshots of life (which is really what they are) would have to include more than just the peasants themselves. It would be impossible, for example, to understand peasant life without reference to the priests and the seigneurs. So it seemed more sensible and more honest to give those ubiquitous country figures, and others as well, their proper place in the book. As a result it is not only peasants who appear in this incomplete (though sometimes perhaps over-detailed) sequence of sketches, but I have tried to keep them as straightforward as possible so that my growing grandchildren and those of my non-specialist friends who enjoy reading history may perhaps one day read them without boredom or frustration.

I must also confess that I set myself a wager. I tried to encompass the whole of the French peasantry from Flanders to the Pyrenees and from Brittany to Provence by drawing together all those characteristics which they had in common, but it was always the diversity, the contrasts of language, customs, work, ways of doing things, food, and play which made the strongest impressions, making the attempts at centralisation – or 'absolutism' – which mark the seventeenth century a little more than previous ones (though much less than later centuries) look almost risible. At least every province, and every *pays*, should be recognisable in this book, and the descendants of their former inhabitants, having glimpsed something of what they used to be like, will be able to turn to the already large number of books which describe, often very eloquently, the regions in all their original individuality.

I

A bird's-eye view
of the French countryside

Apart from the angelic hosts, their satanic counterparts, a few witches looking for sabbaths, and Cyrano de Bergerac's balloon-traveller drifting towards the moon, nobody in the seventeenth century could have seen the kingdom from this height. It would unquestionably have been a frightening sight, as at this period everybody, except a few (urban) poets, saw mountains and forests as wild and hostile, and regarded nature as something dangerous. But if an inhabitant of twentieth-century France agreed to go up and have a look he would see that, by and large, little had changed in the disposition of the countryside.

The main outlines

There were the same expanses of great bare plains dotted at regular intervals with large villages, the same woodlands as were there until the recent reallocation of the land, with their few scattered hamlets, the same water-courses, except that there were only two or three canals, almost the same stony, sandy, and marshy areas (with some exceptions); there were the same snow-covered high mountains, and lower mountains covered with forest, huge woods, and pastures that were already much-used; the same towns, for the most part, stood in the same places, although they were smaller, and still surrounded by their walls; there was the same pattern of roads and paths, although there were many more of them, and they were much less straight. All this could easily be observed from a considerable height.

The only difference is that none of the mountains except the Massif Central was then entirely French, and in fact a part of the Massif still for a time belonged to the King of Spain, who was Duke of Charolais, until Louis XIV reached a peaceful settlement with him. The Vosges were part of Lorraine, and therefore belonged to the Holy Roman Empire, only the short Alsatian side having become French in 1648. The Jura were part of Franche-Comté, and therefore Spanish, until 1678; all the main peaks in the Northern Alps, including Mont Blanc, belonged to Savoy, and then Italy, until 1860: their glaciers and snows reached lower than they do nowadays, because of the 'mini ice-age' which lasted through the sixteenth and seventeenth centuries. The *comté* of Nice and its alpine hinterland remained in foreign hands for longer still. And the recently rechristened Atlantic Pyrenees had only been French since the King of Navarre's reign, while the Spanish–Catalonian Roussillon and Cerdagne only became French after 1659.

All round the coast, wherever the land was unsound because the ground was marshy or sandy, Henry IV had brought in the best engineers in Europe, the Dutch, to dry it out, desalinate it, drain it, and build polders with their canals, locks, meadows, and low farms, many of which still bear their names today. This kind of work was carried out on the bay of the Somme, on the meanders of the lower Seine, in Normandy, and round Mont Dol, as well as in those much more extensive regions, and those where the famous areas of salt marsh were retained and remodelled – the 'bay' of Bourgneuf, which supplied part of western and northern Europe – the Poitou marshes, the *palus* of the Charente and the Gironde, which effectively took on their modern appearance at this time; the great ponds of the Languedoc, part of la Crau, and lower Dauphiné began to look different, and even some of the lakes of Auvergne began to be filled up. It was a vast undertaking, now almost completely forgotten, and it did also involve some 'ingenious' Frenchmen, like the Provençal Adam de Craponne; however, they were not yet able to tackle the big malarial zones such as the Sologne, the Dombes, or the 'Lannes' (i.e. les Landes). But this is the period when both the geographical outline and the human aspects of the kingdom of France took on the pattern that we recognise today.

The ancient system of roads is no longer there. They were

Gaulish, Roman, medieval, timeless, and the system was much
denser than that of today, made up of 'ways' (one cart at a time),
tracks, and footpaths, hardly any of them paved except a few roads
into and through the towns, and the 'high road from Paris to
Orléans'. They formed a complex yet natural network linking one
village with another, a village to its pasturage, summer pastures to
winter pastures, one grid of plots of land to another, one bridge
(probably said to be Roman, but in fact medieval and much
repaired) to another or to a good ford, and old Roman cities to
others, often starting from Lyons, the capital of Gaul, then from
Paris, the capital of the kings of France. It was in the eighteenth
century, the century of bridges and highways – after the short-lived
works carried out under Sully – that the roads were straightened
out, at considerable cost (even in those days the state had to pay for
the compulsory purchase of land!), and were broadened and
extended; later it was Napoleon who oversaw the building of new
highways.

But whether the old roads were narrow or wide, they were full of
activity, although it went at a slower pace than nowadays. There
were people walking with a hoe or a spade over their shoulder,
going to 'labour' in the vineyards or the fields; small groups
converging on their way to the local market, carrying baskets of
eggs, chickens, a 'warp' of serge (to be finished off by weaving),
newly made clogs or needles; young men in their best clothes
attracted by the feast, the gathering, the patronal festivities – and by
the promise of games, wine, and dancing; fish-carts, or itinerant
potters, driving mules loaded with 'fresh' sea-fish, and earthenware
bowls and cooking pots; pedlars with bundles on donkeys or on
their backs, with needles, trinkets, sacred or profane booklets, holy
(and not so holy) pictures, and also bearing all the local news. On the
wider roads, there were wooden carts with iron axles, moving at the
slow pace of the oxen which (more often than horses) pulled them,
carrying stones, wine, sheaves of corn, hay, dung, or wood,
depending on the season and what was needed. Now and then could
be heard the muted trot of a diligence, or more likely a stage-coach,
struggling through the sand or mud; less frequently, the light trot of
a chaise, or an elegant carriage; more dangerously, the frenzied
gallop of the king's horses going post-haste (they were the only ones
allowed to travel at this speed) from one stage, or one inn, or one
relay to the next. But there were relatively few of the heavy

waggoners' carts which were already known as *camions* (waggons, lorries), because it was still usually cheaper and easier, if slower, to transport everything except light and costly goods by water. The highroads were seasonal substitutes, or permanent links, between different rivers.

The first canals were just being built, inevitably by the Dutch, linking the Loire and the Seine, at Briare and Orleans; then, at the time of Colbert and Riquet, these were followed by one between the Garonne and the Mediterranean, the 'canal des Deux-Mers'; and soon after that, the canal network in the north was improved, on the Flemish model of course. Everywhere, even on the smallest rivers, fragile wooden boats which would look minuscule to our eyes sailed with the current, or were hauled upstream by powerful horses, along towpaths that are still visible (where they have not been washed away by the current); peacefully, they carried stone, gravel, bricks, and sand to build towns and ports, wheat to provision them, wines for their inhabitants to drink, and less often people to live in them. Scarcely less slow were the passenger-barges used by great ladies like Mme de Sévigné, and on the Rhône by the great Cardinal himself. And almost everywhere there were ferries wherever there were no fords, or where these had become submerged. Every so often there were obstacles to be traversed: rapids, sand-banks, sunken boats, or a toll-gate, where a bridge-keeper or a toll-collector levied his right of passage; these were usually fairly small, but sometimes a substantial fee was charged, as at the powerful customs post at Ingrandes on the border with the duchy of Brittany, which was so high that it (fortunately) forced the wine producers upstream to make nothing but superior quality wine. Even beyond the reaches navigable by small boats, rivers in the seventeenth century, whether they were royal, or seigneurial (the smallest), were an integral part of the lives of those who lived beside them, and their neighbours: they drew their water from them, fished in them (even without permission), and refreshed themselves by swimming in them, until the clergy turned into the upholders of a new sense of public modesty.

Then there was the forest, which took up so much of the view of our hypothetical astronauts. Marc Bloch long ago described those woods, which had been occupied and to some extent civilised since the Middle Ages: they were full of clearings, under cultivation, at least temporarily, with wood-cutters, wood-gatherers, and charcoal-burners, game and livestock grazing or crunching acorns, sometimes legally and sometimes not, with women and children surreptitiously driving their cattle there; and hunters, and poachers, and people gathering fruits, and a few wrong-doers, but many fewer robbers than in the streets of Paris. Then with the new foresters, and Colbert's legislation, the great forests were surveyed, recorded, and protected, and access to them, as far as it was possible, was prohibited: timber for ships, for construction work, and for burning was valuable capital which needed to be preserved from the peasants who seemed to think it was all theirs. The overall area of forest, however, was not very different from that in the twentieth century, although the trees themselves were different, with far fewer conifers.

There may be little alteration on the large scale, but there are a multitude of changes in detail. The old towns, of course, were all in the same places, all fairly small in size, with only Paris having a population greater than 100,000. The towns were still clustered within their walls, although kings now left them to crumble instead of demolishing them. They would all have had ten or so church towers, sometimes many more, and here and there there would be strange empty spaces: an uneven square, a green for arquebusiers or archery, areas for walking and exercise, orchards, small pastures, a walled vineyard, cesspits, and 'shambles', the forerunner of our abattoirs; these towns were permeated by the country, including livestock, and a few houses also stood outside the town gates, which were closed each evening, beside the main roads, or down rough tracks.

Those old French towns which escaped the industrialisation of the nineteenth century could not have looked very different, before the introduction of concrete in the late twentieth century, except that there would have been fewer church towers and suburbs, and the walls would have been turned into boulevards. As far as the peasants were concerned, they were still the sites of fairs and markets, justice and administration, the place where the notary and the 'bourgeois' landowner lived, and where they came to meet people, to discuss matters, perhaps over a few drinks.

There was no town, just as there was no river and certainly no 'cart road', which was out of the orbit of the peasants of the seventeenth century.

Yet their lives were focussed on their everyday place of work, their land, and we shall understand that better if we look at it first from above.

If the rural historian's hypothetical aircraft came down to 200 or 300 feet he would no longer see things in terms of lines and masses; instead he would be perceiving the simple or complex, often harmonious, sometimes unexpected, always intelligent architecture of one of those microcosms of human society known to our forebears called *terroirs*.

A *terroir* meant a locality, which included all the buildings, courtyards, gardens, vineyards, fields, open or enclosed, meadows and pastures of all sorts, wasteland, moorland, woods, forest, not forgetting the network of tracks and streams, which all made varying contributions towards the existence, survival, and prosperity of a group of human beings which might be as large as a big village, or a small one, or just a single, isolated, farm. There was obviously an infinite variety of these localities then as now, although naturally most of the component elements are fairly universal.

Let us look at some.

Terroirs in the north

The best known, and obviously the most common, is found in at least a quarter of the kingdom, including the north, the east and part of central France, as far as the wooded country. The landscape here is mostly flat and expansive, on the edge of the Great European plain, where fertile alluvial soil reaches, at some points, to beyond the Loire.

The landscape can be described in a few words; a village concentrated at the centre of cornfields, which are divided by old cart-tracks and bounded by sparse woodland, with perhaps one or two windmills on a hill, or a large fortified farm. It is typical of Picardy, the Beauce region, the drier parts of Champagne, and the greater part of the Brie region.

However, in the seventeenth century it did not much resemble the seas of corn, rippled by the wind, beloved of later poets. There were no fields, as there are today, full only of tall wheat freed from weeds by the advances of scientific agriculture, nor any beets or maize. Different cereals alternated, with oats here, barley there, and weak stems of wheat usually mixed with rye and scattered with cornflowers, poppies, wild vetch, and other plants which neither improved its quality nor made it easier to keep. Far from reaching to the horizon in all directions, the different colours of cereal, with their different purposes (barley for making beer, oats for the horses, *bledz* (wheat) often *mesteils* (mixed) for men) did not even cover all the available and workable area. A third, or perhaps less, was fallow, sometimes 'green', sometimes pasture, sometimes ploughed, according to the season: it was fallow because it was thought, quite reasonably at a period and in places where there was little manure and fertilisers were unknown, that the land had to be rested one year in three, even in these naturally fertile plains. So here and there we would see a group of fields, or a farmyard, or a topographical feature where the grass grew, grazed by small, yellowish sheep – the 'wool-animals', the *bélinal* (ram) and *brébial* (ewe) – often guarded by a shepherd and one or two dogs, to keep them out of the neighbouring fields where crops were growing. At other times, in spring or autumn, the *sombres* (the local name given to the fallow fields, especially in Burgundy) would have been ploughed up, either to break new ground or to prepare it for sowing new crops, and the land would appear in shades of brown or black earth, often full of nodules of flint, or turned-up fragments of chalk.

Without the unbroken vistas of wheat we have come to expect, we are reminded of another fact which the amalgamation of farms and reorganisation may have made us lose sight of. The arable land was almost always laid out in strips, generally ten times as long as they were wide but sometimes longer; this is sometimes, though not fully, explained in terms of adaptation to the use of the wheel and mould-board plough, and the need to share inherited land equally (in accordance with local custom). These pieces of land were normally bounded by a furrow larger than the others (and which had twenty different local names: in Anjou it was called the *rèze*), and by large stones dug well in at each end, and they would be served by one or more tracks which grouped them together, so that it was naturally in the interests of those cultivating them to grow the same things in the same way, especially when it came to harvesting. Layout and custom both inevitably led to collaboration, and these agreements often became enshrined in provincial custom and practice, which carried the full weight of law within a locality or a region, and which had been set down in writing in the sixteenth century, and had to be complied with.

Interrupting this dominant pattern of long straggling fields, squarer patches of better land would often appear, extending over several *arpents* (an *arpent* being a frequently used measure, something between a third and a half a hectare); these were usually the best fields in the seigneurial domain. They would either be close to the château, or to its *basse-cour* (which would be a good field, almost next to the courtyard itself, which belonged to the seigneur, literally as well as figuratively), or else much further away, at the edge of the locality, where we shall encounter them again.

Roughly at the centre of the locality would be the hundred or so houses where the people who cultivated it lived. In the middle would be the church, with the cemetery and presbytery adjacent to it, and the square nearby. Not far from there would often, but not always, be a château, or a manor or some big house. From above it all looks very simple.

Some villages seem to have had a circular or clustered pattern, with two concentric roads and several radial tracks. Others were stretched out along a stream, or along both sides of an ancient roadway (which was less likely to be Roman than people thought); some had two central foci, which sometimes corresponded to two places of worship, or more uncommonly to two minor seigneuries, or to two smaller localities which had amalgamated, or occasionally to a village which had been partly burned and rebuilt on a slightly different site. Whatever their shape – and the commonest were grouped together or linear – they created islands of greenery in the bare expanse of fields of crops interspersed with fallow areas, with roofs nestling in it or emerging from it. Here in the north, almost all the roofs were thatched with wheat or rye-straw, long, tough stems cut close to the ground, providing the houses with coolness in summer and some warmth in winter for almost no cost (beyond the strain of arms and backs), though with the ever-present danger of fire and burning. Two or three houses, though, the richest, were roofed with tiles, or slates, depending on the proximity of slate to be quarried, ease of transport, and the possibility of heating ovens to fire clay.

In addition to these visible signs, every village in the north and east possessed some sort of legal and customary status of which various concrete indications were visible. First of all, it had boundaries, which would often be marked physically, for example by a circular road which went behind the gardens or the enclosed fields. Beyond this point were the fields, which were not considered to be part of the village, but had a different status. Another way of marking boundaries was to plant wayside crosses, or large trees, such as pear trees, at what could be termed sacred places, on the four or five roads that converged in the centre of the village, by the church; raised stones and artificial tumuli were also used. Crosses, which were later given new uses, particularly by the catholic and royalist missions of the next century, were the most usual markers, and old documents speak of villages *intra cruces*. Within them, therefore, a different set of laws obtained and the cluster of houses takes on the aspect of a land of liberty, where people could grow pretty much what they liked in their gardens, and enjoyed a degree of freedom or exemption, too, because they paid a lower rate of tax on the surface area of their land to the seigneur and the church; sometimes even being immune from tithes.

In reality, every northern village – and often those elsewhere – boiled down to a collection of contiguous *manses, mazures, meix* or *mas* (the meaning of the latter shifted in the south): all these words stem from the Latin (*mansus*: a dwelling place, in the primary sense) and they are found almost universally. Included in the *manse* would be the house itself, the yard where the dungheap stood and the fowls scratched and where the tools lay about, the outbuildings joined on to the house or close to it for beasts or storage, the garden (almost always enclosed), and sometimes another field close by and well-manured, known to the seventeenth-century Burgundians as the 'wing of the *meix*' or the 'house field' (which was no doubt the most important of all). Living in a *manse* also gave rights over the land in general as well as over the commons, where they existed: these were communal pastures which were often mediocre but useful for the poorer inhabitants.

Nothing of this would be visible from above, beyond the bricks and mortar, except the fruit trees and the carefully-tended beds of 'herbs' (usually green vegetables, leeks, and cabbages) and 'roots' (the only root vegetables of the period were carrots and turnips, which were far from tender). There would be no sign of the twenty different sorts of beans and 'peas' (our dried haricots: in the seventeenth century 'haricot' meant not beans but a stew of lamb and turnips), stomachs fed (if at all) on the plainest food.

If we now gain height and leave the village in order to look down on the wheat and fallow fields to try to pick out the livestock, we will find some surprises. Apart from large flocks of thin sheep grazing together over stubble fields, the sparse common land, and those fallow fields not yet ploughed in preparation for sowing, we might well see several strong teams of heavily-built horses – two, four, or sometimes six to a team – pulling a heavy plough with wheels, coulter, share, and mould-board, or an even heavier cart: these would belong to the 'powerful' members of the village; but there would be almost no cattle, except perhaps five or six cows grazing in front of the house if there was a sort of grassy bank (although often overgrown) between it and the road. And we would then realise the grave weakness of these broad plains of wheat: the frequent absence of pasturage, and therefore of cattle – *aumailles*, as they were often called – in any significant numbers, and thus of dung to fertilise the fields, which sheep cannot do adequately. So whenever a small river ran through a locality, the water meadows were tremendously valuable; their principal function was to provide hay, and beasts were not generally allowed on to them until a second harvest, an 'aftermath', had been cut: they were a great help, nonetheless. However, if there were some poor outlying fields at the edges of the *terroir*, too stony or too rocky to make it worthwhile sowing them, these would at least provide some indifferent grazing, usually communal (although sometimes claimed by the seigneur), where everyone would try to take at least one cow, in the permitted seasons. And where there was practically nothing to support weak and expensive cattle, we can more easily understand how the fear of a shortage of wheat (no substitute known for it) could drive populations to put all the available acreage under cultivation without keeping any space (except village gardens) in reserve for other crops or speculations. These vast reservoirs of grain also had to feed the great northern cities, especially Paris, which meant 3–400,000 mouths at the beginning of the century, and 500,000 at the end.

Towards the edges of these plains localities there was often a small wood, one or two windmills, and a large farm. The woods, which belonged to the seigneur, harboured countless rabbits, small rodents, and birds of all kinds, which in principle only the seigneur was allowed to hunt, but resourceful poachers also took advantage of this small-scale reserve, which functioned as both dovecot and warren. More importantly it provided plenty of timber and firewood, and the many different kinds of berries that were used for making drinks: but there were endless difficulties and conflicts involved in gathering them. It was easier to get them from the great forests, but they were often too far away. This was the reason for the scarcity of wood, and therefore its high price (it was the one commodity to rise steadily and steeply throughout the century), which constituted one of the inescapable weaknesses of these broad northern localities, and made them appear richer than in fact they were, save for a small privileged number.

We shall come back to the windmill later, and that real character, the miller, but we need to look now at those great fortified farms, placed at the boundaries of two or three localities, in the middle of maybe 100 hectares (seldom more) of adjacent lands, which can still be found today in Picardy or Brie. They were large solid buildings (for beasts, food stores, tools, and people) arranged in a square or a rectangle round a vast courtyard, with the dungheap in the middle and the dovecot at one side or above the monumental gateway (sometimes, as at Thiérache, fortified), the dovecot revealing the seigneurial nature of a very long-established settlement. It seldom dated from a romano-gallic villa, as people often like to think; but it may well have been the continuation of some clearance and settlement set up around the twelfth or thirteenth centuries by an abbey, a group of monks or canons, who were much more likely to keep documentary records than great lay nobles.

There is scarcely any need to say that while hundreds of localities of the type described above were to be found in seventeenth-century France, there would also have been some which had fallen into dilapidation and others which were more complex; and that a great forest, even if it was half a league away, could considerably alter aspects and styles of life in its neighbourhood; or that even a small river or pond could make a beneficial addition to the area in terms both of grass and fish; or that a few slopes planted with vines could make a noticeable difference to both landscape and rural activity. But we shall be dealing with vines and vine-growers, and forest and foresters at a later point.

Let us first look at some localities over in the west of the country which are so different that they could be out of a different world entirely.

The wooded country in the west

We move now from the plain (in Normandy called the *plain*, in Touraine and Berry and other places the *campagne* or *champagne*) to the fields and woods of the west of France, and to some extent elsewhere as well.

Seen from above the landscape formed a kind of tapestry, mostly green (in spring and summer), and divided into squares, rectangles, and trapeziums of different sizes, each surrounded by dikes and ditches (the two words are often synonymous) planted with hedges, bushes, and some larger trees, sometimes pollarded. The fields were thus all fenced round (with a movable barrier for access), and people and animals travelled along hollow grassy lanes which crossed the countryside in straight or curving lines: the broadest, called green roads, usually led to the main pastures. From a distance and at an angle it would all have looked rather like one large forest, but there are in fact no forests in this part of France; Brittany (which had just become a not very enthusiastic part of the kingdom) was then, as it still is, one of the least wooded parts of France. It would soon have been apparent that there was plenty of wood and pasture for beasts; and a closer look would have revealed three or four times as many cattle per *arpent*, or acre, than there were in the northern plains. But here and there we would also see some fields of corn, divided up into strips as elsewhere, but surrounded by carefully formed dikes; in Brittany there is even a name for them: *méjous*.

In this terrain there were very few large, centralised villages: where they did occur, they tended to be more like small market towns. Village in these regions meant hamlet, especially in Brittany, and several of these were linked together in fairly extensive religious units or parishes. The villages might number about a dozen houses, set perhaps in a row, or haphazardly, or organised round a small square, with a cross and often a chapel. All round the village, the *terroirs* were laid out in roughly concentric rings or ellipses, with the heath on the horizon. This fairly complex pattern of landscape can best be grasped by a closer look, for example, at Cornouaille in Brittany.

The buildings were low and simple, constructed of the ubiquitous stone, thatched with straw or reeds near the coast (and perhaps sometimes with furze?). The houses consisted of two or three buildings, but people and animals shared the same one, which the animals helped to keep warm; sometimes there was a manger for the cattle; always a sty for the sow and her litter of *gorins*. At one end of the building there would be the oven that the peasants had risked building despite the customary seigneurial monopoly. Under a crude shelter there would be a rudimentary home-made plough with an iron coulter and share made by the local blacksmith, a few rudimentary carts and perhaps one larger one for longer or more important tasks. Another shelter would be used for storing wood, straw, brushwood, furze, and bracken. Between these low buildings there was an open space, well-trodden (by feet?) and cleared for use as a threshing-floor on which ripe grain was beaten with heavy, dangerous flails. Nearby, and always mentioned in texts, was the *port à frambois*, the dungheap, oozing everywhere (and thus losing the liquid manure which is the most efficient fertiliser), and a little further away, the *leurquer* or *placitre* (small square) with a cross beside it, a place of meetings and intersections.

Next to the area where the *aitres* (hearths?) and other buildings were, a second zone would begin: *courtils* (cottage gardens or small fields), enclosed by hedges or ditches (ditches in Brittany always in fact being dikes). There might be as many as three or four of these, each with its own particular use. One would provide vegetables for the household, who carefully fertilised it with their night-soil. Another would often be an orchard with a number of different sorts of trees whose fruits were stored in trays in one of the rickety outbuildings (in the seventeenth century the apple had only just been introduced from Normandy and would almost certainly be replacing the strong, old pear trees with their small, speckled fruit, a good proportion of which was used to produce cider (*sydre*), which later came to be known as perry). There were still a few vineyards, but they were mostly in what is now Morbihan, where the Rhuys peninsula normally produced a sharp green wine (leaving aside the Nantais, Muscadets, and others which are Loire wines rather than Breton ones). Honey-bees temporarily in captivity here and there provided, in addition to the only kind of sugar known in the countryside, a sort of Breton mead, the effects of which were very powerful (but people were already showing a preference for wine which could easily be transported by sea and river).

One of the fields would almost certainly be given over to hemp (*chanvre*: also called *chenevière*, *chanvrier*, *chenavier*, etc.) which, when it was cut, would make the pools where it was left to steep stink unpleasantly, before the mature hemp occupied the days and evenings of the breakers and spinners (both male and female). This work (and also similar work on the more delicate flax) enabled the whole of the northern area to live in relative comfort, and provided one of the great riches which the Duchess Anne brought to the King of France on her marriage.

The largest of these fields, enclosed like the others, contained the corn-growing area, which here in Cornouaille meant wheat destined for sale, and which could be grown almost every year, given the abundance and proximity of dung and fertiliser. This sort of household field provided and contained a measure or a measure and a half of good grain, here as almost everywhere the unit of capacity corresponding rigorously to the surface area and vice versa, which thwarted all the early 'metric systems' (in neighbouring Anjou, a *boisselée* was the area of ground sown by a bushel (*boisseau*) of seed, and as the ground varied so did the measures; it was the same in the Auvergne).

This band of cottage fields was productive and important, and the areas of corn at its edges bordered on the *terres chaudes*, or 'hot' fields. These were also planted with cereals, but the main crop was rye, the staple of the popular diet (in the form of porridge and bread), which could be replaced or supplemented by buckwheat in some regions (its cultivation calendar is different: it is a later crop, and so can make good any failures in the earlier rye; also, it seems that buckwheat could be ground by hand at home without contravening the seigneurial rights over milling). Hay was grown too, and provided the best possible food for the fine, small Breton horses whether ponies or post-horses. These fields were arranged in very large enclosed areas, and divided into *parées* made up of *seillons*, often (though not always) in strips, those being units of labour and surface area, the two being linked. *Seillons* and *parées* were marked by boundary stones and each one might be held by a different peasant: the net effect was of little pieces of wheat country set down on good land in the middle of wooded country, and not far from moorland; the earth was well-manured and fertilised as there were plenty of cattle, and the sea, with its seaweeds, algae, and *maerl* (a mixture of shells, sand, and seaweed), was not far off, so cultivation could proceed almost continuously, with only occasional fallow years.

Beyond the ring of household fields, and the outer ring of 'hot' fields, although not usually more than a quarter of a league further away, we find the *terres froides*, the 'cold' fields, which were virtually reserved for cattle. Some of them were still enclosed and were just used for grass, which was cut once or twice a year (depending on the summer), after which the hay was carefully gathered, and the livestock put in and safely left. The other 'cold' fields, some enclosed and some open, were poor pastures of various sorts situated on the mountains (the *menez*) or rocky ground, virtually moorland, which was 'swaled' (i.e. burnt) from time to time, a process which enriched the soil and enabled a crop to be sown and harvested for a year or two. Moorland it may have been but (despite the foolish sneers of Arthur Young, who passed through the area at a gallop 100 years later) it was managed moorland, consciously given over to furze, or broom, or to bracken, which as well as being used as litter for livestock could be compounded, after beating and blending, with the residue of one of the more solid grains to provide food for the Breton horses. Beyond this cultivated moorland, included in the 'cold' fields, there were more common lands which might belong to one or to several villages, where anybody could gather bits of wood, gather acorns for the pigs, and take cattle at certain times of the year, in accordance with established custom.

All around what we might call a Cornouaille-type village, there-fore, we find agrarian land which was anything but unproductive. There was a far greater variety of resources than in the plains of the north: wood and game both usually abounded, and with no shortage of food there was always an abundance of livestock too. Indeed, the poorest peasant would have his cow and his farrowing sow, and the average tenancy might well have two horses and a good half-dozen cows, which of course also made a substantial contribution of dung and foodstuffs (here, in a province where salt cost almost nothing, this included salt butter and salted meat). This, and the use they made of the sea, and of hemp and flax, reveals a practical and organisational intelligence on the part of the people who lived in this landscape, Bretons or not, who also had the advantage of perhaps twice as much land as they could use.

But why, in an age where already most of nature is man-made rather than natural, did the landscape take the form of wooded countryside here, rather than broad, almost bare, plains? There were many reasons: the climate, the nature of the soil and its imperme-ability; the density of human habitation and the power of the towns, both of which were much less substantial in wooded country; and, with the help of archaeology, we may also speculate about origins. Perhaps, too, enclosure is natural, spontaneous, in some way inherent in man: after all, it brings with it decided advantages, cutting down the force of the west winds, protecting crops against livestock, the hedges providing a habitat for a host of useful wildlife, providing welcome supplies of dead or standing wood, as well as fruits and wild berries. Seen from this perspective, it is rather the huge cereal-growing plains, deficient in so many respects, which pose the problem.

Problems of this sort probably can never be solved: all we can do is raise them by describing the landscapes. They do not become visible on their own, especially in this period when there were scarcely any agronomists, and where everything was governed by tradition, and the landscape was a given which nobody dreamed of changing, so that any possible innovator was in danger of being thought sacrilegious.

Mediterranean contrasts

If anybody had been able to fly over the area around the Mediterranean, between the mountains and the sea, in the seventeenth century, they would have seen the original, forceful features of a landscape that is now either blurred or completely obliterated. In those pre-tourism days there were fertile river basins, and plains, divided into odd-shaped or quadrangular parcels, most often separated by dry stone walls, all set in surroundings which might be marshy and wet, or almost bare and rocky, or covered in scrub (*maquis* or *garrigue* depending on the soil) and against the background of vivid terraces climbing the nearby mountain slopes like giant staircases; in some favoured parts there were magnificent forests, a few traces of which remain, like the chestnuts and cork-oaks of les Maures, to give some idea of what they were like. There was none of the wooded country typical of the west, though, and very little of the open country found in the north, and in addition to these differences, the inhabitants spoke different languages.

In the plain of Languedoc and the Provençal basins, where the river-banks had not been destroyed by the fast-moving rivers, the villages were often grouped together with their lands in the form of

enclosed fields reminiscent of others we have seen, and these lay
fallow every other year, as the Midi was too dry to support spring
cereals. Once the sheep left the fallow fields, the peasants would try
to scratch a few crops of beans from them, while on the other half of
the land the main crop (apart from some winter barley) was the solid
southern grain, *siesse*, until the arrival of Italian durum wheat. The
great flat expanses of low vines which have transformed the
landscape since the nineteenth century were quite absent: the vines
there grew on the slopes or in gardens and owed their reputation
largely to the Muscat and Malmsey grapes that were introduced
from Spain, leaving aside, of course, the Hermitage wines, as old as
the Romans, or the Châteauneufs, which like the popes were outside
the region and the kingdom. Olive trees, on the other hand, were
almost ubiquitous – but they suffered in the frosts of 1709 – and
water had only to appear, or be laid on, for amazing growth to
appear – plants, bushes, trees, what the Tuscans and Umbrians call
coltura promiscua – creating what were in fact large oases.

Another characteristic of the Mediterranean region (and one
which is also found between the Loire and the Gironde) is the
frequency and extent of marshland and salt marshes, too, composed
of pools, mudholes, reed beds (like the ones near Aigues-Mortes),
half-dead rivers, and treacherous sands. At this period, they still
covered a considerable surface area, as the Dutch brought down by
Henry IV – and some others – had only just started their work of
infilling and draining, and it was only on the Atlantic coast that
marshland had been turned into real meadows. The population was
semi-amphibian, and lived in huts made of mud or reeds or poor
wood, catching fish and eels, extracting salt, and being overrun with
mosquitos every single summer. It was a world of its own, but one
which was to be found all round the Mediterranean.

But the really distinctive feature of the Mediterranean localities
occurs nearer the mountains. The Cévennes and the Alps alike were
terraced to a height of 1,000 metres or more, like huge steps. In the
seventeenth century these terraced fields, variously known as
restanques, faisses, murettes, accols, and *traversiers*, and by many purely
local names as well, were enjoying a renewed period of success:
decades of work had gone into reconstructing fields which had been
abandoned during the great plagues and their aftermath, tireless
work that is almost impossible for the outsider to appreciate. The
incessant labour involved both careful masonry and the trans-

portation of soil which needed to be brought up all the time on men's backs (less commonly, by mule), especially when a sudden downpour and a large storm forced them to stop everything else and go back to the seemingly endless task, the heavy baskets of soil balanced on pads on their heads. And of course for grass, barley, rye, vegetables, and the tree which was once Athena's to grow on these often dry, and sun-drenched terraces, they needed water. This would be collected higher up the mountain and then diverted and controlled so as to reach one *restanque* before being transmitted to the next, and, in some cases, notably near Mauguio, plunging down to the sea. As in the gardens we shall be looking at later, this gave rise to a whole number of specialised ways with water and intricacies of irrigation. Skilled specialists controlled the flow of the precious liquid, dredging the channels, moving the stones, bulwarks, and mounds that governed the flow, and tracking down 'water-thieves'. All of which must have involved countless changes of location, all by foot, steep climbs, and controlled slides down, especially when the village was some distance away, as it often was.

These southern villages sometimes looked more like fortresses perched on a rock or a pointed ridge, a high point that cannot be used for cultivation, overlooking its small, fertile river basin, not too far from the high terraces and perhaps the *garrigue*, clearly prepared to defend themselves against the Barbary pirates from North Africa who continued to make attacking raids on the islands and coastline of Provence up until the time of Molière (who indeed made good use of them to bring his plays to their dénouement). The typically tall, narrow houses leaned against each other for support, leaving shadowy passages in between, or else stood around an uneven vaguely baroque square, surrounded by tall elms, or sometimes lotus trees (though no plane trees yet). There, too, would be the *maison de ville*, two or three chapels, and perhaps as many churches, and at least one of those open-sided bell-towers for ringing the *campana*. A few of the houses had thatched roofs but most of them had round tiles, with shingles or roofing-stones (*lauzes*) at the higher altitudes. The whole village would be surrounded by strongly built, thick, old walls, rebuilt where necessary, and with two or four gates which would be shut and bolted at night, although there would be a secret postern-gate for late-comers, early arrivals, and probably also for lovers. Very few houses would be outside the walls except perhaps a well-built farmhouse, another chapel, and a few stone huts belonging to the vine-growers. It was not until much later that the villages would start to come down to the plain, after order had been brought to the Mediterranean, and the minor trade roads were more reliable and used by more people.

Despite the walls, some of the villages managed to sustain typical Midi gardens, either within the fortifications or spilling down the hillside behind their own high walls. These gardens would be copiously watered by a system of channels, or by the old-fashioned noria or *seigne*, a sort of well with a wheel and scoops worked by a mule, blindfold, such as could be seen not far from Béziers, like an echo of Africa or the Middle East. Everything combined to make the gardens luxuriant and full of colour; the *fauiolo*, the haricot bean, which came from Peru via Italy, peppers and tomatoes from Mexico, huge pumpkins, possibly from Naples, garlic and onions from Catalonia or Spain, peach trees and plum trees from Asia, and different kinds of fig trees from all over the place, the orchards of golden fruit, oranges, citrons, lemons, and the rest – they all seem to have originated outside the kingdom. Such gardens would have been inconceivable to a peasant from Picardy, but they were useful experimental sites, and staging posts, for many Mediterranean, oriental, tropical and American fruits, some of which gradually became established further north. In reality, this characterised only the very best *huertas*, fertile sites with plenty of sun and water, developed with intelligence and good fortune; places like Comtat, Orange, Nîmes, and a few others. More usually the common fields of the Mediterranean villages supplied beans, green cabbages, purple turnips, bristly cardoons, and thin leeks, grown in the shelter of an old fig or olive tree. They were a valuable support but one never achieved without hard work with spade, hoe, and hand, and a combination of sweat and hard-earned experience.

The most noticeable feature of these Mediterranean localities, though, was bigger than the crowded villages and the irrigated gardens and the fertile basins with their crops and trees, bigger even than the great amphitheatres of terraced fields: it was that whole area which the Romans called *saltus*. But leaving aside the forests themselves, which, after Colbert, were increasingly brought under proper management, and which are anyway fairly local to Maures and Cévennes, we shall look at the chalky, short *garrigues*, at the dense, prickly, impenetrable *maquis*, and at the stony heathland which peasants were driven by force of numbers to bring under cultivation at least for one year out of three or four or more in periods of expansion, particularly the sixteenth century, and which provided wood and firewood and, more important, pasture all the time. The pasture supported sheep and goats, and sometimes small donkeys, easy animals to keep as they did not reject the very short grass and prickly shrubs which were no more suited to herds of fat cattle than the climate was. When summer came and the *garrigue* got dry and burning hot, the great flocks of Languedoc and Provence began their long march to cooler pastures along the broad stony tracks of transhumance – the *drailles*, some of which can still be seen – which led them finally to the high, flowery meadows of the Alps or the Cévennes. During the summer months the *garrigue* would sometimes be deliberately burnt, because after the fire the grass would grow again more richly, ready for the sheep and goats on their return from the mountains in September. Yet for all this, some of the more desolate areas, particularly the Crau, remained impossible to use for anything except hunting, and to inspire fear and stories, despite all Adam de Craponne's efforts to drain and irrigate the Midi.

The *terroirs* of the south of France, then, completely different from the rest because of the climate, the mountains, and the land itself, contained both the best and the worst, the barren land and *huertas*, the latter constructed entirely by generations of ingenious, exhausting labour; and as much labour was also expended on the farms, the vines, the gardens, and the giant steps which surrounded the whole domain. It need hardly be said that, with the additional characteristic of speaking their own language, they were not always terribly keen on things that came from the north, particularly from Paris. But that is another story . . .

Other *terroirs*, in other provinces, could no doubt also be described. For instance there were villages in newly felled clearings, *essarts* or *gasts*, in the middle of forests or woodland where, in a rough oval, houses and gardens were at the centre, surrounded by fields which had constantly to be cleared of stones and undergrowth, won from the grass and bushes that surrounded them, often in the form of terraces or shelves, like the pockets of agriculture of a very rough, wooded, pastoral Massif Central. Or there were other *terroirs*, similar to those recently described, in a 'herring-bone' pattern, where in a kind of elementary geometry houses stood on both sides of a cleared road, behind a sort of bank of grazing, rubbish, and dung, with a garden-cum-orchard at the back, and a long cereal field beyond that, reaching as far as the fringes of the forest, where the last traces of cultivation met the first stretches of grass and undergrowth, half cut-back, half kept in its natural state. Then there were the vine-growing localities – which we shall be returning to later – with their small, two-storey houses with a storeroom or cellar for the vats, tuns, and barrels; these were long-established on the banks of the big rivers, particularly the Seine, the Marne, and the Rhône, and on the hillsides of Ay, Vertus, and Chablis, but were more recent arrivals in the otherwise ordinary landscape of the Beaujeu, where the unfailing thirst of the inhabitants of Lyons and Paris was just starting, in the seventeenth century, to build up a fine series of vineyards: as for the ones in Beaune, Vienne, Condrieu, Tain, and Tournon, they had been there almost for ever.

Vine-growing districts need to be treated separately because they pose particular problems of their own, but nonetheless each type of *terroir* almost always comprises three main elements, in varying proportions, which Roman writers on agriculture long ago identified and gave names to.

The *ager*, the worked earth, the basic nutritive field, comes first: it may be open or enclosed, and is given over to the production of *bled*, black, grey, white, or yellow which is the almost universal basic food, providing bread, porridge, and pancake. Also universal is the *mansus*, a unit of family life that includes the *hortus* or garden, which provides necessary or additional ingredients for soup, mainly fruit and vegetables. The *saltus*, a word with a considerable breadth of meaning, really refers to everything that is neither *ager* nor *hortus*, primarily the grasslands or heath where cattle can graze and where hay of varying degrees of richness can be grown for the cattle when they are brought in for winter, but also to the uncultivated areas of scrub, brushwood, woodland, and forest which provided people and animals with many of life's necessities.

As we have seen, there is an enormous inequality in the distribution of these three ancient categories among the different regions. The north and the east have far too much *ager* and not enough *saltus*, or in some cases none at all. In other, mountainous, regions, both where it is too dry and where it is too wet, the opposite is the case. Brittany and the Mediterranean Midi are oddly similar in that both seem to have achieved a kind of beneficial equilibrium, although with very different plants and livestock. At all events neither province appears to have suffered to any severe extent from the shortages and even famines which hit so many other regions, including those of the north, the east, and the Paris basin.

Most peasants probably never questioned the structure or origin of things, and for them the form and the organisation of their localities must have seemed facts which they received by virtue of life and consciousness, and which were as obvious and unchanging as the sun, the moon, and the seasons, or as the saints of the calendar or the local church, or as angels, demons, and witches. They were far more interested in what linked them to the land, and the way they 'held' it.

2

Peasants and the land in the seventeenth century: possession and 'holdings'

Even before the Revolution and the formulation of the Civil Code it was commonplace to talk of France as a 'nation of small land-owners', with a peasantry which 'was very settled because of their material attachment to their native soil': that these are basic truths is taken for granted, and they have become clichés which are always being reiterated in speech and writing. As usual, there is a certain amount of truth in them, although (with a few exceptions which I shall come to later) as generalisations they are very imprecise.

A different mode of ownership from our own

Unlike in England where every owner of land owned their plot 'from the centre of the earth to the vault of the sky', the French peasant had no claim whatever to the sub-strata which, although they may once have belonged to the seigneur, now belonged to the king, who from time to time sent out the poor geologists of the period to prospect for minerals (though not yet for coal). But the average Frenchman, especially in the countryside, was not much troubled by such simple curiosity.

What is really important, however, and much more difficult to grasp, is the old Roman idea of what used to be called 'quiritarian' property: total ownership which, until it re-emerged powerfully with the Revolution and the Civil Code, had disappeared except in a few regions thought for a long time to be unusually 'backward'. In

those places there is a fairly continuous pattern of absolute ownership of plots of land, designated 'allodia' or freeholds, which do not
recognise a seigneur. We find them in Bordeaux and Guienne at the
end of the Middle Ages, and although there was constant pressure to
get rid of them they survived. Researchers have discovered them in
northern Burgundy after 1685, and there they included houses,
gardens, vineyards, enclosed land, and old fields. Others survived
into the middle of the eighteenth century in lower Auvergne and the
Allier valley; nor were they historical curiosities, as they accounted
for up to 30 per cent of localities. In Provence and Languedoc they
could not have been out of the ordinary either, even though they
were gradually absorbed; in these provinces the land was assumed to
be 'free', thus allodial, if the seigneur had not produced proof of his
seigneurie, or that, at least, was what the jurist Caseneuve maintained in 1645. And although Louis XIV haughtily proclaimed an
edict to bring all surviving freeholds under his direct seigneurie, in
August 1692, it obviously did not make a great deal of difference.

More than 90 per cent of the kingdom, nonetheless, either did not
know about allodia or else had forgotten the existence of what was
the sole form of complete ownership, although almost all peasants
acted exactly as if they were absolute owners of 'their' land, selling
or letting it, and bequeathing it, exchanging it, even giving it away.

But they did this with the consent of the seigneur, and they had to
pay for it, often heavily, for the privilege. The peasants probably
had little use for theories (and practices) which maintained that the
seigneur was the 'eminent (and only) owner', and that they were
simply enjoying the use of it, 'holding' it by paying an annual rent:
copyholders, in short. The law of 'no land without its seigneur' was
absolute throughout at least two-thirds of the kingdom, and was
broadly respected elsewhere, despite the reverse adage, which by
the end of the century was coming to lose its meaning, 'no seigneur
without title'.

The term 'copyholder' (*censitaire*), which is occasionally replaced
inaccurately by 'vassal', is a deeply significant one, designating
somebody who, on a fixed date each year, pays the seigneur the
so-called recognitive rent, by which he acknowledges that he holds
his lands from him. Many of these rents were of very long-standing,
and represented no more than a few sous, but although Charlemagne's sou had been gold, and Louis XIV's was merely bronze, the
payments had lost none of their significance; some, however, were

shrewdly fixed in kind, usually hay, which provided a cunning, if unintentional, indexation to the cost of living; others were embellished with 'surtax' of a few extra centimes. But even though many of the rents were indeed light, paying them did not give peasants control over the land. At each change of seigneur – or every thirty years – they theoretically had to 'acknowledge' and 'enumerate' (at their own cost) all their holdings, although in practice they often pretended to forget about it. These were trivial matters in themselves, but tangible reminders of their obligations, which also made themselves felt whenever son succeeded father as tenant (the only right of succession that was recognised before the changes introduced by Louis XIV).

Other reminders of seigneurial power were less pleasant. Every time peasants sold land, for example, the seigneur routinely levied what was called *lods et ventes*: this was a right to exact what was sometimes as much as the *quint* and *requint*, a fifth plus a fifth of a fifth, theoretically 24 per cent, although sometimes it was reduced to half that amount; always provided, of course, that the seigneur did not exercise his right of 'withdrawal', by which he substituted himself for the buyer (who would be unable to protest) and bought it for the same price, which he would promise to pay some time.

What was called peasant property, therefore, was almost always encumbered by the superior authority of the seigneur and seigneurial laws (which were removed by the Revolution). And the peasants were lucky if, in some regions, vastly higher dues were not levied on some land – the land most recently brought into cultivation – and sometimes heavy champarts which as part of the harvest were a burden on production rather than property, but which brought the value down nonetheless.

It is worth adding here that in some provinces, particularly in Franche-Comté which was annexed in 1678, there were still some peasants subject to mortmain who were so powerfully tied to the seigneurial land that they were unable to move out without abandoning their possessions and forfeiting their rights. This survival of serfdom also meant that peasants were not permitted to marry without the seigneur's consent, nor to bequeath their possessions to any except children 'living and eating at home' with them, otherwise it was the *échute*, and all goods reverted to the seigneur. M. Arouet de Voltaire, the son of a lawyer and the great-grandson of a money-lender, was a seigneur in the eighteenth century and he denounced barbarity of that sort; yet it was still very common in the Jura and the surrounding plain (particularly among the 'gentlemen' of Baume), even occurring – though in less extreme forms – in Burgundy and the lower Auvergne.

The peasants were less inured to the hardships and harassment they suffered from the seigneurs than might be supposed and, as they could hardly conceive of changing the system, let alone do anything about it, they resorted to various forms of trickery; mock ignorance and passive disobedience were (even in those days) the weapons they preferred, and which they brought into play at times of disorder, or when the seigneur was absent, old, or senile, or when the succession was in dispute. But in almost all instances the time came when a vigorous steward or a young seigneur would set about re-establishing the old rights, and often looking for new ones, showing that the past was far from dead.

The peasant's share

Under this system of seigneurial ownership, with its limitations, its tolls to be paid, and the deference that had to be shown, the French peasants nevertheless did own their goods, their 'own' things, even if they never owned property in the twentieth-century sense. What proportion of the land did they in fact 'hold as their own'?

A great deal of very rigorous and painstaking analysis has been conducted into regional patterns of land-tenure, but despite this very little is known for certain about the subject, except for the Midi where excellent old land registries have been preserved (although even these are descriptive and estimated, with very few plans). But it is reasonable to suppose that peasants owned (in the seventeenth-century sense) a good half of the land, all of which of course they cultivated (which probably represents some kind of record for Europe then). The church almost certainly owned at least 10 per cent of it: much more in the north and east than in the south and west. The nobility had well over a quarter; and the bourgeoisie were naturally well-provided in the immediate neighbourhood of the towns.

Peasant property itself was very unequally distributed. The proportion was predictably low in the areas around towns, especially large towns (between about 20 and 30 per cent of *terroirs*), and was also low in those areas where powerful families of the nobility, both old and new, had their seat, and where there were large abbeys, with a great deal of subdivision. A host of very humble people, sometimes gardeners, often vine-growers, would hold at most 2 hectares each, and sometimes less than half a hectare; very few could obtain a secure living from their plot, and had to take on additional work as small tenant-farmers, day-labourers, seasonal masons, weavers, handymen of every kind, or by selling whatever they could, such as medicinal herbs or simples.

But there were huge areas in the centre and south of the country, and among the mountains, where two-thirds or three-quarters of the land was under peasant 'ownership' (limited though that term is); there were usually a very few substantial landowners, with a dozen or two hectares (the name of which varied from province to province), over against a scattering with 4 or 5 hectares, and the great bulk who owned very small plots of land, humble people who were probably very proud to own (or think of themselves as owning) a primitive cottage, with a garden, two or three plots of land, and possibly common rights as well, and who as a consequence were very deeply bound to their native soil with a kind of intensity which meant they seldom left it except for major family occasions or a visit to the market in the nearest small town. This almost fierce, visceral bond between the peasants and 'their' land (for it was only the Revolution which finally gave them the right to own it fully) is probably one of the most deeply rooted characteristics of the French, and it is already clearly present in the seventeenth century, especially in its more difficult periods. And as the peasant's inherited land was not usually sufficient to feed him and his family, even though, as we shall see, this was not usually very large, the basic, hereditary passion was to enlarge his holding by whatever means he could.

In the contemporary sense, then, the peasants owned, albeit unevenly, a good half of the cultivable land in the kingdom (although a much smaller proportion of meadow and forest), and of course did the work on all of it. Under what conditions?

In this context, the apparent precision of the nineteenth-century terms such as 'direct development', 'tenant-farming', and 'share-cropping' masks the loss of much of their older meaning. The first term, *faire-valoir direct* was unknown in the seventeenth century. The second was applied to anyone who signed a lease, whether it

was for levying taxes or supplying armies, the largest being distinguished by the epithet 'general'. The third could be used to refer to
almost anything: in Maine and Anjou, for example, a share-cropper
(*métayer*) was somebody who farmed on a fairly large scale, about 15
to 30 hectares, called a *metairie* simply on account of its size (the
smaller ones were called *closeries* though they were not necessarily
enclosed, or else 'tenancies' (*locatures*) though they were not necessarily rented).

The peasant proprietor

For a long time there has been a myth about the 'jolly farmer', even
the 'rich farmer' (aware of his approaching death, adds La Fontaine,
who knew very well that not all farmers were rich by any means),
living in a solid house, with one or two pairs of good horses, plenty
of equipment, one or two children helping him, and sometimes a
servant as well, directing the cultivation of well-grouped pieces of
land – which actually belonged to him – and taking no rent, or
almost none.

But in fact in all the great cultivated plains of the north and east it
is very uncommon to find a truly independent farmer; and they
grow fewer in number as the seventeenth century progresses. To be
independent the farmer required not only the large, wheeled
plough, heavy carts, and teams to pull them, but also fields of his
own to provide subsistence and pay taxes which were much higher
than twentieth-century ones; at least 5 or 6 hecatres 'à la sole' (in
rotation: a first strip of maslin, not too rough, the second of
spring-sown hay or barley, a third for livestock, some peas or
lucerne). And all those things are not found very often. On the other
hand, especially in Champagne, there were numbers of 'half-
farmers', with one horse, 8 or 9 hectares, and a half-share in
equipment often owned jointly with a relative; in the area around
Paris, the same phenomenon occured and here they were known as
sossons; further north there were the *haricotiers* or *haricandiers*, not
pure cereal growers but growing a bit of everything, including some
indifferent grass on which to support two or three cows, and the
same number of pigs, along with some hemp and flax, and working
for a few days each year as a day-labourer or doing odd jobs: in
short, proprietors on a small scale who could turn their hands to
most odd jobs to make ends meet, at least in normal years. When the

weather was particularly bad, though, or they were hit by an epidemic, or perhaps by an invasion of soldiers, then the fragile balance of this way of life could break down under the weight of famine or debt, to the benefit of the richer farmers. This is a process which seems often to have occurred in the seventeenth century, particularly in a broad band round Paris, where it was the richest Parisians and their local dependants who profited.

In other parts of the country, more central or more mountainous, the land was obviously less fertile but there was enough variety for quite large families (comprising several generations, or the households of several brothers: we shall see more of these later) to live without too much difficulty off 40 or so hectares. A fairly small part of this would be given over to cereals, usually rye, to feed the household; most of the rest would be pastures of various quality – good water meadows for hay, less rich but enclosed pasture for about twenty cows, particularly young ones which could be sold, and then further away some fields under cultivation which could be used as supplementary pasture, some scrubland for the 'white beasts' (sheep) and sometimes for a few goats, although these were treated warily because of their evil reputation and their wicked teeth, and last, they would hope to have some oaks to provide acorns for the pigs. Owner-farmers such as these lived principally by livestock: but unfortunately we cannot always assume that the animals belonged to them, which is something that would make a tremendous difference to their position.

The situation in the south of France is less well-known for the seventeenth century than for the sixteenth or eighteenth, but there seems to have been quite a considerable percentage of independent proprietors there. Pierre Deffontaines, a long-forgotten geographer, described the *pages* (from *paganus*, a peasant) as proud owners of a large domain: like minor seigneurs they had rights to the stone-pines, and could keep a dovecot; and they employed small farmers (*métayers*) and large numbers of needy peasants in lower Quercy and the Agenais. Throughout this part of Aquitaine strong houses, uniting the father and the intended 'inheritor', profited from good family estates which had just been given additional security by the introduction of maize (in the 1730s). In lower Languedoc and lower Provence (e.g. at Roquevaire) a good number of the peasants – sometimes called *ménagers*, sometimes *maîtres de mas* – tried to live off their own land by practising intelligent polyculture and making both garden and *garrigue* yield their maximum; but it seems that only a third at most were economically independent, and that in the end was the only significant independence. But the others did some farmwork on top of their own cultivation, for a townsman, or somebody from the village who had married away, for one of the small plots owned by the local church or the parish 'fabric'.

There was one quite different type of small proprietor who lived fairly easily on a small estate – the vine-growers or vignerons of the Seine valley were once a familiar example. They had 1 or 2 hectares of vines, plus a garden and a small field, and by working intelligently and hard they supplied the taverns which flourished outside the gates of the larger towns. This was usually fairly profitable, as the taverns did not pay tax and the population of most such towns doubled, at least, between 1600 and 1715, with a commensurate rise in the demand for wine. But we shall be coming back to the vignerons, as well as to other, rather different growers, who are really no more than vine share-croppers.

The dominant form: share-cropping (métayage)

Leaving aside the great wheat plains, where they are not known, the 'half-crop agreements', which I refer to generally as share-cropping, must have affected the great majority of estates and, thus, of tenants. The principle was very simple, although it is rarely applied in its pure form: the lessor provided the capital in the form of land, and at least half the livestock and seed; the lessee provided labour power, implements and equipment (often called *cheptel mort*), part of the livestock, almost always the smaller animals (poultry, pigs, goats, sometimes sheep); costs and profits (though not always losses) were strictly shared, half and half, and these included grain, hay, increase in stock, trees, and orchard fruit. This was the basic plan, the theory, on which local custom and social rivalries worked hundreds of variations; few of them benefited the lessee, the share-cropper, who in the Midi was called *métadié*, *bourdilei*, *mégeur* or *miégeur*, and twenty other names which no longer have the same meaning.

In some cantons in northern Burgundy (and possibly also in upper Brittany, under another name) we find contracts of *renterre*, which give the lessee no more than a third of the fruits (i.e. fruits of the earth, from Latin *fructus*, harvest); a careful reading of the wording shows that the *renterre* is fixed: so much per *journal* of land;

and while this could be readily borne in good years, it could become a heavy burden in bad ones, when the produce sold for a higher price. This kind of subterfuge, which at first sight appeared generous – and indeed could afford to be, at no risk – appears in many other situations.

All the royal taxes, the seigneurial dues, and the church tithes generally were the responsibility of the lessee. Particularly in the case of grain, it is always specified that the share should be worked out *sur l'ayre* (at the threshing) after the tithe had been paid; and the tithe, as we shall see, could be considerable. In general, too, the share-cropper did not have the right to touch the trees, not even saplings in the hedges; he might only take dead branches (wood was very expensive). In addition, in wooded countryside, he would have to remake part of the embankment each year, at his own expense, and plant new trees, and graft them. Sometimes the master would set aside a small pile of (good) grain before the share-out; often, too, the use of a good meadow for *aumailles* (cattle) would be his. When it came to sharing the poultry, he would choose first, and probably choose the best (in mitigation it may be said that papers relating to quarrels which have been preserved show that the share-cropper could conceal part of the total). If there were losses on the livestock, the share-cropper often had to bear these himself, as being due to his negligence or incompetence. In brief, the two halves often turned out to be somewhat unequal.

In addition to these complicated and disputatious shares, there were other, sometimes quite substantial, payments. To take some examples from the marshland in the Poitou, the Gâtine: to the more or less equal shares were always added *suffrages* and cartage. Each lessor requested, at fixed dates, a dozen woodcock, a hundred crayfish, one *daim* (a newly castrated young buck); less unusually he also requested young kids at Easter, chickens and goslings at Whitsun, pigs for St Michael's Day (29 September) or All Hallows (which was then a festival, rather than a day of mourning), fat geese at Christmas, cheeses according to the season (some fresh, some dry), baskets of apples or broad beans at harvest, tow or thread of hemp or flax, and even a few cartloads of broom or heather faggots – all to be delivered to the home of the lessor. While these various *suffrages* may represent the master's share in the poultry that had been reared by his share-cropper, and in the increase of his garden, orchard or hemp field, transport was quite a different matter. It meant taking out of commission, time and again, carts and oxen, because almost all the contracts insisted upon 'transporting wine' which had to be fetched in Saintonge or round Thouars (on the borders of Anjou), and then delivered to Parthenay or Bressuire. At the beginning of the seventeenth century the share-cropper was still often forced to mow his master's meadows and carry in the hay (and his wife would have to take part in the *buel*, the great seasonal washing of household linen) as well as the 'discretionary carts', misused clauses which disappeared in the course of the century, as the *suffrages* became somewhat less burdensome during the next.

This pattern of share-cropping is still fairly simple; but there were others – in Centre, Berry, the Bourbonnais, Nevers and Brittany – which our twentieth-century terms can scarcely do justice to. For instance, some include one element which was something like tenant-farming (so many baskets of grain or a sum of money), another element which involves share-cropping (livestock held and shared on a roughly equal basis: butter, cheese, poultry, meat, leather, etc.), as well as the ritual offerings on major holidays, reminiscent of feudal obligations. These astonishing contracts are by no means oddities: there were many others, like the dismissible estates in lower Brittany, which it would take a dozen or more pages to explain.

What can be said for certain, though, is that the old pattern of landholding in France, especially in the seventeenth century, was primarily one of *métayage*, of share-cropping.

Tenant-farmers (fermiers)

The farming lease was almost universal in the great wheat plains of the Paris basin, the north and east: to my knowledge, there is no share-cropping at all. The principle of the contracts is not basically any different from the ones we have just been looking at.

In former centuries, up to the sixteenth, there were odd contracts, which ran for twenty-seven years, or fifty-four, even ninety-nine, years, or for 'several lives': these involved gradually rebuilding a farm and its crops – at shared and very reasonable cost – after it had been abandoned or ruined in the wake of war, plague, or poverty. All that came to an end with Good King Henry. Thenceforth, leases often ran for six years, or for three three-year periods (with the possibility of termination at the end of each three-year period, which coincided with the three-year rotation); towards the end of the century, barring accidents due to exceptionally bad years (such as 1694 and 1709) the nine-year lease became the usual one. The owner rented to a man he knew well, who would provide at the least his own equipment and horses, and often his livestock too. The rent was payable in kind, in money, or in a combination of the two. At the beginning of the seventeenth century, landlords seem to have preferred the rent in wheat, the price of which was rising steadily. When the price subsided (whether after 1635 or after 1663) the landlords tended to prefer payments in money (in gold or silver coin of the realm, and nothing else) which is not hard to understand. In the first few decades of the century, the rent paid annually (or, more often, in two terms or four 'quarters') was augmented by a number of vaguely feudal offerings: capons, lambs, and, in the districts where it was woven, fine linen. As the century wore on, these customs vanished until in the more practically minded eighteenth century money was the only currency used. Leases of this sort called for long-established farming families, marrying among themselves, of the sort particularly to be found in the neighbourhood of Paris and Lille (which only became part of France in 1668). We shall return to these groups later, as they merit closer examination. Elsewhere brothers and brothers-in-law joined forces to take large farms, often quarrelled, failed, and lost livestock and equipment by distraint, in addition to the rare sums of money they could call their own.

Others, less bold, were content to farm a few fields rented from a burgher, merchant or shopkeeper, or a churchman or a widow who had more land than they could use themselves. Sometimes, for a few livres, a peasant undertook to look after one or two cows (seldom sheep) ensuring that they were fed and sharing their produce, often in a most complicated way (people of this period have little inherent simplicity); these were known as *baux à cheptel* (leases of livestock), or simply as *baux de vaches* (leases of cattle); it would be a good investment for the lessor, and (as long as no accident befell the animals) it could help the lessee's finances. These *cheptels* (called *acaptes* in the Midi) are found in most parts of the country, even in areas where share-cropping is the main pattern. Sometimes a garden was also leased, with a few rows of vines, a terraced field, a marsh, or even several together.

Thus for most of the 'average' peasants (or 'middling' as they were called), the daily reality of their work was divided among an unequal mixture of small plots of their own, small leaseholds, *cheptels*, of which they owned more or less 50 per cent, seasonal work – days harvesting, wood-cutting, working as a builder's mate – and of course household tasks, particularly in the winter and in the evenings – spinning, knitting, cutting or carving wood, all the small jobs which principally need skill and patience.

At an even humbler level there was the smoky cottage, a garden, day-labouring, and working cloth or wool: this was the fate of the *manouvriers*, the day-labourers, the poorest of all the peasants, if we except the disinherited, abandoned widows and 'imbeciles': the really poor and the beggars, whose habitual skill led them to charity. They did not know, or no longer knew, the many different ways of earning their bread in the countryside.

Pure leasehold farming was the simplest and least widespread form of farming; exclusive cultivation of one's own land was even less common. Seventeenth-century France was mainly a country of share-croppers; mainly, but not entirely. We shall be looking at some typical characters, the most familiar of which is the vigneron. But first we need to see how the peasantry lived, what kind of shelter they made for themselves to inhabit.

3

Houses: outside and in

Just as there was never one type of French peasant, particularly in the seventeenth century – Jacques Bonhomme is a literary creation, and by no means a harmless one – nor was there ever one type of rural housing, even one characteristic of a particular province, any more than there was one type of furniture or clothing. Attempts to suggest the contrary usually make use of pictures of opulence or comfort (the 'old' farmhouses of the Midi, the seigneurial farms of Brie, or 'the' house of 'the' Burgundy vigneron), or else the later creations of the nineteenth century. The gleaming costumes put forward as 'traditional' (a word that covers a multitude of sins, and that never carries a hint of a date!) are less than a hundred years old, like the Breton coiffes, the best-known of which, the sugar-loaf *bigouden*, is a fantasy even less old than that.

About one seventeenth-century rural dwelling in a thousand must have come down to us intact; and we have a description or an inventory for perhaps one in a hundred. The houses that have survived are naturally the finest and the strongest; those, in the main, which were the richest, and the ones that were built or cut out of stones that were unbreakable, or which could be easily cut with good tools. Certainly, some French artists, like the Le Nains, have left pictures and sketches but the record they present is of dubious reliability, and never reached the level of realism of their colleagues in Liège, Belgium, or Holland. On the other hand, beneath the dust in the archives there are numerous and exact descriptions, although they have a great deal more to tell us about the internal layout and furniture of these houses than about their architecture and external appearance. In fact, we are almost too lavishly provided with the most detailed enumeration, and the most succinct description, of furniture, linen, clothing, tools, and accessories: in the case of the richest households, we are not spared a single saucepan or skirt. For this we must be grateful to the clerks of the seigneurial courts and the notaries' copyists. Without them, we would be driven to idle, or at best superficial, speculation.

The house seen from outside

Of the many factors affecting the construction and position of the seventeenth-century peasant house, two are predominant. It hardly needs to be said that the prime consideration is simple geography: the soil, sub-soil, and climate; and the other, equally obviously, is the wherewithal to build or maintain the building, the rich in this respect being better placed than the poor. Legal and customary implications also need to be taken into account, as well as the main use to be made of the land belonging to the house.

These obvious but necessary preliminary remarks help to show why a granite house makes more sense in Brittany than in Champagne, or why open sheds or large threshing-floors (*airials*) make better sense in dry regions than in the north or west, and why slate or stone roofs are more likely to appear in exposed regions if the raw materials are to hand and can easily be removed. Similarly, daub – the technique of using dried clay, or mud, to stop up most of the gaps in the wooden framework on a more solid foundation of flint modules or rubble – is more often the result of a dearth of stones large enough for building than of artisanal or artistic research, although the latter may be there as well. Choosing building materials was only a problem in important towns (Paris, for example, was still at the stage where the direction of its expansion was determined by the proximity of limestone and sand, plaster and brick-clay) or for the great houses of the nobility, the wealthy, or the church, for whom the cost of transporting materials was of no great significance, especially if they could come by water.

Nonetheless, even building or repairing a house of flint, wood, and clay often called for specialist skills such as those of the mason or the carpenter. In the country, it is true, many ordinary peasants, according to documentary evidence, at certain times of the year became *massons de terre* (builders) or thatchers (but never carpenters, which was a job requiring real training), although itinerant artisans and their mates occasionally looked over their work, or gave them a hand, or the benefit of their experience. In the same way, where the soil and quantity of wood permitted, plenty of brickmakers' mates and wood-cutters (charcoal-burners too) turned out to be no more than seasonal incarnations of adventurous peasants who, not having much land, found it a profitable secondary occupation (as well as a more or less clandestine source of bricks and firewood).

From thatched cottage to seigneurial farmhouse

Beyond these material contrasts – and contrasts of material – which are fairly simply explained, all seventeenth-century rural dwellings must have reflected the degree of wealth or poverty of their inhabitants.

The humble day-labourer, with a garden, a plot of land, a couple of sheep, working seasonally for other people, spinning or wood-working at home, would live in the classic cottage, the *chaumine enfumée* (smoky cottage) specified by La Fontaine, and these would certainly have been the commonest dwellings in France at that period. Made of stone or daub, depending on the region, but always with a solid chimney, stone surrounds for door and windows, it would be built around a simple frame of local wood, and roofed with reeds, rye straw, heather, or fern, topped with some large stones to protect the thatch from the wind. Inside there would be a single room, square or elongated (sometimes with the stable at one end). Beneath its occupants' bare feet (they put on clogs to go out) would be a floor of trodden earth, sometimes strewn with reeds or branches, all pretty well soaked with rain, damp from the walls, and chicken urine and droppings. The 'hearth', the heart of the house, usually had a hook and a pot; there they warmed themselves, when the door was not open to make the chimney draw. Wind, rain, small animals, and every sort of parasite – creeping, scratching, jumping – came in all the time. Apart from cold (which they could protect themselves from by means of old cloaks, flea-ridden blankets and *poches* (sacks)) their chief enemy was *arsin*, fire; a frequent danger but one which at least meant exemption from taxes. Fire was made worse because the thatch burned so quickly, and the nearest spring or well was often some distance away, with at best a single bucket (of wood, with iron bands) in which to carry the water.

Such hazards could not of course affect those cottages which were entirely stone-built, such as the *bories* of what is now Vaucluse. These were made completely of stone, or cut out of the rock, and were still inhabited less than a century ago. Each part of the house acquired its own special function – kitchen, scullery, sitting and dining room, pigsty, sheep-pen, hayloft, and granary – a development that was never found in the small thatched cottages, with their rustic, tumbledown outbuildings, half-stables, half-sheds, which never housed anything much.

Another sort of house which was similarly safe from fire were the cave-houses found along the banks of the Cher, the Vienne, and the Loire in Touraine and Anjou, and a few other places. These would be built in a cave in the hillside, with a good stone façade, and the chimney projecting into the grass or undergrowth of the plateau that served as the roof; often they would stretch quite a long way back, but though they were certainly dark, they were probably no darker than other houses (candles were always expensive), and they stayed cool in summer and warm in winter, were almost immune to fire, and did not encroach on to agricultural or grazing land, nor on to the vine-growing slopes. And it was always possible to hollow out one or two small caves nearby for casks, or for a donkey, sheep, or cow.

Usually there would be a sort of small courtyard in front of these houses, sometimes fenced in, where the small dungheap stood, unfortunately letting its valuable juice, liquid manure, ooze away – often in the direction of the well; a few fowls might peck about, but not many as they tended to find the valuable corn. There would also usually be a few roughly-made outbuildings, often in extreme disrepair, for storing tools, livestock, and – in theory at least – provisions, but more often faggots and straw. Pieces of wood and *potain* (broken earthenware pots) – which post-mortem inventories never forget to evaluate – would inevitably be strewn about. There might not always be a well (they were often communal, like the fountain and the oven – or else seigneurial). If there was an oven, this would be situated either at one end of the house or in a small building close by. Sometimes there might be a pond, dirty and dangerous, as that would be where the hemp was left to rot down, adding its own unspeakable smell to those of the dung and filth. There would almost always be a garden, too, the domain of the woman after the man had dug it over, with beds of cabbages, turnips, and broad beans, and a few fruit trees, often half-wild (the art of grafting seems not to have been universal).

Seventeenth-century peasants, like their descendants, were almost constantly on the move between these and other places: fetching water, wood, herbs, and other plants, taking out the cow, bringing it back in, or occasionally cleaning it; going to the field or the village oven (this latter once a week or once a month), to wash (less often still, sweat and dirt being seen as warming and almost clean), to the woods (and to do some poaching), to do day-work for the local farmer, to take part in the great collective labours of harvest and vintage, as well as going to the market in the neighbouring town at least once a fortnight (as long as there was veal, lamb, chickens, or eggs to sell). These routes were almost ritual, marked by familiar trees, old walls, bramble-bushes, a boundary, a cross (cross yourself as you go past), the seigneur's dovecot, the presbytery, the church and churchyard . . .

Regular journeys and frequent outdoor work raises the question of who stayed in the house, and when. The old? As we shall see, they were not around for long. Children? If they were small they went with their mother and if they were older their father set them to work. The house was chiefly the place where the family ate in the evenings – in the middle of the day less commonly – and where they slept, huddled together to keep warm; they seldom stayed up after dark – candlelight was too expensive; in winter it was where they made love (in summer they could do it outside); and it was where they were born, and where they died.

The kind of scene that has so often been described, as well as painted and engraved, must sometimes have occurred in the biggest and most well-established houses, belonging to well-off peasants and farmers (those who could afford maids and footmen: the master presiding over a full table of guests, the women by the fire with cooking pots; evenings of work (and sometimes chit-chat, where everybody has plenty of room, and fire, and light. This was not, however, the usual pattern; it was restricted to well-established houses on the best farms, and they will be considered in their place.

Peasant interiors

Whereas we have to reconstruct or imagine the exteriors of all but the exceptionally fine or solid seventeenth-century houses, we can be much more certain about their interiors, which are described in far greater detail and abundance. When the clerks came to draw up an inventory of everything involved in the succession of an estate, to protect the rights of children who were still minors (there were nearly always some), and sometimes in preparation for an auction, as the objects described in the inventory would almost always be valued, in accordance with strict custom, all this would be done with such thoroughness that not a bowl, or a blanket full of holes, or a pound of wool to be spun would be omitted.

The poorest peasants – the majority – did not usually have very much 'movable furniture' as it was called: one or two beds, a table, one or two benches, one or two three-legged stools, and a chest or two. There were no dressers or cupboards, although the latter began to appear in more well-off Normandy households towards the end of the century.

The bed, which would be made of more or less contiguous wooden planks, would contain a *lict* (which corresponds roughly to the modern mattress), made of some coarse material stuffed with straw, or, in regions where the poultry-yard was of more significance, as in the south-west, with feathers (in which case it would be called a *couette* or feather bed). There might be sheets but these tended to be kept for ceremonial occasions, and for use as shrouds; there would always be blankets of some sort, and a number of them; often there would only be the one bed, in which case everyone would share the same warmth, the same fleas and the same outpourings: nonetheless there would fairly often be two beds, one described as 'for a child'. Does this mean a cradle? Cradles are rarely mentioned, so it seems reasonable to suppose that they used hanging grape-baskets, or a few planks roughly put together: there are hardly any mentions of the true cradle, rocked by foot, in the country, until later than the seventeenth century.

The contents of the chests (one of which might, luxury of luxuries, have its own key) are always specified. One would contain provisions: wheat or flour; salt in one pot (obligatory, as it was sold almost everywhere by agents of the crown); some, probably rancid, pork fat in another. The other chest would hold the *hardes* and *nippes* (garments): at best, these would consist of a pair of hempen sheets; very occasionally a table-cloth or napkins; two or three grey or black skirts, and the same number of *corps* or bodices (as our grandmothers called them); a few hempen shirts, one or two for children; no underclothes; a few scraps and pieces of old material, and that was all. Clothes in current use, such as cloaks, smocks, or aprons, hung from nails or pegs; all would be well-worn, never washed, passed down from one generation to the next, mended and patched with whatever was to hand, such as the sound bits of a garment which had finally given up the ghost. On the bigger farms, of course, there are more – and more varied – clothes, but it was not until the next century that women, at least in the north, would begin to dress better and more colourfully, and to collect together a small amount of personal and household linen.

As far as cooking arrangements are concerned, there was just the fireplace, a few cooking pots of various sizes, usually earthenware, sometimes cast iron, some plates, bowls, and basins of wood or earthenware, wooden spoons (pewter for the richest), no forks, except at the royal court, and a few individually-owned knives, which would be wiped on the sleeve or the thigh after use. The crockery would be washed when possible in a sort of wooden tub made from an old cask cut in half and crudely patched up; there would be all sorts of barrels around the house, frequently empty ('mouth-open' as they called it), which could be used for collecting rainwater (if there was a gutter), or for filling with apples, or fruits and berries gathered from the lanes and the woods, which could be left to make 'drink' after water had been added and they had steeped for a while; there would not normally be any wine or cider, either because the fruit had not been gathered, or because it had already been sold or was too expensive.

The most surprising item on what, after Balzac, came to be known as 'valuers' inventories' are the weapons: not just heavy knives or pitchforks but arquebuses, then muskets, particularly what was simply referred to as a 'gun' (*fuzil*). At first one tends to imagine peasants collecting more or less useless trophies from nearby sites of battle; battles were, after all, fought in most parts of the country during the wars of religion, and the Fronde, and, slightly later, on the frontiers. Yet there are altogether too many arms for us to believe that they were all abandoned or sold by soldiers (although many certainly were sold); and we continue to find guns in the eighteenth century too, when – apart from a few local and short-lived skirmishes – there was neither civil war nor invasion. It does not, however, follow from this that the guns were for hunting (nor, to a lesser extent, for defence against wolves, which were numerous, and bandits, who were not), because although poaching was so easy and widespread that it was many years before people in the country started to keep rabbits, it does seem to have been carried out by means of snares, traps, lures, and similar devices rather than by guns. So a certain degree of mystery remains, and tends to suggest that life in the country was not idyllic, or devoid of danger.

Another fact about most households is less surprising: even in houses well-provided with clothes and furniture, the heirs declared that all the *argent-monnoie*, the money, had gone on the expense of illness and burial: there was never a sou left. It is interesting, though, that these unanimous declarations of impecuniosity hardly ever occur before the middle of the century (when taxes soared to an astronomical level). Every peasant, in reality, except the utterly poor (and they did not have houses) possessed a few copper coins, even some silver, enough at least to pay the royal tax (and some other smaller taxes), and in the end they would be forced complainingly to hand them over, sou by sou. In many cases, there would be lists of debts, rather than money, and these too were declared and described: debts to a richer farmer, a relative, the seigneur or to a local money-lender, recorded on scraps of thick paper and signed with the deceased's 'mark'. It clearly made more sense to declare debts than assets!

The above inventory of peasant interiors is strictly derived from archive documentation and can be interpreted in several ways. It only refers to the poorest (but not the completely destitute) and least 'specialised' (insofar as that is a meaningful term in the context) members of the French peasantry; these were by far the most numerous, and accounted for easily half the king's subjects. Naturally, therefore, this description fits less well with even marginally specialised groups, such as vignerons or market-gardeners, or to peasant artisans who worked as weavers, blacksmiths, and menders, or to innkeepers or millers; and it applies even less to the large farmer-collectors who, on their 100-hectare estates of wheat, occupied large buildings with an enclosed courtyard flanked by outhouses, sheds, cow-sheds, sheep-pens, stables, and a dovecot, and furnished them in a manner that was almost bourgeois. We shall, however, encounter a good number of these more specialised categories in the course of the book, in their proper context and their own milieu.

But before we leave this area, we need to try to obtain a glimpse of the men themselves, and their families and descendants, so to speak, in the flesh.

4

Birth and survival

The mechanics

It was generally expected, perhaps too readily, that the first child would appear ten to eighteen months after the wedding. But this is only an average. The actual time between the first sacrament and the second (baptism) could be anything from two months to three or four years. The shortest gap indicates what our delicate-minded demographers call prenuptial conceptions: these are uncommon in the seventeenth-century countryside, although there are some interesting local variations. The longest gap probably represents cases of sexual difficulties, most probably one or two miscarriages, often close together, which can be identified from trustworthy but infrequent sources, where they are referred to as 'accidents'. For the rest, the average, especially the frequency tables for first births, which are easy to establish, point overwhelmingly and quite explicably to the period between the ninth and fifteenth month.

After the first, further children followed every two years on average, or slightly longer, until the woman was well into her forties, or one of the partners died. This could mean eight or nine births in less than twenty years of fertile marriage: of these, two or three would not survive the first few months, and others would die in their early years; three or four, sometimes more, sometimes fewer, reached the age where they themselves could marry.

These unsentimental, abstract, overall figures are the product of the very precise work done by demographic historians, and they are particularly accurate for the northern half of the kingdom during the second part of the century, where hard work, good sense, and good source material (parish records) have provided us with a very full picture. These facts are beyond challenge and related specifically, for once, to the rural context; but they fail to reveal not only the slight regional variations, and differences between individual instances, but the actual reality of everyday life.

Conception

One of the hardest things to accept was sterility. Today we know that about 6 per cent of couples are destined to remain childless because of one partner or the other, or some failure in their union. The proportion in the seventeenth century has been set a little higher, when, of course, nothing could be done to remedy the problem. This estimate has been reached by following the fortunes of young married couples, who we know anyway tended not to move away from the area. This is one of those 'natural laws', like the preponderance of boys over girls at birth (about 105 to 100), which is always visible in sufficiently large samples, or like the greater strength of the 'weaker sex' (who in fact live longer), or the constant percentage of one set of twins in every 110 births.

These factors, however, were unknown in the seventeenth century, and after a couple of years at most the visible sterility of a young couple would start to provoke anxiety, almost shame, among their family, and derision and an unhealthy apprehension among the other villagers. Everyone knew, of course, whether the marriage had been consummated, but the proof was not exposed to the public view as it was in Mediterranean countries; so the terrible risk of 'knotting the lace' had been avoided, or overcome, or exorcised. (This is a reference to the practice of casting spells during the marriage ceremony in an attempt to prevent the marriage from being consummated, a practice which was widespread and so generally feared that most episcopal instructions ordered it to be zealously tracked down.) A well-balanced mixture of pagan and religious rituals could sometimes succeed in unknotting what only an evil demon could have knotted up. Most young married women, though, managed to get pregnant quite quickly without the help of God or witchcraft. Those who did not, normally turned to the saints to intercede on their behalf: these varied from one region to another, but the Virgin Mary was the favourite; they would go on special pilgrimages, wear medallions or lockets, rub themselves with some clearly masculine relic or piece of statuary, ask for advice or information from older experts, and in the end ask for a philtre from the omnipresent but unobtrusive witch.

If this produced no result, they had to accept their unfortunate place as 'barren' women, regarded with contempt. There was no possibility of a divorce; there were only annulments, or more precisely statements of nullity in the event of non-consummation, and these were only for sale to well-off couples, at the end of a sordid and not necessarily honourable inquiry. Neverthless the unproductive couple may perhaps have been able to bring up an orphaned nephew or niece, or to hope, after being widowed, for a more fertile second marriage.

Once pregnant, would the young peasant wife – who would normally have passed her twenty-fifth birthday, given the late age at which marriage took place (as we shall see in the next chapter) – become the focus of affectionate interest? It is very difficult to say with certainty, but probably not. But her mother, sister, friend, and local opinion were more than ready to offer her advice of varying usefulness about what she should eat, the cravings she should satisfy, and the fears she should avoid in case they afflicted a new-born baby; what talismans, amulets, or medallions she should wear; and about a ritual pilgrimage to one of the many shrines to Our Lady of Delivery in each province. All these peasant customs relied on magic to some extent, and even in the late twentieth century, they are still far from extinct.

At the same time it is clear that the mother-to-be continued to play her usual part in the work of the family, not only in traditionally female areas of house, garden, and livestock, but also in the major tasks of summer – haymaking, harvest, and the vintage – even when her pregnancy was very advanced. This frequently resulted in 'accidents' or 'injuries', two modest contemporary terms for miscarriages (never abortions, which carried the death penalty and were unheard-of), which indeed most often happened in the summer, as the often harsh details entered by the priest in his register attest. Harsh, because for the priests it was a question of whether there was sufficient time to baptise or at least *ondoyer* (give a form of emergency baptism to) any prematurely born infant who gave some sign of life, in order to save what they called his soul; whereas they tended to care much less about the dying mother, even though she was sometimes given the last rites despite being impure. The advent of a new christian, even an incomplete, temporary one, meant a great deal more than the fate of a doomed mother.

Childbirth and survival

Even when there were no accidents of this sort, and they were due as much to physical weakness as to overwork, the birth of a first child still presented more danger than subsequent births (as to a lesser extent it still does), especially in the rural, but even in the urban, conditions of the seventeenth century. We now know that in the south of Paris around 1600 one primipara in eight died. No doctors were present at labour, nor surgeons, both of whom might have been able to help matters (Louis XVI had a surgeon for his mistresses); in fact no men seem to have been allowed to be present, particularly not the father, let alone the priest. Childbirth was a woman's business, especially old women (over fifty), those matrons who were now and then referred to as 'wise women'. Every village had long had several, a sort of Greek chorus of old women, semi-witches, who 'knew'. In the seventeenth century there was normally only one per village, though, and she was nominated, or in some cases (in the east of France) actually elected, by a positively Aristophanic gathering of women, who were looking for experience and skill as well as a knowledge of herbs, amulets, and recipes. The priest quickly endorsed the choice; when he could he advised on it. In any case, he had to vouch for the 'good life and habits' of the wise-woman, especially her ability to administer a proper emergency baptism to weakly neonates. This connection quickly gave the appointment a degree of official sanction, stemming from the bishop himself, who of course would never come to verify it – one more example of the way the imperious catholic church of the counter-reformation penetrated into all areas of life, even this one.

There is little direct evidence about the physical conditions of childbirth, but there is an abundance of material criticising them produced by doctors, hygienists and kind-hearted reformers during the next century, not all of it balanced or disinterested. We can be almost sure that the mother gave birth sitting down, with her clothes on, and strongly supported, and that the midwife worked in unimaginable conditions, with unwashed hands, fingers, and fingernails, preparing dressings which were the reverse of sterile, containing spider's webs, pounded leaves, and insects and dried dung. Fortunate the women with strong constitutions, normal presentations, and healthy babies. It is worth noting in passing that twins were almost always foredoomed, and their mothers with them. Where there were serious difficulties, the sole important concern was to baptise the child, whom people were almost always ready to assert had shown some sign of life, in order to ensure his entry to Paradise where he could pray for his parents, so that he would not have to wander the uncertain world of limbo or run the terrible risk of being buried in unconsecrated ground. It must also be firmly added that in those days a child or a woman were easily replaced: less than a year for the former and less than three months for the latter seem, from examining parish records, to have been the usual periods.

These records also show that the mortality rate for women aged between twenty and thirty-five was far higher than that of men of the same age, contrary to the pattern for all other age-groups. And they show that new-born babies were particularly at risk in the first days and weeks of life, less so in the months that followed. All the same between 20 and 40 per cent, according to the region, did not reach their first birthday. The national average calculated by the demographic historians at the I.N.E.D. is over 280 per thousand – and is even higher in the splendours of the early eighteenth century – which defines the massacre and to some extent ratifies it.

The reasons for these figures are clear enough, although not always recognised. Unnoticed malformations, traumatism during birth, mishandling suffered during the first few hours, the harmfulness, or absence, of maternal milk, and such like, provide the main explanation of 'endogenous' mortality (i.e. the soonest to strike). The custom, which later became an absolute obligation, of baptising the child in its first twenty-four hours, or at the latest by the next day, probably led to more premature deaths, as the font might well be some distance away, the weather cold, and the church unheated. Any child who was fortunate enough to be fed on his mother's milk (or as fairly often happened by the superfluous milk of an aunt or neighbour) was protected against attack by many of the 'exogenic' causes of death. But children were still liable to simple accidents, as mothers could not watch them all the time, nor was it easy to find anyone else to do it, as almost all children were born after their grandparents had died, and there were not always older sisters who could look after them. 'Heat stroke', which occurred when the swaddling clothes and bands were too tight (and not often changed), was a common phenomenon; not to mention the danger of suffocation in the family bed (the word used then was 'overlaying', and it was a topic which the church – again – was deeply involved in for vaguely moral reasons); and then there were the more serious dangers of terrible attacks of entero-colitis and gastro-enteritis in summer – green diarrhoea – which leave the parish registers for August and September full of 'little bodies'.

Suckling

The problem of maternal milk was an extremely serious one. It reflects the mother's health, of course, and her degree of tiredness, and this could be considerable during the periods of hardest work; it also reflects the quality and to some extent the quantity of her food, which consisted too often of a basis of cereals and starch, with few dairy products, practically no meat except a bit of rancid fat pork, and a small amount of not always ripe fruit: not a pattern of eating likely to recommend itself to dieticians today. The major crisis arose when the milk supply diminished, for all sorts of reasons, often due to debilitation; or else when it dried up altogether, particularly, it seems, when the mother found herself pregnant again, a situation which posed additional, almost insoluble, problems, as we shall see. A child who survived thus far would have been carried in arms, settled and warmed in his parents' bed, or occasionally placed in a cradle (although these were expensive unless home-made) or in a sort of hanging basket. He would have been dressed all the time in a bonnet, the nappy, swaddling clothes, and bands kept tight to protect his body and help it grow properly, while the whole ensemble marinated in urine and *bren* [dialectic word for faeces] (the words 'shit' (*merde*) and 'shitty arse' (*cu brenneux*) appear in the learned *Dictionnaire Francoys* by P. Richelet, dating from 1679) which were thought to be beneficial, and which only added a slight extra whiff to the powerful odours of the peasant dwelling, something that did not offend the peasant nostril in those days (or, indeed, until quite recently).

The day came, however, when the child who survived all this

began to cut teeth, then to walk, and to be weaned from his mother, bringing him so to speak into a second age. By that time a younger brother or sister had usually been born, or was due.

'Slow' couples and 'fast' couples

It came as a surprise to demographic historians (and historical demographers) to discover, in the 1950s, that there was a gap of two years or more between births. Expectations were based on the myth of annual childbirth, backed up by a few exceptional instances or the tireless biographies of the great bourgeois and parliamentary families of those days (not so much the nobility), where apart from anything else it was not always the same mother who officiated. But tens of thousands of examples no longer leave the true situation in any doubt, though there are of course exceptions which we shall look at. The main reason for the length of the gap seems to have been the universality of breastfeeding, particularly in the country-side, which made a good number of women temporarily infertile (some doctors suggest a figure of 60 per cent); their infertility would be supported by the occasional presence of various taboos (still found outside France) forbidding men to 'approach' women when they were breastfeeding (probably something to do with the belief that this would spoil the milk). A counter-proof is provided by the fact that women who lost their children soon after birth statistically (and therefore on average) became pregnant more rapidly than other women, the gap between the two childbirths being reduced from about two years to twelve months or even less.

If we look more closely at the history of specific couples (which we can do for those, often the majority, who did not move away from their place of birth), it becomes clear that they fall into several categories. One section, maybe one couple out of six, or more in some provinces such as Brittany, are notable for their 'rapidity'. For a good ten years robust women could give birth every ten to fifteen months; after, the pace would slow down somewhat as they approached the menopause, which seems to have come relatively early, almost always before the age of forty-five. It is among these exceptional couples that we find the few very large rural families in the seventeenth century, assuming that a good proportion of the fifteen or sixteen children born actually survived. This rarely happened, however, as the most fertile women often lost many of their children at or soon after birth, which helps to explain the speed with which they became pregnant again.

At the other extreme are the 'slow' couples. To some extent these are to be found in all parts of France, but they are particularly common in the south-west, and this raises a question. Could it not be that the peasants of Aquitaine practised – timidly, irregularly, and clumsily – *coitus interruptus*? It was not in fact unknown, but tended to be avoided either through laziness or fear of sin, as the church in its wisdom was quick to thunder (in Latin) against what it treated as the sin of Onan: but would priests in the depths of the country have taken that view? Childbirth, for whatever reason, occurs less frequently in that part of the country, perhaps as a result of these onanistic practices: an interval of two years, followed by one of three, then four – whatever explanation is advanced, the fact remains. These couples may have lost fewer children, but there is no real proof of this.

Another factor to be taken into account when considering the average position of the majority is the understandable case of couples who had (only) one, two, or three children and then no more. While the desire to restrict the family cannot be passed over as an explanation, there is no proof for it – whereas there is abundant proof of it in the late eighteenth century. The customary explanation is in terms of the illness of one partner or the other, usually the woman, who might be injured by a clumsy or brutal midwife, or struck by some gynaecological trouble then unrecognised or ascribed to magical causes.

At all events, the general law remains: after the first child, another would be born every two years up to a total of eight or nine, if the couple survived that long, and of these, three or four would reach adulthood. But this needs to be qualified straightaway by looking at the number of couples in which one partner died before the wife was over thirty. We know the statistics for this: scarcely half achieved fifteen years of marriage, either because the wife died (in the first few years) or because of the death of the husband, whose strength began to fail at about forty and who was much weaker by the time he was fifty. The net result is that, although the fertility of the rural population then was some three times ours, it only just managed to maintain its rate of reproduction, adding a few per cent overall, but also suffering drastic falls (whose effect became clear in the following generation) as a result of savage epidemics and famine.

Now let us leave the safety of statistics and look at the life of a child who actually survived.

Dressing and weaning

In the first tenuous months of life the child appeared to have a largely vegetative existence, particularly in the eyes of the mother, and we may assume that little attention was paid to him. His loss was not deeply felt; many priests omitted to enter such a small burial in the register, or, if they did, it was in one or two lines, mentioning that only the sacristan and gravedigger were present, seldom the father. Those few, rich, peasants who kept records in the family Bible did not even devote a line to it. The name was often given to the next child, although one cannot say what this perseverance or thoughtfulness might mean. When the child began to prattle and take his first steps (guided by his mother or elder sister?) he probably began to command some attention. But the crucial time was the *robage*, when the child passed from wearing swaddling clothes to the frock worn by both sexes, and weaning. In preparation for this they probably gave the child some kind of cereal porridge, chewed and moistened by the mother, as is done in many parts of the world today.

The transition to adult food pure and simple, even if it was only soup and porridge, or wheatcakes, must have involved some difficulties; and in addition there was the fact that the child was no longer protected by breastfeeding from the various viruses and infective agents which were now free to attack his organism. Children between two and four years of age fell victim to a variety of little-understood epidemic diseases: from occasional clues we can surmise outbreaks of croup, typhoid, rubella, measles, and scarlatina (referred to generally at the time as 'the purples'), horrifying 'upsets' of terrible diarrhoea, and, with dreadful regularity – every five or seven years – deadly smallpox which attacked peasant children and royal offspring alike. Not all who caught it died, but they were all scarred by it. Nonetheless, most escaped it, partly because they did not fall into the hands of ignorant and pretentious doctors.

Once he was independent, we do not know whether the peasant child in his frock was the object of much affection: there has been a great deal talked about love and non-love, with no evidence to support it. Children do not seem to have been made much of except in the rich families that Ariès so much enjoys looking at. Yet we can imagine the young child growing up in the one and only room of the house, maybe under the eye of an elder sister or, extremely rarely in the seventeenth century, a surviving grandmother, who would make him or pass on to him timeless toys such as rag dolls, or a horse made out of a stick with a head stuck on, or rough barrows or carts; later on, he would have hoops, tops, a tame bird in a cage (taken originally from its nest). Or he would follow his mother around the yard, to the dungheap, to the cow-shed, to the garden, down the lanes, to hoe the fields or pick stones, trying to keep out of the way of the animals' hooves, the edges of tools, the pond, and the well. Very quickly, by the age of five, he would join in small tasks both inside and outside the house: washing dishes, moving rubbish, pulling up weeds, keeping an eye on the chickens (which were always trying to get into the cornfield and the vegetables); and occasionally he would use an improvised broom or a needle, even a distaff. But by this time he would be approaching the crucial age of seven.

The age of discretion

The church called it the 'age of discretion', later the 'age of reason', and the number seven is prophetic, magic, or sacred in almost all religions, however old, along with three and twelve.

For a start, boys and girls began to dress in recognisably adult clothes at that age: hemp shirts, breeches and leggings (not always the latter) for the boys; bodices and several skirts for the girls (with nothing underneath), with some kind of old lined cloak for bad weather, clogs (but not always, or only for Sundays), and a hat or bonnet to keep off the sun. All the clothes were very plain and very crude – their unwashed skin could put up with the roughest cloth and material – shaped and reshaped by the mother out of old clothes of parents or older brothers and sisters, or of those who had died (who were buried naked in roughly made bags), much patched and undyed, dull, dark, the colour of dust, mud, and sweat: it seems only to have been in the eighteenth century that clothes, especially women's clothes, began to include some colour and elegance, at least among the poor and middling peasantry (leaving aside the better-off, as usual).

Just as the children's clothes were smaller replicas of those of their parents', so were their tasks. The girls most often stood in for their mother in the (often quite rudimentary) tasks of cooking, house-work, and looking after any younger children; they also helped a bit with the smaller livestock, raked the garden, and helped with the distaff, reeling, and sewing. A daughter's realm was the house, and she would seldom go out until she was grown-up, and even then only under the strict supervision of her mother, elder sister, or a neighbour, who acted as rural duennas, or worse still that of her father or brothers, who were merciless about her obligations and her honour – save in the small number of aberrant families, those of drunkards or unmarried mothers (the latter pattern often repeating itself in subsequent generations).

The boys were freer and had time to run around with others of the same age, playing with tops, running races, fighting, perhaps playing off-ground tig or blind-man's buff, if these were indeed rural games, or had become so; but more often they would be robbing nests, looking for mushrooms or wild strawberries, start-ing to do a bit of poaching (tickling a trout or setting a rabbit-snare only required a little dexterity). Most of the time, though, a son had to join in the work of the family, becoming a sort of apprentice in the shadow of his father by whom he could be quite roughly treated. Affection does not seem to have been very widespread, and the master's superiority over the son was frequently achieved with slaps and beatings. He would quickly have to take on the job of cleaning the livestock and, closely watched, the setting up of the family dungheap; also he would have to use the hoe, the billhook, until such time as he was strong enough to manage a spade or pick, or lift up a laden pitch-fork; he also had to see to moving and guarding the livestock (when there were any) and do some legal or clandestine wood-gathering, as nimble and speedy children could more easily evade the attention of foresters and gamekeepers on the seigneurial and royal estates.

In many cases carrying heavy loads and premature hard work led to deformation of the bone-structure (limps, deformed hips, and hunch-backs were common), and also unpleasant *descentes*, the hernias revealed by earnest charitable inquiries, although the medical evidence was not available until the following century. When they were seven, boys started spinning (not a skill reserved for women) and helped the father, as he wove cloth, to fix or guide the threads by sliding under the frame. In towns there are even regulations about the wages to be paid to 'workers' of this age. When they reached the age of ten some would be put with large farmers as shepherds, cowherds, or servants, and there they would sleep in the cow-shed or on the straw, and feed on crusts and scraps from the table, at the mercy of the whims of the other servants and the severity of the master. The only exceptions were a few good households such as the ones described 200 years later in the novels of George Sand – which are more precisely observed than is often thought – and in the forgotten masterpieces of Guillaumin.

For the luckiest ones in the few provinces which were aware (we do not know why) of the possible usefulness of some rudimentary education, seven was also the age at which school began. From the beginning of the century, from Normandy and the Loire to Artois and the Vosges, there were a certain number of village schools, where small boys and even girls were regularly taught not only the rudiments of prayer and piety, but also to read and write, and sometimes to add up, though every peasant who was not stupid could count on his fingers or on notched sticks or tally-sticks. They learnt to read, taking their turn with what was often a single spelling-book, or from a Bible, if the master was able to get hold of one. The masters were far from being specialists at their job, except those who came down from the Durance or the Ubaye, whom we shall return to: they were usually jacks of all trades (including church duties like bell-ringing and doing some of the sexton's jobs) and did some gardening and carpentry as well as making each child in turn read and write then spell out loud as he stood, cane in hand, in some large and draughty room which was either borrowed or rented. Children came to school after the vintage, and left to work in the fields again at Easter or haymaking. The parents jointly maintained the *magister* (he was called twenty or more different names) by giving him a few sous each month and two or three bundles of firewood a year, and by inviting him to eat with them from time to time. The church endorsed his 'nomination' and gave him alms. Rather late in the day and at the insistence of Louis XIV, who had grown sanctimonious as a result of his second marriage, the church introduced rigid segregation of the sexes after the age of seven, the general result of which was to exclude girls from education alto-gether. Colbert, with his utilitarian philosophy, on the other hand (in advance of Voltaire who was not good on this issue), began to concern himself with peasant education, as did all the best minds of the time.

The most surprising thing – and if they read official printed documents, historians ought to have known this for more than 100 years – is that between 1686 and 1690 something like half of the men signed their marriage certificate, and less than a quarter of the women: but this only applies to the north-east corner of the kingdom, from Cotentin to Alsace, and the southern Alps, and is a special phenomenon of the high valleys, which produced school-masters in the way other places made clogs. The most distressingly low levels of literacy are found in what became the departments of les Landes and Morbihan. The huguenot regions were always in the fore, as protestants did not like illiteracy.

Facts such as these, supported by tens of thousands of examples, naturally require an explanation, but there is no very obvious one. Some people have adduced the length of the winters which curtailed labour in the countryside (though there was always plenty to be done indoors), but this hardly explains the high level of illiteracy in Limoges or Auvergne. Others have pointed to the benefits of clustered settlements, but they could equally well foster ignorance; the good influence of the church has been mentioned, yet Brittany was uneducated; it has even been suggested that there are special qualities inherent in the French language, but this was very little spoken in northern Lorraine, Alsace, or the western part of the southern Alps. A more likely explanation, it seems to me, is the hypothesis of a degree of economic progress, and the possibility of rising up the social scale in the provinces which had schools. In fact, parents must have wanted their children to go to school for three or four winters, and have been prepared to pay for it, even if this amounted to only a small sum, and this indicates a desire for social advancement. What possibilities were there of that?

The only ways to achieve social advancement were by means of shrewd small-scale trading in grain, smallcloth, and particularly in wood, which presupposed an ability to count and read contracts, or by taking on a good farming tenancy, or share-cropping agreement, which required the same abilities; the only other route was by joining the church, which needed patronage and an obligatory annual income of between 50 and 100 livres – a sum not to be found 'under a horse shoe' as they said, although a horse was neither a common animal nor a cheap one. In any case, it being only in fairy tales that shepherdesses marry princes, labourers' sons were not the ones who rose in the world in this way – unless, as sometimes happened, one of them married a rich farmer's widow. But school was only a way up for very few.

Even the provinces with less than one school for every ten villages were not necessarily condemned to backwardness, as every child between the age of about seven and twelve had, in theory, to go to a catechism class which was meant (along with the school, where there was one) to impart the rudiments of the true faith and prepare them for their first communion. Responsible priests in responsible dioceses (were these a majority before 1650?) did what they could to provide this religious education, with the simple and sincere knowledge of matters of faith which was theirs. In other places there was just a false pretence, a few fleeting gestures, or nothing at all. With the catholic revival, followed (after 1650) by the slow establishment of seminaries, and the gradual disappearance of the fanciful, ignorant, and scandalising priests tolerated under Louis XIII and Mazarin, the catechism on the whole had to be treated more seriously, although it necessarily remained at an elementary level. This did not prevent the continuance of simple faith, particularly its practical manifestations, but wakes, folk tales, gossip of witches, worship of a superfluity of saints and holy relics were gradually forced into retreat or underground. By the end of the century the influence of settled priests who were better-educated, more respectworthy, and more authoritative had produced a faith which was more regulated, perhaps sadder and more fearful, and stifled the more extreme of the old manifestations. There is too little evidence in this realm for historians to offer anything but possibilities and intuitions, often founded on documentation, which either cannot be taken as authoritative or can be regarded as being too one-sided: there are very few properly controlled and established statistics.

The age of communion

When children reached the age of twelve or thirteen, they took their first communion (not then called 'solemn' communion) and thus entered a sort of fourth stage, that of adolescence, in which they were at last seen as full christians, and begin to be recorded in censuses and parish registers and to be 'assessed for salt' in the many provinces where the *gabelle* was in force; a year or two later they were confirmed, when the bishop happened to be passing through. At all events, they now had the semi-official status of communicants, and had to attend church at Easter and the other so-called holidays of obligation. They could also now work as adults (though in practice many already did) and were just about allowed to marry according to the decrees of the church (which set the age of puberty at fourteen for boys and twelve for girls, ages regarded by doctors in the next century as at least three or four years too early). The young men were also allowed to join *sociétés de jeunesse*, societies of young people (where these existed), such as the now well-known *bachelleries* of western central France. These presided over rural festivals, under the direction of a vaguely elected 'king', to celebrate the May, the Midsummer's Eve bonfire, or the patron saint of the parish. The societies demanded dues in money or kind from the newly-weds of the year, and organised noisy mock serenades when a 'foreigner' went off with a village girl, or when an old man (forty or so) remarried a young woman, especially if he was a widower (or worse still if she was a widow). A young man would continue in this way, serving as an unpaid apprentice to his father, until some land fell vacant either upon his father's death or that of his father-in-law or step-father, after which he would leave the *bachellerie* and become part of the circle of married peasants. Then the cycle would begin again.

Charivari

The only exception was where a young man (seldom a girl, unless she was going to go into service) was driven by poverty, ambition, or a sense of adventure to set off to the town, a shabby bundle on his shoulder, in the hope of finding his fortune. There he might work for a stonemason, and become a master mason himself; he might become a footman, and rise in that small hierarchy; from showing a bear or marmots, he might progress to working as a tumbler, or even an actor; he might start off working as potboy in an inn and end up married to the *patronne*; he might start out hawking almost anything in the streets – baked apples, wafers, banquet leftovers – and become a shopkeeper; as a beggar, he could become a soldier or leader of beggars; or else he might sink finally into lockpicking, theft, or mendicancy, become a 'blind' beggar or pretended cripple. Of the girls who left or ran away, few could expect anything but squalid or lubricious domesticity with no chance of wealth, even if they escaped prostitution: only in Paris were there as many as 20–30,000, but everywhere there were a large number of casual prostitutes who also worked as seamstresses: there are no examples in the seventeenth century of transformations like that of Jeanne Bécu, who became the Comtesse Dubarry.

The sons and daughters of peasants, if they survived the dangers of childhood, almost always remained peasants themselves: they in their turn bore peasants from whom, in the end, most Frenchmen are descended. It was not really until after 1840, with the coming of factories and railways, that at first a few, then many groups of people began to leave their ancestral fields in search of a less wearing life in the suburbs, in small businesses and minor public offices, a pattern that has only ended with the enormous upheavals of the late twentieth century which have finally meant the death of the old rural life – a process which the oldest of us have been able to observe as it went along.

5

Peasant marriage

Everything that concerns marriage in peasant society seems to be fairly well-known now, even if it is not always very well understood. This is partly explicable in terms of the very different sources of curiosity and 'questionings' which come together in the study of marriage. The subject concerns lawyers, because marriage involves a contract, whether written or not; theologians, because it is a special sacrament; it concerns demographers who have access to long series of often very detailed seventeenth-century marriage certificates; it also interests sociologists – although they do not usually go so far back in history – because a group is being created which has to be fitted in with other groups; it concerns folklorists who collect ways and customs which they have to assign dates to; it concerns those ethnohistorians who are not too incomprehensible to the ordinary reader, and are eager to find elements of rural attitudes and culture, which are often precisely and reliably recorded; and it also interests the currently fashionable sexologists, quite justifiably, although it permits all kinds of divagations.

Of much greater importance are the documents that have made the investigations into peasant marriage possible, and provided a foundation for what has been written about it. Millions of marriage certificates have been preserved in old parish registers, with which France is almost as well endowed as Italy; tens of thousands of marriage contracts are kept in the files of notaries; there is an even greater number of probate papers applied for where marriages were broken (by death) but where post-mortem valuations were often preserved in the judicial or seigneurial archives; there is deceptively simply canon law legislation; there is a legislation based on custom and practice which contains a staggering amount of variation; then there was the imperialism of the royal legislation which, after a few false starts, tried to dictate in sacramental matters and beyond (though not with complete success) and in civil contract. In addition there is all the material to be gleaned from the various forms of literature, from the most controlled to the most rambling: from moral miscellanies to drama, from the novel to farce and from fairy tales to crude bawdy (the latter often spread by the small pamphlets sold by pedlars). There is a great wealth of material available to anybody prepared to gather it: what then has to be done is to organise it and focus it on the seventeenth century.

A curious sacrament

For peasants as for everybody else marriage is a sacrament, but one which in principle needs neither priest nor church as the young people concerned administer it to each other *par paroles de présent* (by exchanging promises), to use the contemporary phrase. This sacrament is not 'perfect' or complete until the physical act has been performed. The priest was there (at least at the first ceremony), but only to verify it by responding with the witnesses where necessary (there were usually two witnesses for each side); and the nuptial blessing was for a long time more of a formality than anything more solemn, and was never really indispensable. For the sacrament to take effect and be complete there needed to be no obstacle in its way – the principle ones being to do with kinship, even quite distant (cousins needed a special dispensation, which was always granted, at a price), or spiritual relationships such as godfather and god-daughter, or previous engagements. These were therefore considered early in the proceedings, and the practice of publishing banns 'on three consecutive Sundays' in the parishes of those about to get married seems to have been universal. It is scarcely necessary to add that parental consent was absolutely obligatory, even for those who were of age (usually those over twenty-five), although they were allowed to dispense with it after three respectful (written) supplications.

Once the couple were outside hallowed ground, the sacrament

was not valid until the *copulatio carnalis* had taken place. Was this verified, as it was for the French kings? Written records are very discreet on this topic, oral tradition less so: but whatever the case, those close to the newly-weds probably knew what to believe.

All that, as we are very well aware, was accompanied by rejoicing, feasting (not all Pantagruelian), and rituals of one sort or another involving the family and the villagers, all of which have been frequently described, but as it were *en bloc*. Their main function was to celebrate the transition of the engaged couple from the *bachellerie* (*bachelier*, like bachelor, means an unmarried person) to the circle of married men and women. They also emphasised the couple's entry into a 'house', whether they thereby constituted a new economic unit or fitted into an already existing, large (sometimes very large) family (and economic) group.

Like the earlier rituals, these are simple observations, but they demonstrate at what point the apparently simple act of marriage can permit of a number of complex aspects which need to be discussed. Let us, however, be content with a description of the actual reality of it.

The establishment of a statute of marriage

Oddly enough, the familiar statute and customs of marriage seem not to have been firmly established in France before the mid-seventeenth century. For several decades the church, on the one hand, and the state, on the other, tried to change the old customs. The church was largely obsessed with engagements and the state with parental consent.

Engagement or *paroles de futur* – a reciprocal promise of marriage after a sometimes unspecified length of time – seems to have been the custom in many of the provinces of France and in the rest of Europe. According to canon law, the *verba de futura* could be made part of the sacrament of marriage as long as the *fiancés* went on to the second phase of the sacrament, sexual union. In some provinces, and to a greater extent in England, the couple's bed was set up in the middle of the main room, and sometimes a period of trial marriage even ensued. Without going as far as that, it seems that originally nobody minded how far the engaged couple went, sexually speaking, although there was no guarantee that *paroles de futur* would become *paroles de présent*. But the church, which began to grow quite obsessively prudish after its first internal reforms and the first decrees of the Council of Trent (1545–63), felt a need to clarify this state of affairs. It had to move carefully so as not to arouse too much trouble over what were often very long-established customs, and so in its wisdom it fulminated against the 'cohabitation' (even where this was not sexual) of engaged couples, but at the same time gradually reduced the gap between the date of the engagement and the nuptial blessing until, in the last days of Louis XIV's reign, it became obligatory to get engaged only the night before the wedding. Honour – or what was seen of it – was saved.

It was between 1560 and about 1640 that the state won the battle over the necessity of parental consent. The church was not so concerned with this aspect, as in its eyes the sacrament was constituted by the words and deeds of the young couple themselves, as long as they had passed the age of puberty. This clearly led to abuses, especially among the better-off, with some young husbands demonstrating their chief interest to be in the fortune and 'expectations' of their wives (they always found a priest to register their 'promises'): there are sober records containing allegations of abductions and rapes – sometimes renowned actual cases – which were a constant fear. About 1640, the joining together of the two tutelary powers provided reassurance for the fathers and mothers of well-to-do families. Very few had any serious worries anyway as parental, particularly paternal, authority was carried to a point which the young people of the late twentieth century would find hard to imagine: unpaid labour, no pocket-money, no time off – or what little there was strictly supervised – and corporal punishment at will. This continued until the age of majority, usually twenty-five, although this was fixed by custom rather than law; even after reaching this age both sons and daughters had to obtain the authority of their parents if they wanted to get married, in writing if necessary, and if this was refused they were forbidden to proceed until they had presented three 'respectful notices': even then daughters sometimes had to wait until they were thirty! This suggests that marriages were arranged by the parents in a good number of instances.

The revolution in the age of marriage

We can find out at what age people married when it becomes possible to compare certificates of baptism and of marriage for the same person, which – because women moved away from the village where they were born less often than men did – is easier to do in the case of women, and in the parishes where marriages were customarily 'solemnised'. We know from studies of the Paris region and in La Bresse (where the source material is of unusually fine quality), that women there were getting married at the age of eighteen or nineteen in about 1560. Analyses based on a broader sample show definitely that they were about twenty in the reign of Henry the Good, and that their fiancés were about twenty-five or older. Women gradually got married later and later. Except for Centre and Charente, where the old customs continued (for reasons I shall try to explain below), in the reign of Louis XIV, women married at twenty-three, twenty-four, or twenty-five, and quite often more, while their husbands were frequently more than twenty-seven, and quite often over thirty.

This undeniable change has been interpreted in different ways. Some historians have seen it as providing a form of contraception by continence or asceticism, as in practice a delay of this magnitude in the marrige of women (who are the only significant ones in this respect) leads to them having two fewer children (given, as we have seen, that childbirth occurs on average every two years). It may also be that people got married later under Louis XIV simply because it was more difficult, in what was a fairly depressed period, for newly married couples to find land or a house that were vacant, as the density of the rural population increased particularly sharply, and the French countryside appeared almost 'full' in terms of what was possible at that period. It would seem, in short, that young people put off getting married for essentially socio-economic reasons. This interpretation is borne out by the evidence of central France, where, in the large family-based communities, one of the newly-weds was simply welcomed into a large farm already in existence (that of the spouse), and the earlier age of marriage was retained. It has also been suggested that, with the reinforcement of the power of their parents, the engaged couple waited until the age of majority before they married. Frustratingly, none of these explanations can be proved; the second, however, seems the most likely one.

Pre-marital sexology

Given that illegitimate births were very uncommon in the seventeenth-century countryside (1–2 per cent of the total, although some were concealed in neighbouring towns), that unmarried mothers were treated with general contempt by their families, the church, and the parish, and that 'prenuptial conception' remained uncommon too (5–10 per cent at most), late marriage would seem to pose problems of sexual continence – a topic for which some authors have shown a particular predilection. Seen against the rather unbridled climate in England, with its wealth of bastards, engaged couples making love, and babies arrived hard on the heels of wedding ceremonies, France looks like an island of good behaviour, or dexterity, or else hypocrisy. But for a girl the situation was clear-cut enough: she was always watched closely, hardly ever left the maternal home and had good reason to be afraid of a dishonour that would lead to her exclusion from family and village life (remember that abortion was treated as infanticide and punished by death), and so sexual continence was the only answer. The only exceptions were those unfortunate servants who were frequently made to serve the pleasure of the master or his sons. Those who were 'good' – superficially, at least, the majority – could compensate to some extent by engaging in fairly innocent evening pastimes and dancing (which under Louis XIV the religious authorities set about banning with enthusiasm) and other festivities at haymaking and the vintage.

For the boys, who had less at stake, we have to rely heavily on memoirs and stories, of which there were very few, and on a few trial records. A few fairly shocking cases of sodomy and bestiality have been discovered, and these were normally punished with death: the severity of the penalty probably explains the rarity of these 'horrible crimes' (except at court). It also seems likely that some generous married women sometimes accommodated young bachelors, as did the occasional servant, and the unmarried mother who operated in most villages. Plenty of attention has been paid to the manuals compiled for confessors, and the amazing (Latin!) treatises on sexology left by the great specialists of the period, particularly the Jesuits, whose detailed knowledge is absolutely frightening. There is very little to be learned about the inhabitants of the countryside from the semi-intelligible testimony of these very unusual works, which have more to tell us about their authors than anything else. Our forebears (apart from a few eighteenth-century writers of varying quality) have told us nothing at all about the way in which they coped with their supposed continence. Common sense should help us to understand what went on, as well as the recollection of juvenile and adolescent life in the country – even in the twentieth century – before the widespread availability of effective means of contraception, in the days when girls 'were afraid'. One fact alone can be stated with certainty: people married as a rule fairly late during the seventeenth century, and almost never had children before marriage. The fact can be embellished with all sorts of hypotheses, dreams, and attitudes, but they will be no more than that.

But almost everybody got married, which means that confirmed bachelors were rare: the exceptions were the clergy, some servants (who were not always chaste), some who were disadvantaged, and those who escaped from rural life when it offered nothing to them and took the high road to the towns, to a life of migrant labour, vagabondage, and the army. Men, especially if they had some means and not very many children, remarried very soon after being widowed (sometimes only a few weeks or months after the death of the first wife, and preferably to a young woman), and this created complicated families with the children born of different mothers. It was less common for children to have more than one father, as widows found it harder to marry again, especially if they were responsible for a number of children and were somewhat exhausted. These simple and natural facts are supported by vast quantities of statistics, particularly for the reign of Louis XIV.

The when and why

On which day of the week and at what time of year did people get married? Weddings often took place on Tuesdays, sometimes on Mondays, as the latter end of the week was given over to the memory of Christ's Passion, and on Sundays the priest was too busy. The periods of Lent and Advent (roughly all of December) were excluded by the church. And the times when agricultural labour was most needed, particularly haymaking and the vintage, were also no good. May was also seldom chosen, as it was a month which (since Roman times) was regarded in many places as bringing bad luck. Marriage therefore tended to take place in the periods in-between, often in November, January, and February. In those months there was little to be done on the land, and in the parts of France where pigs were raised these, especially February, were the months when one of them would be killed, thus providing some solid nourishment for the guests. There is a superfluity of evidence about boisterous, prolonged, and bawdy wedding feasts, both written and visual, from which it appears that many families spent all their resources on these pagan celebrations. Yet hardly anyone has anything to tell us about what went on among poor peasants – or even those who did not have a pig to kill – and one suspects that their festivities were on a much smaller scale.

Why then did a couple choose to get married? This provoked questions among modern writers as well as earlier ones, and has given rise to a quantity of over-confident speculation. Retrospective investigation into the question may seem more difficult, or less verifiable, because it cannot easily be quantified. Nonetheless, there are several things to be learned from it, often reliable and confirmatory, which have sometimes been adduced. They are dressed up in scientific names of one sort or another, which I shall reduce to the geographic and the socio-professional.

It is proverbially true that in order to get married the partners must first know each other. With the sole exception of a very small number of marginal figures and travelling seasonal workers, journeys in the seventeenth-century countryside were never further than to the next market town, and the next parish was a day's walk away at most, and so most marriages were local affairs – especially for women as the weddings were usually celebrated at the house of their parents. Even in very small parishes, most marriages were to another member of the same parish: parochial endogamy reaches 65, 70, even 75 per cent and more. Three-quarters of those remaining were to people living at two or three leagues distance. A few brave folk from the ranks of rich farmers, rural merchants, and the more itinerant artisans sometimes went further afield in search of a wife who was their equal in social standing and wealth. Anything beyond that borders on the unlikely and the miraculous. Strangers, *horsins* as they were sometimes called, found difficulty in being accepted until they had been observed for some time, if not actually put to the test.

It will surprise nobody to learn that people normally married, not within their class or profession, as the two terms scarcely existed in their modern sense, but within their 'estate'. Which simply means (as almost all marriage certificates state) that unions were contracted between the children of labourers or *brassiers*, between the children of large tenant-farmers or well-established farmers, between the children of vignerons, or gardeners, and between the children of small artisans and the few rural domestic servants, i.e. between people of comparable condition of living standards. What one might call socio-professional homogamy was at its strongest among vignerons, sometimes reaching the almost unheard-of level of 90 per cent. Also the couples' ages are much more evenly matched than in any other area, because they married workmates who had particular specialist skills: consequently in areas, like the Seine valley in particular, where small-scale properties are the norm, it is tempting to say that rows of vines are making an alliance with other rows of vines; in fact, the interested parties themselves go so far as to put it in writing (or have somebody write it for them) when, because they are cousins, they have to obtain a dispensation of consanguinity before they can be joined in matrimony.

This brings the discussion on the reasons for marriage back to the point generally taken to be the crux of the issue: do marriages take place because of inclination, mutual interest, or by parental arrangement?

It has to be said at the outset that all the surviving documentation, or practically all, tends to support the least romantic hypothesis: the law and custom as it related to marriage (and to inheritance, as a marriage necessarily involved considering the possibility of two or three inheritances), the inflexible authority of the parents, and numerous certificates and contracts all show, quite clearly, that everything was negotiated in advance by the two families, and that the wedding brought together fields and meadows, increased the numbers of horses or cattle, and brought new strength to more experienced workers. Princes never married shepherdesses, though they sometimes seduced them, as Henry of Navarre used to, and as rich farmers did their servants.

In a small group of neighbouring parishes, though, where almost everybody knew each other, there must have been some scope for mutual attraction. Presumably, so long as there was not any great discrepancy between the position of the parents, and so long as the parents did not have other plans for them, an agreement could be reached. Moreover, not all official deeds relating to marriages have been preserved; in some provinces they were not even recorded, custom sufficing. These gaps demonstrate that we are talking in terms of probabilities rather than certainties. Indeed, in Normandy some rather touching requests for dispensation have been found, addressed to the episcopal see by, for the most part, cousins who are past the age of majority, saying that they suit each other and enjoy each other so much that they should be allowed to marry. It seems right, therefore, to make a small allowance for love marriages, although it must be said that romance of that sort rarely seems to have had a successful outcome. Every unequal marriage, not just where there was a disparity of ages, but where status was unequal, shocked the community and aroused mockery, derision, and often cruelty which went far further than the noisy, nocturnal, often bacchic ritual charivari. Well-off farmers' wives, prematurely widowed, who married their head servant were exposed to harsh reprisals even if the husband was quite worthy of the position. But examples of this sort are probably exceptional.

There was more to peasant marriage than just a sacrament, a change of age group, a possible sexual adventure (dubious, but who knows?), a variable set of rites and festivities, and the opportunity of arranging, often in writing, precise provisions for the future of the property when the inevitable successions took place, dividing it between parents, if they were still alive, future widow or widower, and any children there might be. It was also – perhaps primarily – the act of creating a new economic enterprise, or the renewal of an old economic enterprise, or (less commonly, as we shall see) entry into an already existing economic community.

It was therefore necessary in most cases – and this is probably the explanation of late marriages – for some smallholding to be vacant, or at least a cottage with some land around it, either owned or rented, on which a new couple could establish itself as the nucleus of a new family. In most parts of France, getting married meant leaving, leaving their parents' dwellings, unless one of them was left vacant by death, a situation which almost always speeded up the marriage. At all events, it meant setting up hearth and home, with the hearth the central fireplace, whose fire was the symbol of life and the (semi-pagan?) spirit of the house. It also meant taking on a tenancy, or share-cropping arrangement, or a smallholding, or a *borde*, or sometimes the parents' own farm.

The day after the wedding – or the day following that for the richest – a new life began, with its many tiring tasks, and the expectation of the first baby, a life that seemed mapped out in advance, for better or for worse – but not always in conjugal closeness, as the types of family turn out to be quite unexpectedly varied.

6

The different types of peasant families

The word 'family' is so loaded with emotional associations (the Holy Family, 'Travail-Famille-Patrie', 'Familles, je vous hais', the Two Hundred Families, and so on) that it is not easy to see the institution itself calmly and clearly. Added to which, so many sociologists, ethnologists, and historians have worked and written on, around, and beside the subject, that, despite a few notable exceptions, it is very hard work reaching the really quite simple essence of it.

In the seventeenth century, as later, the word seems to have been used in two senses, at least in the small half of the kingdom where French or one of its numerous dialects was spoken. In its broad sense it meant all the people united by ties of blood (lineage and issue), and also known collaterals (brothers, sisters and their spouses, uncles, aunts, and cousins). Normally this extensive group excluded anybody who lived far away (which meant more than 5 leagues, or 20 kilometres), and a good half-day's walk: occasionally, however, the family came together for a wedding or a christening (godparents – three at the start of the century, two later – were normally chosen from among these relations), but not, apparently, for burials. They might also come together on the day the parish celebrated its patron saint, or to join in the ceremonies at Christmas or St John's Eve – the sanctified solstitial festivals – or even to help at the start of the vintage, when a lot of labour was needed as the grapes had to be gathered in as quickly as possible. Those of us who were brought up in the country, and are old enough, will remember these festivities, which also sometimes included the opening of the hunting season. These occasions also involved the poor, who were numerous; we do not know what their celebrations were like, but one may suspect they were not very glamorous.

In ordinary usage, the word 'family' was used roughly in the sense it bears today, to refer to a couple, who were then always married, along with their children, occasionally a surviving grand-parent, and on rare occasions an unmarried brother or sister. They were usually called either the 'conjugal family', which is not very scientific, or the 'nuclear family' or 'mononuclear' family – a family with a single nucleus, the married couple. Historians and sociologists have long been at loggerheads over the length of time the nuclear family has been in existence. It has even been maintained that it was the general rule, if not universal, in almost all of Europe long before the seventeenth century. More detailed, first-hand evidence was required, and a number of studies have now been carried out. These have led to the conclusion that things are more complicated than was at first thought.

All the same, it remains certain that if we could draw up statistics on the family for the whole of the French countryside in the seventeenth century, we should find that the nuclear family predominated. But while it was almost the rule in the group of provinces that stretch from Anjou (perhaps from upper Brittany) down to and including Lorraine (and probably Alsace), and from the newly united Flanders to the banks of the Loire, the other regions presented a more complicated character.

The best procedure is for us to examine them, too.

Double families in the Midi

We shall start with that third of the French kingdom where everybody except the ruling classes, who had to be bilingual, spoke only the old dialects of the south, the different forms of the *langue d'oc*: in the southern Alps, Gascony and Limousin.

This first example will probably seem 'eccentric', as if the 'centre' was necessarily of supreme significance. It is drawn from the valley of Barcelonette, which only later (in 1713) became part of the kingdom. But it has been studied by somebody who has the advantage of being both an historian and descended from a long line of mountain dwellers from the upper Ubaye. Let Roland Warion himself explain.

A family was identified with a house. Talking of a junior branch of a family, people would say that they came from house A at place B. It ensured that there was land for every generation of the family . . . Often, house and land went together . . . At all events, the house was a rectangular building made of (local) stone with a vast four-sided roof which sheltered the family, animals, provisions and animal fodder for at least seven months . . . The size of the house was roughly proportionate to the amount of land owned. Every census (the earliest dates from 1702) gives exactly the same number of families as houses, and always gives six people per 'fire' . . . The house also includes all the buildings, plus land, plus the sequence of generations of one family that are born in it, live in it and on it and usually, though not always, die in it. Individuals had to conform to the required 'policy' for the maintenance of the house. This policy was based on a single axiom: never divide or diminish the patrimony. The result of this was that each generation had only one clutch in the nest, so to speak. Only one heir was allowed (even long after the Civil Code was established). The house and its land together comprised an Estate, a family estate like that of the Bourbons or the Habsburgs. The father was as much a ruler as a landowner. And in theory he governed for the greatest good of his house, and its continuation. The heir presumptive worked for nothing while he was waiting for his turn to govern; the daughters received dowries if they married; the younger sons got less than the daughters as they could emigrate (they went as far as Holland in the seventeenth century, and later, even to Mexico) whereas the daughters of an honourable family could not decently leave the area . . .

Widespread southern families of this sort, with a single heir, could only survive where the proprietors were of at least average wealth, as was fairly common in those regions. We know almost nothing about the poor wretches who had little or nothing to pass on to their descendants. All that can be said is that the nuclear family probably predominated, as a small house – even with a garden – cannot support two married couples and a number of other single adults.

Other very detailed studies of communities in Gascony, the Pyrenees across to Auvergne and Limousin show that, allowing for slight regional variations, the pattern was the same everywhere. There is always a fairly sizeable house where two couples live (or soon will live, or until recently did live) with several children, and now and then a brother or two or a sister lodged in a garret and working for their keep. The father, naturally, chooses who shall succeed him. This would normally, but not necessarily, be the oldest child; quite often a daughter would be nominated as heir, in which case care would be taken to marry her to a strong, sensible husband, who would have to be a younger son, so as not to endanger the future of the house from which he came. Almost everywhere in the south, particularly in Gascony, the house meant more than the individual. This can be seen in the way people in everyday life were called by their christian name, followed by the name of the house they came from, instead of using the patronymic: before long, would be added the name of the new house, while not forgetting the original one.

Large families in the central part of France

It might be thought that these double-nuclear families, where a young couple take over from an older one, only thrived in the south, in those large households where an extra child or unmarried sister could easily be accommodated, and where there were always six at the table or round the fire – large family groups who were kept together also by the need for labour on extensive holdings of land. And yet we do not often come across the tidy, conjugal nuclear entity which has been thought of as so typically French, cultivating a small field and garden outside its little cottage, with a pigsty with a (small) pig wallowing in it, a pen with two or three small sheep, and maybe a shed for the (small) cow, if that does not live in the cottage itself. (Livestock then was roughly half the weight it is now, so the epithet 'small' was meant quite literally.)

We quite often discover other instances of large, complex family groups, especially in wooded areas suitable for rearing livestock, in parts of France where they are unexpected.

In La Courtine, in upper Marche (what is now the *département* of la Creuse) there was a priest in the mid-eighteenth century who was interested in demography and genealogy and traced the families in his *cure* back for five generations, and so back to the middle of the seventeenth century. More than two-thirds of his parishioners and their forebears had lived and still lived in loose but complex family groups, which always contained at least two conjugal nuclei (the parents and the designated heirs) plus one or two married collaterals, the surviving unmarried ones, and a fluctuating number of vulnerable children. In most cases the children left the 'family-stock', the normal arrangement being as follows.

One child was kept at home, and the dowry which came with the son- or daughter-in-law was used to compensate the brothers, as the dowry was paid strictly to the father of the bride or groom. Except in cases of incompatibility (which were allowed for in the contracts, but rarely occurred), the newly married couple had to live in the communal house and work there in return for clothing and shelter. The gift to them from the parents of all their possessions was fictional, as they retained the life-interest. A system of this sort naturally forbids marriage between heirs, with the joining of their property, which at least left something for a younger brother; and if there were several brothers, they would wait around, living in some nook of the house and working for nothing, in reserve, in case one or more of the heirs died. In that event second and third marriages would take place, the participants often of widely differing ages, in order to achieve the most important aim, which was to safeguard the household, and of course the land, which must always have been fairly extensive. Such was the 'system' at La Courtine.

It is clear from a family structure of this sort that paternal authority must have reached a very high level, and that the situation of the heirs was humiliating enough, let alone that of the younger brothers, who would sometimes leave in disgust for other occupations and other places. But the majority probably grew resigned and accustomed to what we would call slavery but what they probably saw as the traditional, thus in those days eminently respectable, ways of life.

There is no doubt that this sort of family was to be found not only in the central part of France but also in the west and – though not so recently – in the north, where it would not have been possible for one man alone to work the large farms, even with a wife's help. Various leases (for tenant-farming or share-cropping) which have been found here and there provide the evidence for this. Since the sixteenth century a prudent, resident nobility in Poitou had divided the land into large, forty-hectare share-cropping tenancies, and these needed reliable, well-established peasants to work them, the choice often being joint tenancies between father and son, father and son-in-law, or brother and brother-in-law. Thus in 1545 the 'noble place, tenancy and holding of la Brunetière' (in the parish of Vautebis, Vienne) was let for six years to Thomas and Jehan Pouldretz, farmers, and their mother Perrette Escale. Twenty-two years later, two Jehan Giraults, father and son, take the lease of another one at Saint-Martin-du-Fouilloux (Deux-Sèvres). A century after that, in the parish of Tallud, Toussaint and Mathurin Vernin, father and son, beef farmers, took on a 50 per cent share-cropping tenancy at Besançay. Later still, a married couple and the children of a first marriage who were still under the age of twenty-five (and therefore minors), all farmers who had 'lived together in one community at the Prieur tenancy', moved into one at Boutilly, near Bressuire.

These instances, which are all taken from the admirable work of Dr Louis Merle, an historian of Niort, fully demonstrate that where the farms were of a size to make it desirable, large families lived and worked on them. It is certain that if parts of Brittany and Anjou were studied in similar detail, they would show comparable family patterns; and some have been located in modern Finistère.

Frérèches *and communities of farmers*

One phrase in the third contract from Poitou deserves closer examination: 'lived together in one community'. It once more poses, in an unexpected context, the much-discussed questions of family communities. The main area in which they were to be found was the old Nivernais province, where somebody called Guy Coquille (well-known in his time) made a serious study of the custom, describing the communities and trying to systematise them. Some survived well into the nineteenth century. But people, apart from some amateur folklorists and earlier sociologists like Le Play, normally regard them as curiosities, not to be taken too seriously. But reading the notarial records and the tax assessment books, it becomes clear that they were more widespread than this suggests. 'Family communities' were definitely numerous, powerful, and very much alive, and in the mid-seventeenth century were characteristically found not only in the Nivernais, but also – if less frequently – in the Bourbonnais, part of Limousin and Berry, and perhaps in some neighbouring regions as well.

Despite the rather flattering picture of them that is sometimes presented, these communities consisted essentially of a few simple features. Each would be a large farm, with a good number of pastures of various sorts and qualities, and therefore plenty of livestock, either 'red' (cattle) or 'white' (sheep) as they used to say. In the middle stood a large building, with a huge communal hall, and a number of rudimentary small rooms. Here lived between twelve and thirty individuals, sometimes even more, all related to each other and under the authority of a 'head and master', usually the oldest of the men, who formally elected him to the position. Land, house, livestock, harvest, furniture, farm and kitchen implements, money – everything was held in common, and the master made all the decisions, perhaps with the aid of two of the *parsonnier* farmers (i.e. two who had an interest in the community). But the master alone signed the livestock leases, the farm leases, and even each community member's marriage contracts. All marriages, in fact, were arranged between the heads of two communities who knew each other, one of whom needed a new male or female for his community, usually because somebody had died. So the newly married bride or groom left their own community for good, and joined the new one, enriching it with a dowry. If new members disliked the new surroundings, or became a widow or widower without issue, they were free to leave, but they could take nothing with them except their personal belongings, and a few livres-tournois by way of viaticum. They were free to marry again if they wanted to, as long as it was outside the two communities, which would mean a simple conjugal existence, and probably extreme poverty.

The communal life of so many men, women, and children obviously gave rise to quarrels. The circuitous phrasing of notarial documents often reveals a community splitting up, and the difficulties this involved, especially when those who were leaving were fairly numerous, and not content to take nothing with them but their clothes and a three-livre piece. In the nineteenth century, where the documentation makes it easier to study these matters, many of these communities seem to be rather rich, although of course by then they had become unusual, which they certainly were not in the reign of Louis XIV. The communities were known as *taisible* communities (i.e. tacit, but subject to customary law), or sometimes *frérèches* (where they comprised only brothers and sisters, both married and unmarried, a situation which, of its nature, cannot be sustained in its pure form for very long), and they were strongly characteristic of a good part of central France. Whether they were a majority is uncertain, but in most places they probably were not. The frequency of their occurrence varied. They may possibly have existed in other provinces, particularly in the west.

But it is fairly certain that there were no longer any communities of this sort on the great wheat plains of the Paris basin by the seventeenth century, even though some of the huge farms there, before they came to be run by the great 'cocks of the village' with permanently employed servants and some temporary labour, were farmed by *consorties*, associates, two or three peasant couples, bound together more for economic than family reasons, though often related to some extent as well, because one couple on their own would not have had sufficient resources of livestock or implements to do what was necessary.

The primacy of the nuclear family in the north

From the Sarthe to the Rhine and from the Scheldt to the Loire, the nuclear family was almost universal. Such families are to be found elsewhere, but they tend to be where the farms are not very large, and to be somewhat overshadowed by larger and more complex family groupings, which must once have been even more important than they were in the seventeenth century.

One tends to think of the nuclear family in the north of France at this period either as living an idyllic life, or sunk in the direst poverty. Some would have had very little money, others more, but the evidence for this does not come from the family structure. The popular image, largely the work of the eighteenth century, has a couple with children – lots of children – and a grandfather by the chimney-corner: an affecting picture, which may occasionally have been an accurate representation. But as a general one, it poses problems, the easiest of which to solve is that of the grandparents.

The traditional image, still tucked away in some corner of our memory, depicts the grandmother rocking her grandchildren to sleep with lullabies, reciting fairy tales and rhymes, all the while keeping an eye on the pot, and a white-haired grandfather carving small toys out of wood for them. At the beginning of this century, the historian Lucien Febvre even thought that the grandparents 'educated' the children, and passed on their sound traditions to them. But in fact our ideas of traditional civilisation mostly come from the nineteenth century and it is only then, or perhaps at the end of the eighteenth, that grandparents came into their own. It is now twenty years since Jean Fourastié showed, with the support of statistics, that during the reign of Louis XIV men and women who married between the ages of twenty-five and thirty had only one of their four parents at the wedding, and that would probably be one of the women. In addition, wherever it has proved possible to draw up an age-pyramid for a village or a small region, usually at a date fairly late in the seventeenth century, those over sixty years of age have never made up more than 6 or 7 per cent of the total population, almost three times less than the figure today. Indeed it is enough to read well-kept parish registers (marriage certificates and burial certificates) to understand why a grandfather by the fire was most uncommon, or at best a very short-lived phenomenon. Those who were still alive shared in the work of the house, the garden and the cow-shed, and no particular attention seems to have been paid to them when they lost their strength or became bedridden. The rest of the family probably waited rather impatiently for the disappearance of the useless mouth, and perhaps sometimes helped it on its way. Pity appears to have played little part in the harsh lives of the rural population three centuries ago. (Can we really say that we have passed that stage today?) Yet there also seems sometimes to have been a degree of admiration and respect for the exceptionally long-lived. Octogenarians were readily reputed to be 100 years old, a fact which the priest would duly inscribe in the parish records. Unfortunately, each time it has been possible to check one of these assertions, it has proved to be an exaggeration.

It was also fairly uncommon for there to be more than a small number of children, at least where the same couple was concerned. The average gap between births was two years, with death accounting for a quarter of very young children, and another quarter of older ones. A few 'true' instances may cast some light on this perhaps surprising assertion.

At Auneuil, in the Bray area, somewhat west of Beauvais, Thomas Alépée, labourer (who could nonetheless sign his name correctly) married Antoinette Roblin (who signed hers with a cross), on 11 July 1662. Both lived in the parish, and neither had any parents still living. Their birth certificates have not been found, but when Antoinette died on 8 March 1699 the priest described her as 'about sixty'. He gave the same age for her husband when he buried him, five years later. In thirty-seven years of marriage (which was quite a long time), she was fertile for twenty-two, which suggests that she was not much more than twenty when she married. Her first child was born thirteen months after the wedding, and lived for only five months. Four more children followed every two years: a second, Marie, and a boy, Simon, lived for a few months. The other two, Anne and Françoise, were more resilient, both getting married, at Auneuil of course, one at twenty-four, the other at thirty-six. Anne we know lived to the age of sixty-six, dying in 1733. The last five children were born at slightly longer intervals: three of these died in infancy, the last, Antoinette, at three days old, in May 1684. However, two successive Marguerites grew up and married, one at twenty-four, the other at twenty-eight, and both died in the same year, in 1748. But between the first pair of girls and the second there was a thirteen-year gap. None of them became anything other than ordinary poor peasants, and none of them moved away from the same village, which was fairly large, having about 1,000 inhabitants. The fate of the Alépées of Auneuil (the surname has not disappeared) is representative of many such instances at the time.

Georges Durand has made a more systematic study of another part of France altogether, the area around Lyons, particularly Saint-Genis-Laval. There, for example, the Renard–Mortier household had seven children between 1694 and 1711, but by the latter date there were only three children living. The Ferlet–Jangots despite having seven children only had three live at one time – briefly – in the sixth year of their marriage: in the eight years that followed they never had more than two alive simultaneously, and sometimes only one. The Raymond–Bourgins, Jacquême and Alexis (aged sixteen and fourteen) had to coddle or rebuke Anne (who was seven) and rock or ignore Claude (who was one year old). We may wonder what Etienne Renard, at fifteen, thought of Mathieu, eight, and Marguerite, five, the sole survivors of his six brothers and sisters. No great spirit of comradeship can have existed between them, of the sort that normally springs from the carefree games and confidences of childhood. Separated from the younger ones by six years or more, the elder brothers or sisters were often caught, if not crushed, between the helping or watching over the younger children and sharing the adult tasks in the house and the fields.

These are just a few of a whole set of observations which, taken together, amply demonstrate that houses full of small children were exceptional. They also show that the amount of help which could be expected from children doing small extra tasks in the fields was almost always minimal, belated, and unpredictable. A father could not hope for the services of a strong young man until years of marriage had gone by, and as the father by then would be about forty-five or forty-eight years of age, this became less of a help than a replacement. If none but daughters survived, he had to find a strong, active son-in-law. Until that point was reached, many peasants worked their inheritance or their tenancy on their own, the children being just so many mouths to feed.

Of course, there were exceptions to this pattern. At Saint-Genis-Laval, again, the Prost–Brosse household, married in the last decade of the seventeenth century, saw the birth of six children in thirteen years, and they all survived in what was a very harsh period.

All this explains why it was that, on Vauban's advice, the government made its first serious attempt to carry out a census; they calculated that there was a ratio of four or five between the number of families and the total number of inhabitants. To put it more simply, this meant that at a given moment there were at most two or three children alive and living with their parents. As we know that there were infertile couples (as well as those individuals who were not married), and also some more prolific ones, this gives us a set of snapshots which is not all that different from the modern situation – although of course the social and intellectual context was completely different.

And there is another aspect of the composition of these seventeenth-century families which is not often emphasised, except in Brie, which is that a considerable proportion, possibly a quarter, of families were what have been called mixed or complex families, because they included the children of more than one marriage. Many unions were interrupted quite early on by the death of one or other partner, and a third lasted for less than ten years. Then a new father or a new mother had to be found for the young children, and to take over the running of the house or the land: hence the often speedy remarriages, which often led to more children. Thus if we take some examples from the area round Meaux – from Vareddes, Chambry, Nareuil, Saint-Souplet, etc. – we find Marie Noël, who died in 1683, leaving three girls, Marie, Marguerite, and Nicole, the children successively of her three husbands, Laurent Oudot, Pierre Trouet, and Nicholas Cauchois. Clémence Lucas, who died in 1679, had two children, Etienne and Jeanne, from her first marriage to Jacques Régnier; she then married Michel Charlot, a widower with three children, and had another daughter by him before she died. Michel Charlot, who died in 1680, had time to get married for a third time, to Magdelaine Tavernier.

These complex families, with children of several marriages, accounted for about 20 per cent of the total at the end of the seventeenth century: earlier in the century when more young adults seem to have died, and marriages were consequently shorter, the figure must have been more like 25 per cent.

In most cases these gave rise to problems of inheritance and succession, which the seigneurial tribunals spent a great deal of time settling (as we know from their archives); the children, particularly those who were orphans, tended to be 'lent out cheaply' to some relation who was prepared to take charge of them, sometimes for nothing, or rather for their labour and the small help they were able to give, and sometimes for a small annual rent – a few tens of livres – which was paid out of what little property the dead parents had left, property which these so-called tutors made use of. The negotiations involved in this were carried on in the 'assembly of relations' (the family in its extended sense) before the seigneurial judge, and often must have provided a distressing, if not sordid, spectacle, particularly where the orphans were very young or inherited very little. This all helps to explain or provide some basis for that old and seemingly maudlin fund of stories about 'poor little orphans', who were maltreated, persecuted, abandoned, sold, or subject to fugues.

It is difficult to know whether it is justifiable, on the basis of these exact, verified examples, to say that the fate of the children in the seventeenth century was frequently hard, and that indifference and hardship reigned in most families, where – in the case of nuclear families – there were fewer children than used to be thought. Historians can have a good deal of insight into material situations, but they cannot see much of what goes on in people's souls, and what glimpses they do have tend to be rather shallow. Feelings themselves, if not their expression, usually escape their grasp.

On the other hand, historians know where they are with earthly nourishment.

7

Daily bread

When Breughel or Rubens and a host of less well-known figures painted scenes of feasting, carousal, and fête, they represented people letting go and enjoying themselves at local festivities which might be traditional, pagan, religious, or all three. The pictures are full of cut hams, strings of sausages, smoking-hot joints of venison, great glassfuls of golden or deep-red wine, while the peasants dance clumsily, indulge in sexual horseplay and gluttony. Do these represent lively moments of collective liberation? Or duller northern versions of Gargantuan stories? Or are they a faithful, as well as talented, picture of the 'festive' release of spirits in the richest provinces in the world, with the richest peasantry, Holland, Flanders, Brabant, and Hainault? Louis XIV certainly annexed part of these fertile lands, mostly between Arras and what is now the border with Belgium; but his armies and his supercilious legislation could hardly have been conducive, for the time being at least, to such festivities, which had become very rare in the kingdom of France, despite the Rabelaisian legend.

So is the well-known painting by the brothers Le Nain a more accurate representation of the peasant family at table, with its white tablecloth, golden loaf, light-red wine and the honest simplicity of dress and furnishings? Clearly not, as the cloth and the wine are both out of place, and the bread is far too white. Surely those strict believers, the Le Nains, wanted merely to provide an obviously symbolic, slightly popular, version of the Last Supper, using the bread, the wine, and the whiteness of the cloth.

However interesting the painters, especially the great painters, may be, they do make choices and they change things. So do writers, perhaps to a greater extent, whether they are writing pastorals with shepherds and beribboned shepherdesses or realistically stressing the worst and therefore exceptional periods, when epidemics, plague, famine, or quartered soldiers, or even all of them together, ruled the countryside.

Once again, we need to look at the documents closest to peasant life, drawn up by those who knew them well, to obtain the completest and most accurate information. The principal sources are therefore the court scribes, notaries, priests, and the agents of the seigneur; the government records are less useful as the administrators of the provinces only rarely dealt with these material details. The inventories that were compiled after a death often say what the hearths, the flour-bins, and the chests (when there were any) contained, as well as cellars, granaries, courtyards, the few rods of garden, and sown fields, where appropriate.

Types of corn and types of bread

The words which appear most often in these numerous and humble texts are 'bread' and 'corn'. Corn, *bled* as they spelled it, was defined as any cereal which could be used to make bread. Not only bread, though, since barley, oats, millet, buckwheat, and maize (which was introduced at the beginning of the seventeenth century) were frequently used in different sorts of porridge, *galette*, or thick pancakes, which were not just for the toothless of all ages but in some provinces, such as Brittany and Aquitaine, were for general consumption.

Nevertheless, bread remained symbolic both of basic religious and physical nourishment, even among well-off country people; and the breaking of the bread was for long the solemn, almost sacred gesture with which the paterfamilias signalled the start of each meal. For some time now it has been established that expenditure on bread and flour absorbed easily half a poor or humble family's income. To this it should be added that an adult consumed three pounds of bread a day, or more. The reason for this is entirely obvious: bread was far and away the cheapest source of calories.

But what kind of bread? When and how did they eat it, and what did they eat with it?

When most people in twentieth-century France talk about corn, they mean wheat, and when they talk about bread, they mean white bread: the return of 'country-style bread', especially in the large towns, is an inept gesture from our wasteful civilisation towards the great grey loaves of our ancestors. In the seventeenth century, to a greater degree than the eighteenth and even the sixteenth, the corn that was sown, and thus the flour and the bread, was an uneven and unpredictable mix of wheat, rye, and sometimes winter barley. Around Paris they called it *mesteil*, and in the provinces there were twenty words for the same thing. Sometimes a more precise name indicated the proportions in which the grain was mixed: from two-thirds/one third to three-quarters/one quarter, with rye, of course, being the larger part. Rye on its own does not make good bread, and was only used in those regions where local conditions required it, in the mountains or where the ground was too cold. The grain was threshed with flails, a long job which called for strong workers, either in the open air, as in the Midi, or more often in barns, as in the rest of France, which was fairly wet. Then the grain, often badly sorted and badly kept (prey to parasites, damp, and fermentation due to overheating in the granary), was taken to the mill sack by sack and came back having lost at least a sixth of its weight (that was the current rate taken by the miller, though he ritually tricked customers out of more than that), but still with some of its bran. The next stage was the kneading and the cooking, which constituted two separate acts, and in which women played a prominent part. In some places the cooking was done in a communal oven or in one belonging to the seigneur (which had to be paid for), and in others in individual ovens which were sometimes built on to the end of the house: it varied according to the province and the relative power of the seigneur and the collectivity. Cooking was done for a week at a time at least, often for a fortnight or more, and enormous round loaves were produced, with thick crusts when the flour was good enough, so that these ten or twenty pound 'wheels' would last without going too hard. Stale bread was always consumed, out of economy, and, besides, hard bread was much better for pouring soup on to.

Not everybody had soup, though. Substitutes are found here and there, depending on local resources or the ingenuity of farmers, though these may be relics of earlier times. The *milhade* or *millasse* that is found throughout the south-west, a porridge of improved maize, may have taken the place of one made of millet when the American plant became established between 1630 and 1650. This coarse millet, *milhoc*, had an almost undreamed-of yield, 30 to 1 instead of 5 or 6 to 1 for ordinary corn. Its introduction enabled famine to be brought under control, and enabled quantities of sacks full of good wheat from Aquitaine and Languedoc to be exported by river, by canal (from the Midi), and by sea (soon to be sent to the Antilles), as the peasants were now able to spare it.

A similar process occurred in Brittany, a major exporter of wheat, whose inhabitants had had to put up with rye until buckwheat became established, in the sixteenth century. (It had long been grown in the sandy and cold parts of Germany and Britain, and in the mountains, whence it may have been introduced.) Its slow growth cycle enabled it to succeed where other crops failed (and sometimes, perhaps, vice versa). Because this black corn was exempted from the seigneurial mill, the peasants were able to install small individual hand-mills, to make metal sheets called *galetières*. They wiped these with a scantily buttered rag before pouring on the porridge and spreading it out with a sort of spoon called a *tournette* – all these utensils are listed in the inventories – to make the buckwheat pancackes called *galettes*, which have recently become famous, but which must have tasted like eggless omelettes, thick, heavy, and tending to lie on the stomach. The peasants were not able to wash them down with a basinful of cider, either, as apple trees were only just being introduced into the Breton-speaking areas, from Normandy.

A less striking but to some extent similar situation is to be seen in Limousin and the surrounding areas, and perhaps in other places too. The basic food (with some salt pork, fortunately made possible by a plentiful supply of acorns for the pigs) was provided by rye and sweet chestnuts, usually boiled and mashed. The two could complement each other or take each other's place, since they grew in entirely different conditions. Nonetheless, it did occasionally happen that both failed in the same year, even well into the eighteenth century: when that happened the traditional emigration intensified, and the (many) animals were sold sooner. But they had some very thin soups.

Soup

It seems that, in most places, soup was the main food at *déjeuner* (eaten in the morning, breaking the nocturnal fast), at *dîner* (in the middle of the day), and at *souper* (in the evening). What we would call stock cooked slowly in the hearth, over a fire of wood or cinders in a pot that was more likely to be earthenware than metal, hanging from the inevitable chimney-hook, the very spirit of the hearth. Into water fetched from the well, the river or the pond (fortunately boiled!) they put whatever they could find in the way of herbs and root vegetables from the garden or the open fields, where small squares of catch-crops were grown in the ritual three-year rotation. These would not include potatoes (except in some mountainous areas in the east at the end of the century), but there would be plenty of radishes – of a hard, yellowish variety that seems to be almost extinct today – a few carrots and turnips (these were often kept back for sale), sometimes a leek or two, not many of the green vegetables we use today, although there were twenty or so local kinds of cabbage which still survived at the beginning of this century, and plenty of almost forgotten farinacious foods of the pea and bean variety (field-beans, *favelottes*, yellowish and greyish peas, the only survivor from which is the chick-pea, and in Picardy the unpleasant *bisaille*, a mixture of peas and vetches, which surfaced again in the years after 1940). These did not often all appear together as they were dependent on good harvests and effective storage; and there would not have been nearly so much during the miserable winters of north and central France as in the summers.

In those relatively rare parts of the country where pigs were kept, a piece of well-salted fat, old and therefore somewhat rancid, swam in the broth, staying there for several days before being taken out and chewed between the remaining teeth of the paterfamilias. On feast days in the regions where olive and more importantly nut oil were produced, they added a few drops of the precious liquid (the first pressing would have been sold); in Brittany they did the same with some well-salted butter. There was also a great variety of herbs, so-called *fines herbes*, growing wherever the climate and the time of year allowed, and very different in the south from in the country round the Loire: chives, spring-onions, tarragon, sage, savory, thyme, basil, shallots, onion stalks, crushed or whole or cooked garlic; all these, separately or together, could give flavour to the pot and its contents, the true *potée*. When it was ready everybody brought their earthenware or wooden bowls to the hearth, or to the table if there was one, and the father or mother cut the bread into each receptacle and then poured over an amount of broth appropriate to everybody's age and needs. The soup would be rich in autumn, but considerably less so by the end of winter.

Near the sea or large rivers, a fairly thick and highly spiced fish soup was less a culinary speciality than the mere utilisation of the fruits of fishing and gathering: it went by various names, such as *bourride*, *mouclade*, *pauchouse*, and *bouillabaisse*, and was the maritime or waterside substitute for the 'earthy' peasant soup.

After the soup the peasants did not usually have anything. Perhaps sometimes there might be a bit of extra soup, or a crust of bread rubbed with garlic or onion, depending on the region, or in the richer households spread with something more solid, such as butter or dripping; there might be some of the less saleable fruits or berries, in season; in mountainous and very pastoral areas there might be some hard or slightly rancid cheese. The poorest would have no more than a hunk of dry bread.

This very widespread absence of dairy products, fruit, and especially meat (except for special occasions or among the rich) can be explained by two simple facts which are seldom, however, noted, one regional, the other social. They are facts which intrude time and again in this series of descriptions.

The majority of the poor in the countryside farmed only two or three acres, and tried to live off this land completely, which they were more or less able to do as long as the weather was kind and the harvests were good. But they were all forced to find money with which to pay the royal taxes (which went up sharply after 1635), as they had to be paid in coin, as well as to pay seigneurial and other dues. That is why they always had to take their eggs, young cocks, butter and cheese, and the best of the fruit and vegetables to market, or to the neighbouring big house, seigneurial or not. They could keep little for themselves except what was strictly necessary or unsaleable, like the overripe fruit which they threw into a barrel half-filled with water, along with a few leaves that were deemed 'tasty', to make their unappetising daily drink.

Meat was hardly ever seen except on feast days. Horse was never eaten as its meat was thought to be tainted. If there were cows, then any calves would naturally be sold, as would any lambs; old beasts too were sold rather than eaten. Which leaves the 'mystery' of the rabbit and the pig. Pigs foraged, burrowed, and were greedy enough to eat anything, but basically lived on acorns and sometimes beechmast (there were never any left-overs for them, as everything was always eaten), and they were kept in quite large numbers in wooded, forested, or mountainous regions, or where there were enough oak trees growing individually or in thickets (often the property of the seigneur). In the broad plains of the Paris basin and the surrounding area pigs were scarcer: fewer than ten per village. But elsewhere everybody – except the poor, and they were fairly numerous – kept at least one, usually a sow so she could litter, one boar being sufficient for each village. The meat was salted, but not always very adequately (except in those provinces such as Brittany where salt was freely available), and this was used, a little bit at a time, the only regular meat in their diet, and not very nourishing at that.

The rabbit, which has been such an important element in the diet of the poor in the last two centuries, was seldom bred outside large towns like Paris (where Boileau cites it scornfully in his 'repas ridicule'). There were no hutches or domesticated rabbits in the seventeenth-century countryside, nor, probably, in the eighteenth. What was the point of feeding rodents which swarmed all over the woods and fields anyway? Hunting them was naturally forbidden, as being yet another seigneurial privilege. But snares were certainly used universally. When a couple of gamekeepers were sent out into the countryside, there was a constant stream of reports of poaching. There is no need to have looked through one of the old registers kept by the Waters and Forests administration (carefully reorganised by Colbert after 1669) to believe in peasant wisdom on this point, much less when it was the remains of a dismembered boar or deer that were discovered. Quite apart from the pleasure of poaching, wild rabbits must have gone some way towards supplying much-needed animal protein. Cats may also have served that purpose, when there happened to be more of them than were necessary for keeping down mice in the granaries and barns.

The number of days of abstinence, the *jours maigres* – Fridays, Lent, and others – came to well over 100 a year, but what must have seemed some sort of penitence to the rich gourmands of the towns was no hardship, nor indeed anything out of the ordinary, for poor or average country-dwellers. They did not even have to go out to the fishmonger to buy cod or Dutch herring. All they had to do was stick to their normal pittance. If they wanted to eat fish, there were rich, tempting stocks in pools, ponds, and rivers (and in the sea for those who lived by it). Nonetheless, there can have been few rivers like the Dordogne, with its thousands of shad, lampreys, and salmon, not to mention the small-fry like grey mullet (sold at 2 sous each), and gudgeon (sold at 3 sous a pound). In that situation they must surely have kept some back for their own use. In principle, of course, the fishing rights belonged to the seigneur (again), but he frequently either let them out or allowed people to fish there, depending on the finances, as he could not catch or consume everything himself. There is no doubt, though, that river poaching (and poaching in ponds, too, which were sometimes emptied by bands of peasants) was a well-established practice. A perverse sense of fun and the pleasure of the exploit itself (sometimes they put the fish 'to sleep' with 'drugs') must have been as important as the desire for different, and good-tasting, food. Here, too, the registers recording contraventions of this sort are very far from empty.

The food at feasts

In the rustic and provincial cuisine we eat so much of with so much enjoyment, dishes tend simply to be called 'traditional' without an explanation of what the tradition was, where it came from or, most important, when it dates from: and so far we have seen no signs of it. These dishes are by no means legendary, however, except perhaps in the extent to which they are said to have been used; but they would never be found in the cooking pots or basins of the humble peasantry who made up the majority of the country-dwellers, and with whom we are concerned here. They are only to be found on feast days, or in those large stone houses, stoutly half-timbered beneath slate or tile roofs, with their barns, granaries, stables, cow-sheds, sheep-pens, pigsties, and a courtyard full of fowls. Each house would have a store-room or cellar stocked with full barrels and barrels waiting to be filled, with tall earthenware jars, bulging pots, and asymmetrical opaque bottles, in which were kept oil, wine, cider, fat pork, maybe some veal, preserves, and some fine hams would be hanging from the ceiling. In the main room, near the hearth, would be brass or cast-iron utensils, copper pans, plates of earthenware (or later faience), and a set of pewter cutlery for important occasions.

There the stews were redolent of fat pork or even ham, and butter, oil or lard, with cabbage, or peas (i.e. haricot beans – a curious name, given that a *haricot* is a stew made of small pieces of meat mixed with ordinary vegetables), or sun-ripened tomatoes or other vegetables, depending on the region. Then there would be dried sausage, or smoked pork, a hen or capon, a fat goose at Christmas, a lamb at Easter, sometimes a stewed chicken on a Sunday. All the regional differences can be seen roughly symbolised in what ethnologists like to call the 'foundations' of a cuisine: in the west, this was butter, in the south-west goose-fat, in the Mediterranean south olive oil; in some places they used lard, and in a few they made do with nut oil or rapeseed oil. Then, to round off these feasts or *disners* of the rich, there would be all sorts of crêpes, fritters, *bugnes*, *merveilles*, *pets de nonnes* (*sic*), tarts, *clafoutis*, with spice-breads and brioches for the pre-Lenten feasts of Candlemas and Shrove Tuesday, and for other special festivals. At the foot of the table, the servants and day-labourers sucked the bones, gobbled the offal and finished up the left-overs.

This rich cuisine is found not only among the most well-off in the countryside but also, in the nature of things, in the nearby towns, which lived off the country and its best and freshest products. It was the town cooks, in fact, who improved, enriched, and sometimes refined the simple, plentiful, and tasty dishes and the least poor country people took these over in the following centuries, while the town-dwellers looked for new refinements. It is this style of cooking, half-urban, half-rural, which we get in a more or less adulterated form today when we think we are returning to the cuisine of our ancestors, while the food industry in fact provides most of what we eat.

Drinks

Going back to the seventeenth century, it is obvious that both great feasts and poor gruel must have been washed down with something. In the big houses and the larger share-cropping farms, the master would have had local wine, or wine from a neighbouring province (or on the coast of Brittany, Spanish wine, sent by sea!) at his table, at least from time to time. But except in times of extravagant generosity, servants would not be entitled to any. Ordinarily they made do with *buvande*, *boisson* or *demi-vin*: this would be made of water poured on to the well-pressed grape stalks, pips, and skins, or else a crude decoction of leaves and berries. The apple trees which, by the seventeenth century were just beginning to spread from Normandy into neighbouring regions to the east and west, provided a drink of varying strength (sometimes taking the place of the older perry), which came increasingly to be appreciated, and although it was bad for the teeth and the digestive tract the peasants could probably get used to anything. Beer, an old Gallic drink, was only drunk in the north and east; the best would be kept for feast days, the more usual drink being 'small' beer which was light and probably fetid.

But the most universal and the most frequent drink, especially among the least well-off, was water: river-water (even in Paris), pond-water, and water from wells that were only a couple of paces from the dungheap or the flax-retting pit. This water was infinitely more polluted than ours, though not in the same ways. It carried every imaginable miasma and virus, and was probably responsible for a large number of epidemics of digestive and other diseases, the effects of which were multiplied by the complete absence of hygiene; this situation was also responsible for the greater part of all deaths among recently weaned children. That is why drinking wine (or cider) was long seen as conferring biological and social benefits, and its medicinal properties were taken very seriously.

When the feast days came round, the poor threw themselves on the wine, as well as the food, in a kind of frenzy. Christmas, Shrove Tuesday, with all its revenges and 'reversals' (if such really occurred), Palm Sunday, Easter Sunday, blazing, solstitial St John's Eve, often Michaelmas (29 September), always the village saint's day: all provided an opportunity for festivities that were sometimes of Pantagruelian proportions, dreamed of through weeks of fasting, brief moments into which had to be crammed all excesses, all the letting off of steam and getting their own back. In physiological terms, it was not very wise to suffer 350 days of abstinence in order to enjoy 15 days of feasting of a kind that the country weddings could, until recently, give some indication of. But, taken with the brutal transition from starvation to satiety, it could explain the hours of violence that followed the months of stultifying labour, and the frenzied reactions of natures that were alternately excited and depressed. One of these opportunities for excess which continued for a long time, and perhaps still exists in some parts of the country, was the quasi-ritual killing of the pig at the onset of winter. For this, the family grew to include cousins and sometimes neighbours, for there was plenty of work to be done, and some of the savoury products had to be eaten quickly: the blood, in the form of black pudding, some of the offal, the first pâtés, and whatever else they wanted. All day they ate, drank, sang, danced, and the whole event ended in sentimentality, copulation, or a free-for-all. Very often, particularly in Limousin, marriages were arranged at the same time as these pork-feasts: some sharp tongues compared the sacrifice of the pig to that of the bride, or brides, as the one animal was enough for several weddings. There might be something there to amuse modern psychologists, if they were interested.

But whether they were religious, pagan, or matrimonial, these feasts were no more than a moment in peasant life, and an enjoyable event in the history of nutrition. There were other phases in this history, more frequent and more widespread, which gave less cause for rejoicing.

Famine and scarcity

In the course of a life which might be prolonged by good health, financial security, or luck to sixty years or so, everybody who lived in the country would several times have encountered, in various degrees, what the old texts call bad years, years of high prices, scarcity, famine, and mortality. Then there would be fewer rural festivities, or none at all; or else they would take place behind the closed doors of those families who were still rich, or who were growing rich at the expense of those who were suffering. And over the whole of a province, or sometimes even a large part of the kingdom, thousands and thousands of poor people would face the problem of finding their daily bread. Only rarely was there no bread, or flour, or grain: but the doubling, trebling, or quadrupling of the price might render it almost inaccessible. Then, in those parts of the country where few people grew enough to support themselves (and in the towns, too, although there, there was more relief), they started to look for bad flour, flour that was dirty or a bit mildewy; they took barley, rye, or oats and mixed them with all sorts of things: half-germinated seeds which they dug up, crushed beans, vetches, acorns taken from the pigs, cabbage stumps, fern roots, every kind of leaf, even the bark of trees. There are dozens, hundreds of instances in records both official and private, lay and ecclesiastical, literary and simple: the Great King himself admitted it in his *Mémoires* for 1662, Bossuet proclaimed it from the pulpit, and many priests entered it in their parish registers. The worst examples of this kind of diet are cases of peasants driven to dig up the carcasses of dead animals, or to hang about near urban slaughter-houses to lap up the blood and devour the guts of the beasts that were killed to feed the rich; but the likely consequences of such poor diets can be imagined without recourse to such extreme cases as these: dozens of digestive and other diseases were rapidly spread by infected water and human waste, and left thousands dead in their wake. Sometimes there was starvation. Any of the properly kept registers of burials show at once that for some months the normal death rate was increased three or five times, occasionally even more. Despite this, some over-fastidious or glibly dishonest writers have suggested that insufficient and poor food may not have been the cause of these deaths, which is like doubting whether night follows day. There were, certainly, other dreadful phenomena which laid waste the countryside, and the towns; but we are not concerned here with plague, smallpox, influenza, or typhus, nor with the arrival of soldiers (which we shall come to later), only with food that was inadequate, infected, and sometimes non-existent. Why and how this arose, where it arose, and what the consequences were, is the immediate question.

Harvests were often the most important element in the lives of peasants and administrators, or at least a recurrent obsession; the outcome of harvests was dependent on many factors, the chief of which was the weather. It is a cliché to talk about the unevenness of the harvests, and we know that in ordinary years they could vary enormously, one year's being twice the size of another's, or more. There were bad winters, most notably the appalling winter of 1709, but it was not so much the cold which threatened crops, nor even hailstorms or cloudbursts – which were always localised – as wet summers, which prevented the grain from ripening, and mildewed and rotted it. So as far as it can be calculated, the kingdom of France produced about enough in an average year for its needs, but with nothing in the way of surplus. If, therefore, it became apparent in May or June that the harvest was going to be poor, anxiety started to spread, the price of the bridging stocks rose, the richest laid in extra supplies, and the usual sellers – nobles, chapter-houses, convents, dealers in the towns, and the largest tenant-farmers – stopped sending grain to market, waiting until the scarcity they created sent the price to the highest possible level. It is now accepted that the speculators (monopolists and hoarders) always intensified any approaching crisis, which in all cases benefited them, and them alone. If the harvest did turn out to be bad, the prices would rise even higher, unless there was an abundance of spring barley, or unless (as rarely happened in the seventeenth century) the neighbouring province, not hit by a bad harvest, decided to make good the shortfall from its own stocks. So the mechanism was set inevitably in motion; and of course if there were two bad harvests in succession, matters grew even worse still.

What people nowadays have difficulty in grasping, particularly after the experience of the 1940s, is that people in the country could be short of corn, and thus of bread, and suffer severe want, even famine. It must be remembered (and I shall come back to this point) that at least half of them were lowly peasants or day-labourers, unable to produce all the food they needed for a year, and that they were therefore forced to work or to produce something else in order to buy it. In bad years they were hit by a number of factors at the same time: their own small harvest was reduced, the price of grain roughly doubled, while their wages, whether in money or in kind, not only did not go up but often fell. Farmers and large tenant-farmers, whose harvests were also reduced, employed fewer people in harvesting and threshing, and they tended to pay them less, as there was a superfluity of labour desperately needing to work. Additionally, the smallcloth and other products that could be made at home found few outlets, as the neighbouring towns were also affected by the price of grain, and their non-food consumption was proportionately reduced. It did not take long for this set of circumstances to destroy a family: a few months, until the winter or the first cold weather, and the exhaustion of the few reserves of food, were enough to break down most resistance.

What options were open to them? First, they could try to borrow – some wood here, some flour there – but that meant finding people to borrow from. The large farmers, shrewd townsmen, and generous or self-interested seigneurs customarily played that role. They very seldom did it for nothing, only lending to those who had signed a piece of paper saying they would repay it 'before August, *foi d'animal*', sometimes in the form of labour, more often pledging a plot of land or some vines or even the house against 'bond, undertaking or promise to pay', which was properly valid in law. If the borrower could keep going, and the next harvest was a good one, he could redeem his pledge. If not, then distraint followed, with the help of 'justice', after which he would quite often be taken on to work the field or garden which previously belonged to him, as payment of his rent. The dusty files of the old tribunals are full of bonds like this that have become possession orders.

Sometimes a man had nothing to pledge except his labour, and this was not always enough: then all he could do was hope, look for a job, leave, beg, or steal. He could put his hope in the charity of the seigneur or the 'cock of the village', or the priest (who would be quite well-off, but not able to provide for more than twenty or thirty people): finding these sources necessarily limited, he would then send his children out begging, and the older ones would lead the younger (more emotionally affecting) ones along the highroads, to convent gates, to the gateways of towns, and inside them, if nobody drove them away. As their poverty worsened, the parents too would take to the roads, beginning as honest beggars, but soon becoming more dangerous. Small bands tried to attack carts and boats, dug up seeds from the fields, killed animals, or merely cut wood illegally in order to sell it in towns as canes or firewood. They were chased out of the towns, already over-burdened with their own poor, by evil-tempered vergers known as *chasse-coquins* (rogue-hunters), and ended up forming bands of thieves, or brigands, or else enlisting as soldiers of the king (in return for a bounty). It is not hard to imagine what became of wives and nubile daughters living in the neighbourhood of regiments in their winter quarters, or in the large towns. Sometimes death from starvation, cold, or permanent dysentery provided an easier solution to the burden of a family.

The picture presented above is not an exaggerated one. It could have been made more extreme by including even more horrible illustrations, such as the rare instances of cannibalism. But it should be made clear that such a state of events never affected the whole of the kingdom at any one time, and on the occasions when it happened, lasted for only a couple of years at a time, or, in all its aspects, accounted for five or ten years out of the century. Even in the great winter of 1709, Brittany's mild, wet climate meant it escaped largely unaffected. The unspeakable horrors of 1693–4 were hardly felt in the Midi, nor in Brittany. The brutal accession crisis (1662) principally hit the northern half of the kingdom, particularly the Loire. The catastrophic epidemics, military occupations, and bad weather during the Fronde again missed the west and the Midi, and the miseries of the Thirty Years War (1635–1648–1659) fell mainly upon the north and the east. The whole of the south-west managed to hold out, thanks to maize. Relief corn could be more easily distributed to the areas around the major ports, where there was also fish to be had. The Mediterranean south, particularly Provence, seldom suffered these problems, for predictable reasons, and also because of the amount of sunshine it enjoyed (by far the best curative of the period) and the general good health of a population who lived largely out of doors; this did not, however, guarantee them entirely against the severe epidemics which were carried by sea. But that is another story.

Hunger, then, in the seventeenth century was always a social phenomenon, always a provincial phenomenon, and, while it lasted, always a horrible experience. The lavish feasts were also a social and provincial phenomenon, but only happened on rare occasions. To use an eloquent, if vulgar, expression, one could say they were occasional, well-balanced 'blow-outs' which with ups and downs sustained the sixty million or so country people who, for three or four generations, lived and worked between King Henry and the regency of Philip of Orléans.

8

Labourers at work

Let us now take a closer look at what we know of the details of these people's work.

A poor peasant

A labourer (*manouvrier*) was somebody who worked with his hands, and, by extension of course, with tools which, though rudimentary, were made for very specific purposes. They were usually made of wood, with a minimum of iron, which was very expensive; spades for example were often only overlaid with metal, while forks were sometimes no more than a suitable branch selected and cut down because it had a fork in the right place. Sickles, on the other hand, needed a lot of metal, whether they were serrated or plain, narrow or generously curved. And scythes, which were much rarer and usually imported, commanded almost unattainable prices. Handling a scythe, the labourer used more than just his hands and his arms (labourers were also called *brassiers* from *bras* meaning arm), but his body and legs as well, in a sweeping motion. But in any event, work had to be carried out without the help of beasts, whether for ploughing, pulling loads, or carrying heavy loads, and other general drudgery. Horses were costly and delicate, and labourers did not use them anywhere; nor would a labourer have a pair of oxen, for the same reasons (and, besides, how would he feed them?), nor even a donkey, except in some mountainous regions in the south, where the *bourrique* could forage for plants among the rocks.

By the same token, a labourer was somebody with no particular aptitude, but this is not surprising at a time when specialisation was a meaningless term outside the world of fine craftsmen and skilled artisans in some of the larger towns. Yet although they had no specific specialisations, they had a number of abilities, applied skills, and minor talents, rather like rural handymen.

Labourers lived above the most extreme poverty line, often making up the greater part of a rural community, and, as we have already seen, they 'held' a cottage with a garden and a plot of ground – a few perches or ares – which was usually rented *en bloc* from somebody richer than themselves or from a family that had left to settle in another parish. They would thus be both house-repairers and gardeners, and so would their wives. In the garden they would first try to grow peas and beans, for basic nourishment; then cabbages and turnips, and leeks and spinach-beet, and perhaps some culinary herbs, if they liked them. If they were brave they might risk planting a small square of rye or barley (although as these were tithable crops, they were not entitled to), and a few vines, whose shoots, branches, and tendrils could climb or grow against the length of the walls, or up pear, plum, and apple trees if there were any (their disadvantage was that they created too much shade). All the crops would be planted in earth which had been well-turned and dressed and enriched with all the available dung.

There were probably always half a dozen hens and a cockerel in the yard, kept well away from the garden to prevent them destroying the vegetables. This was about the optimum number: any more, and the greedy, scratching birds posed a threat to anything sown, growing, or stored; any fewer, and they would not have the eggs, chickens, and capons they needed to sell in the market to collect the coins they had to have to pay the tax-collector, sou by sou.

There is a familiar series of sentimental stories about the 'poor man's cow', or like the story about the ham shown to Rousseau by a Savoyan mountain-dweller, who said he had nothing.

But it is clear from both common sense and archival material that cows or pigs could only be kept where there was enough to feed them on. The average labourer living in the flat, corn-growing regions could not possibly have kept either: he could not hold pasture of his own, and there was not normally any common pasturage; if there was, it tended to be monopolised by the rich, the seigneurs, or both. The poor man's cow is something encountered in regions of pasture, heathland, common, and uncultivated land like in Brittany, or in the wet mountainous areas (in these areas, though, the term 'labourer' may not have quite the same connotation). Pigs in those days were more black than pink, brutal, ravaging animals, and they needed acorns, or at least beechmast, which meant there had to be plenty of oaks or beech trees. So pigs, too, tended to live in wooded or mountainous regions, and one can search through old papers forever without finding a mention of labourers in cereal-growing areas owning them.

The animal most commonly owned by poor or average households was a sheep, or a couple of sheep. They did not need much attention, as they were able to browse at the roadside, or on waste or fallow land, and for a few sous a year could join the communal flock. In the winter, though, they had to make do with straw. Nonetheless, they were steady suppliers of wool, which was shorn, washed, spun, or worked at home. Every year, having been well served by the communal ram, or one belonging to the seigneur or even sometimes (in the east) to the priest, they would produce a lamb, which was normally sold unless it was a ewe-lamb, in which case it would more often than not be kept. The milk was not much drunk, or only by young children, and was made into cheese which was kept and dried for a long time, making it very strong, and so more economic; this, too, like the eggs and chickens, was usually sold.

Six hens and two sheep, which were never eaten, and a few baskets of apples, turnips, beans, peas, and cabbages, and a few sous, were obviously not enough to support a family of five which, as we know, ate a huge amount of bread, porridge, and pancakes. Most labourers rented or owned two or three plots of land, never more than a hectare altogether and often less than half that, and after ploughing these once or twice (which was not enough) with a yoke of oxen borrowed from the local farmer (if he agreed – payment to be in labour) they almost always sowed them with one of the poor man's cereals such as rye or maslin. It was hard work, weeding by hand and harvesting with a sickle, but after the grain was gathered, after all dues and other payments had been made, and after it had been through the hands of the miller – sometimes the seigneurial oven as well – there was usually enough to provide bread for between three and six months. For the rest of the time, the labourer had to make the most of what talents he had, and of his capacity for hard work.

Day-labourers

The two terms 'labourer' and 'day-labourer' or 'journeyman' were almost interchangeable. Labourers did a day's work for somebody else, a day lasting from dawn till dusk, with a short break at midday, particularly in the summer. These days might be worked for the seigneur or his tenant, or for a large ecclesiastical landowner or his tenant, or for a large farmer who owned several ploughs and a few dozen other implements. Because there were no machines, there were some times of year when farmwork had a kind of precedence, when the size of the task to be carried out, and the urgency of it, required a large quantity of manual labour: the harvest was always one such, of course, and in many places there was also the vintage, and haymaking. From the end of May until October men, women, and children from all parts of the country, and from the town as well (people left the towns for *aoust* (August) which was synonymous with harvest), converged on the harvests. They were days of exhausting and rewarding work, with everybody stooped or bent double for hours at a time scything grass, cutting and binding corn, or amassing grapes, constantly under pressure from overseers or the threat of rain. The long days were broken by short but filling meals of stale bread and cheese, tripe, and offal, washed down with thin or vinegary *buvande* – almost never with wine – and sometimes when the work was finished there would be a rustic supper.

As well as food, which was always welcome, labourers thus earned a 'wage', although the word *salaire* has now almost completely lost its original meaning. Wages meant compensation; it was most unusual for them to be paid entirely in money, and indeed it was not necessary for them to be paid in money at all. For his work on the harvest, a labourer might expect a small percentage of the grain – to store for the winter and to provide seed for the following spring – the acknowledgement of debts repaid (every day-labourer had signed several I.O.U.s for borrowing wood, seed, horses, carts, and so on), and, in addition, a few small coins. Depending on age and sex (women were paid scarcely half the men's rate) and the region in question (places further away from towns paid less), the daily rate was between 5 and 10 sous, which in a normal year was enough to buy the same number of kilos of bread. Assuming labourers carried out between sixty and seventy days of this hard labour during the summer, they would receive the equivalent of between 20 and 30 livres-tournois, which was roughly the amount needed to pay the various taxes, although only if the money was paid in full, and at the time.

Despite the benefits these laborious but necessary summer tasks conferred, they do not seem to have been sufficient to provide the minimum needed by a labouring family, especially if it was a large one (though, as we have seen, this was unusual) or if, as was more likely, it included invalids, or sick or weak members. Other resources had also to be called upon. In many provinces – though not all, and indeed in fewer than in the following century – these were provided by rural manufacture, or, as we would say, by cottage industry, which was far from confined to the village weaver or cobbler.

Subsidiary activities: weaving, wood-cutting, wet-nursing, etc.

The great merchants in the towns had long been aware that labour was much cheaper in the country, principally because there were no guilds there (the word is not used before the end of the eighteenth century, although the institution itself considerably predates the first usage), and many people in the country were badly-off and had quite a lot of spare time, particularly in the winter. For their part, country-dwellers almost everywhere grew hemp – and flax, too, in the wettest areas – and kept a few sheep, so they were used to working in wool and fibres which they had prepared themselves. Most of the family, including children aged seven or eight upwards, would work by candlelight (if they could afford it) or by firelight or daylight, spinning, reeling, and even weaving. Most looms for weaving simple fabrics – serge, or coarse cloth – were fairly easy to make, set up, and operate. The important requirements were space and time. And if some were unable to obtain the wooden stand and, more importantly, the weaving frame and pedals. they could lease them from the merchants, and pay the rent in work.

Labourers in the textile regions usually only made warps for cheap material, using threads well fastened together, or else un-bleached holland which they tried to sell in the market of the nearest town: this was the situation across the whole of the north-west of the kingdom, in a band from Flanders to the Vendée, and to a lesser extent elsewhere as well. Additionally, there was a growing tendency, particularly after the accession of Louis XIV, for the increasing number of wholesalers in towns to order whole pieces of material from the 'serge-makers' or *texiers* of Picardy, Normandy, and Brittany, some of the mountainous regions and the Languedoc. It is clear that these merchants were quite shameless in their exploitation of their peasant spinners and weavers, paying them as little as possible – and in bad coin. Yet the work they provided for the evenings at home and in the winter, and indeed sometimes full-time, gave energetic and healthy workers the small supplementary income they needed to make ends meet.

In other parts of the country, working with wood or metal (nail-making, needle-making) fulfilled the same function, and any areas of the kingdom where people were unable to practise a second trade, or a third or fourth, were very badly-off. But almost everywhere one comes across labourers who could turn their hands to hedge-trimming or ditching, if needed, or even to stream-clearing, a necessary but very laborious task. Others were employed by the day to drain the meadows, either by digging new drainage trenches or by maintaining old ones, and to clear the ground of molehills (and if possible get rid of the moles). Others spent part of their time as masons' mates, but in the rural context, and lacking specialised skills, only 'clay-masons'. Others again worked as thatchers, a craft which, in the seventeenth century, needed at least something of a knack.

The most important jobs, apart from those working with textiles, that could be done near the home were to do with the forest. Forest was not ubiquitous, of course, but there were small patches of woodland – at least – in most regions. It is hard nowadays to imagine the extent to which the forests were inhabited three centuries ago and earlier. Horses had long been bred there, so much so, indeed, that some forests practically constituted a stud. But more recently the monarchy had taken back control from the *noblesse d'épée* of breeding the noble animal for military and ceremonial purposes, and this led, under Louis XIV, to some regions – not just Normandy – specialising in it, and to the building, well into the following century, of the splendid and functional studs which are now ancient monuments, albeit in some cases still operating. At the time of Louis XIV, however, peasant labourers only worked as casual stable-lads, or collected the precious manure.

On the other hand the forests were very backward places, and for some time remained the refuge of charcoal-burners, men who made charcoal by burning carefully sorted wood very slowly within large, earth-covered mounds. Mineral coal was hardly used at this period, and was disliked for its nauseous smoke, and its high price. So charcoal, once manufactured, was conveyed in large quantities by land and by water to the big towns and workshops where it was burned in often considerable quantities. The charcoal-burners themselves blackened with smoke and charcoal, and fairly primitive, gave rise to various legends, and they were generally feared, especially by children. In reality, only a minority of them lived permanently in the forest, in rough huts, most of them being peasants rather like the ordinary labourers who were able to get a few weeks' work with them, usually as assistants rather than technicians, if that is the word to use.

What the labourers did was, in fact, a kind of work with which they were already familiar: cutting and gathering wood. Wood was needed in the country, and even more in the towns, for burning, building, timber, and for making tools, to the extent that it was the most important raw material – and to a point the most important energy source – of the time. This in turn entailed a great deal of hard work maintaining and cutting the wood, moving it (to the nearest passable cart-road), bundling it into the proper number of 'cords' of wood, waiting for the cart, or getting ready to float the trunks in rafts all the way down the Seine and its upper tributaries to supply Paris and the other large cities. Some of this vast amount of work went to specialists, but the heaviest work needed strong muscles and team organisation, and most of this strength was supplied by plain day-labourers who got their firewood and a few deniers out of it.

Towards the end of the seventeenth century – possibly earlier, but we do not know – and in the eighteenth century on a very large scale indeed, labourers' wives earned fairly good money by wet-nursing children from the towns. Women whose milk was plentiful had always been picked by noble or well-off families to live in their houses and feed children whose mother refused to suckle them, out of idleness, snobbery, or for fear that it would spoil her breasts. The wives of successful city craftsmen, shopkeepers, and even master-tradesmen – like the silk-weavers of Lyons – soon began sending their new-born children into the country, by cart or pack-mule, supposedly to be wet-nursed (although they were often fed from rags soaked in cow's milk), but at any event to be rid of the offspring which might otherwise keep them away from shop or work. And, as we know, at least three-quarters of these babies never returned, in the eighteenth century at any rate. It provided, in effect, a primitive and belated form of abortion. About the time of Louis XIV, the general hospitals, where the poor went to die, began systematically sending foundlings discovered on church step, or entrusted to them by errant mothers, into the neighbouring countryside (which could be as much as 100 kilometres away). It is not certain, however, that this activity, which in the eighteenth century could bring in as much as 10 sous, or more than 5 kilos of bread per day, was really established in the seventeenth century.

The French labourer at this period, though, with his bit of gardening and cereal-growing, his few livestock, his summer work, a bit of spinning or wood-cutting, some building work, some wood-carving, and so on, was also always a first-rate poacher, by necessity and probably for pleasure too, and poaching itself was easier than it would ever be again. We have already seen something of fishing or hunting in forbidden places (which meant practically everywhere), and of the peasants' attempts to avoid capture, if necessary by sharing their bag with the gamekeepers, the biggest poachers of all. Rabbits and pigeons, it could be reasonably argued, presented a serious threat to crops. It is not improbable that poached meat more often enriched the pot on its hook over the fire than did salt pork.

So were they happy or miserable, these seventeenth-century labourers? Apart from the fact that, as somebody has said, happiness is a state of mind, it might be felt to be almost shameful to have to pose the question at all. They were never rich, and the probate papers are enough to show how little they had to leave their descendants: assets worth perhaps 100 livres at best (equivalent to a few thousand francs today), a few bits of furniture, worn-out clothes, scraps of paper representing debts, *dettes passives* or liabilities as they were called. Obviously there would be wide variation from region to region, and from family to family (even then there were shrewd and foolish people), and also from one year to another, which could make a great difference. They were hard-working men and women, almost always ingenious, making the most of their resources in the attempt to hang on until the end of the year, but not always getting there.

Yet for all their often substantial appearance and the extraordinary range of their activities, they were often insecure, and seldom in control of their families' destiny, governed as it was by factors much stronger than their will to live.

Weakness and insecurity

First, physical weakness. Men needed to be healthy to carry out such varied, time-consuming activities, and so did the women who had as much work to do as the men – in the garden and the fields, in day-labouring – and who, as well as all the household tasks, had to carry, nurse, and look after the children. Both sexes also needed to avoid accidents at work or in the surrounding countryside (such as falls, drowning, or tools slipping). These may sound like truisms, but it must be remembered that there were no doctors or even surgeons in the countryside at this period, only relatively unskilled bonesetters and that there was no network of support in cases of illness, infirmity, widowhood, or unemployment. In a labouring family where savings were small or insignificant and there was only enough food to last a few weeks, a sick mother or father very soon threatened disaster unless the rest of the family, or, more improbably, some short-lived charity, came to their help: and no help could last for very long. The whole intelligent and hard-working process of survival was thus entirely dependent on the health of the two adults (given that the grandparents, as in most cases, were dead).

A short, serious illness that ended in the death of the father or mother – especially the latter – probably turned out less disastrously than a long, lingering illness which could reduce the energy and output of the family unit by more than half over a long period. A wife's death was almost always quickly followed by the man's remarriage, sometimes within a month (which shows that there were always available girls or young widows); this saved both the crops, which were essential, and the remaining children – until the next ones arrived. A rescue of this sort was much more difficult when it was the man who died, particularly if there were a lot of young children: there were relatively few male candidates for the reconstruction of the family cell, as there were not usually very many available men.

Thus the frequent decline of a poor peasant family, reduced at a stroke to a widow and her children, forced to live either in want or outright poverty, as one person (unless there were grown-up children) could not ensure the survival of the rural unit which two had found hard enough work to keep going. The taxation lists are full of entries for 'Widow X, day-labourer' or 'Widow Y, poor', taxed at a few sous or a symbolic figure (an *obole*, a quarter of a sou), with ten or twenty such entries for each parish. From other sources it becomes clear that widows and their children were sometimes reduced to begging. And all because purely physical misfortune had descended upon a small group of people who hitherto had been far from rich, but energetic.

Other more general misfortunes also affected labouring families particularly badly, because they were not strong enough to resist them. The numerous epidemics (mostly unidentified) which swept through the provinces hit the rich as hard as the needy, and the plague itself was no respecter of persons (although in towns like Amiens it was primarily the working-class areas that suffered). But the poor, who were the least well-fed, clothed, and heated, more easily fell victim to the many attacks of flu, dysentery, diseases of the chest, and so on. And even when children survived the epidemics, they often failed to come through the convalescence, as it was not possible for them to get enough rest or nourishment fully to recover their health and strength. It was usually in the days and weeks after the 'peak' of an epidemic that the deaths occurred among the poor and the badly-off.

Livestock, too, could be hit by disease. The plagues of sheep and cattle, as the epizootic diseases that have since been identified were then known as, were not understood or treated in the seventeenth century, and were sometimes extremely virulent. The correspondence of the provincial administrators for 1714 is largely taken up with one of these catastrophes which, in some regions, killed between a third and a half of all sheep. To avoid contagion people were advised to bury the dead animals as deeply as possible, or to cover them with quicklime – if they had any – which was sensible enough.

Disease of this sort hit the livestock of the rich as well as that of the 'meaner sort' or the poor, of course, but with the important difference that landowners or tenant-farmers could replace the lost animals a great deal more easily than labourers could. In the grassland, where almost everybody owned a cow, its death was an almost unmitigated catastrophe, as there was no way of buying another without going into debt, even if they could find somebody to borrow from. Sheep cost between five and ten times less (a few livres, or three or four days of summer work), and if farmers owned three or four then at least they might save one of them, which would lamb in due course. The loss of a horse would have been almost completely irretrievable although, being so very expensive, horses were never owned by labourers. In fact labourers lived in such fear of some disaster striking their livestock that, overall, they were perhaps more prepared to accept the death of a wife than the loss of a cow. There is a song, dating from the end of the nineteenth century, which says: 'I have two large white oxen in my cowshed . . . I would rather my wife died than they did.' And we may perhaps recall the scene in *La Terre* (written about the same time) where Zola described a woman and a cow giving birth simultaneously, and how he says that for people in the Beauce region at the time the birth of a calf was a more significant event, which may seem rather hard.

Although sickness among livestock – foot-and-mouth disease, foot rot – seems to have been quite common, major epidemics were still unusual. The worst were in the 'bad years' described in the previous chapter. Here I just want to stress that it was the labourers who were particularly badly hit. It only needed one or two wet summers for their already small cereal harvest to become even more inadequate, forcing them either to buy flour or bread at twice or three times normal prices or to borrow, pledging their meagre possessions in writing as security for the loan. There were fewer days of work to be had, and those there were were less well-paid, as the employers, too, had less corn to cut or thresh. There were fewer evening and winter tasks to be carried out, too, as everything went into the search for bread rather than for cloth. When their reserves were finished and they could no longer borrow they had to fall back on poaching or substitute foods, which were often indigestible and sometimes revolting, and which might in the end cause intestinal illness, so easily transmitted, and a whole series of villages might be (in the correct sense of the word) decimated. The last resorts, until better days returned, were begging and pilfering. Dozens of adolescents and old people – the most at risk – lost their lives in those harsh years of scarcity and famine which, once all too familiar, gradually became a thing of the past in the happier reign of Louis XV and of his successors.

In each successive crisis, though – one every ten or fifteen years or more – the poor in the countryside lost at least a part of their scanty possessions. Almost all the historians who have made a close study of the living conditions of the poor in the seventeenth-century countryside agree that they underwent a gradual process of immiseration, and that this was to the benefit of the better-off, and their creditors in general. Yet this does not seem to have been the case in the following century, and the large number of humble peasants seems to have survived from one generation to the next, despite the very real but usually temporary misfortunes they encountered, thanks to their never-decreasing energy, a fertility rate which almost always ensured a slight increase in numbers, and their extraordinary capacity to find and carry out a vast range of jobs.

It was to all intents impossible to escape from the position of labourer, in the eighteenth as well as the seventeenth century, except by very gradual steps, which are difficult to reconstruct. Education could not lead to promotion in a social group which (except in the north-west) was generally illiterate; and where a priest did discover a pious and gifted child and try to assist his studies by finding a patron for him, this was likely to be the son of a rich farmer, as that was really the only milieu in which priests moved, and one from which they often came themselves. Nor was it possible to rise in the social scale through a second trade, such as weaving, or wood or metal work, as the money and the outlets – and often the tools and raw materials too – were in the control of the merchants. We have seen that fortunate marriages, between a shrewd young lad and a farmer's widow, who still had her land, crops, and livestock, did occasionally take place, but they were far from common, and they elicited hostility and difficulties, both from the families and the community. Leaving the village to work in the town was perhaps an escape for the few who succeeded in trade or their craft, and did not become servants, beggars or picklocks, but this was the exception rather than the rule, and tended to take two or even three generations.

In the country it was the richest farmers and the biggest tenant-farmers who 'rose' – and continued to do so for a long time – and not the poor, nor even the *closiers*, smallholders with a few acres of their own.

Nevertheless, although they did not know it, these humble people, in their relative poverty, made up part of the foundation of the wealth of France which the rest of Europe so envied. There were between four and five million heads of family in the country, of whom at least two million were classified as labourers, day-labourers, or *brassiers*, and each one of them might have to pay an average of ten livres in taxes, which comes to some twenty million altogether, or between a fifth and a quarter of Colbert's budget in the 1660s. Add to this half as much again paid out in seigneurial dues and ecclesiastical tithes, and it can be seen that by their agriculture and industrial labour, by their resourcefulness and their courage, these impoverished people provided the basis for the power of the richest monarchy in Europe, as well as the basic income of the richest classes in France (the nobility and the clergy), thus enabling them to shine, to serve, or to do nothing at all.

9

The well-off and the wealthy: or from the farmer to the tax collector, by way of the money-lender

---

The 'biggest' or richest person in the village or the parish was often the seigneur, but he tended to live there less and less in the seventeenth century, and certainly was not often to be seen pushing the plough with his sword by his side, as legend (which is hard to substantiate) asserts he used to in Brittany, where there were numerous younger brothers without much money. But in any event the seigneurs rarely seem to have identified themselves with their neighbours, and it is with those that we are concerned here.

Many people regard the farmer–labourer opposition as the embodiment of the fundamental contrast of earlier rural societies. But we have already seen enough to suggest that that view is somewhat inadequate. Let us therefore begin by defining some terms.

A farmer or *laboureur* possessed a large plough (one with a wheel and mould-board), animals to pull it (preferably two or three pairs of strong horses), and enough land to support them – land which was normally measured in *charrues* (ploughs), each about 20 hectares, depending on the quality of the land. This definition is by and large accurate for the corn-growing part of the kingdom – the north, the east, and the Paris basin, where the northern dialect was spoken.

But the same word is also used in a sustained, vaguely poetic style to refer to anyone who lived in the country. Except for the region around Nantes, though, the word is never used in Brittany where the archives are in French, or occasionally in Latin. Then, although the word is absent from the vocabulary of the old celtic areas, it does often appear in the plentiful archives of the Midi; only there it retains its original Latin (and therefore Provençal) sense of 'labourer', very close in meaning to *manouvrier*, the usual word for a labourer in the north. All of which goes to show how necessary it is for historians to be wary of words, and to restrain their readiness to make hasty generalisations.

The large-scale farmer-collectors in the north

To get the best view of the rich and the very rich, we need to return to the northern plains, particularly to the areas around the major towns like Paris and Lille (which had, unenthusiastically, become part of France in 1668).

To take an example: in November 1694, Claude Dumesnil took over the seigneurial farm belonging to the Dames de Saint-Paul (Benedictine nuns of high standing, successive abbesses having been relations of Richelieu); the farm was at Goincourt, not far from Beauvais, where the buildings still stand today, complete with monumental gateway and emblazoned coat of arms. Dumesnil remained there for thirty-six years, and died there. The farm extended to some hundred hectares, including a dozen of excellent meadowland (it is on the edge of the lush Bray countryside), a vineyard (though the grapes cannot have ripened well, nor the wine kept well), and two coppices, which were perennially useful for firewood and for providing timber for construction and repairs. None of this belonged to him as he rented it, along with various rights we shall come to later, for the substantial sum of 1,200 livres (four times the income of a country priest, or the annual wages of some twelve labourers in Vauban's estimation), plus 40 hectolitres of pure wheat, the value of which varied between 200 and 600 livres, depending on the year.

All the usual furniture, however, belonged to him (and it was of good quality), as did everything that came under the heading of stock, both live and 'dead': ploughs, harrows, numerous carts and their separate (iron) axles, casks, and so forth; and twelve horses, with two permanent carters and two ploughboys, twenty cows and five calves, six pigs or sows (numbers which may appear fairly small to us, but which are not small for the time, particularly when we remember that the young may have been sold), and then a huge flock of 225 sheep, roaming over the fallow and common land, fertilising it as they went. The supreme sign of wealth was the poultry yard, with 188 fowl, including two dozen turkeys, and the same number of ducks – both very uncommon in the farmyards of the region. Additionally, there were eighty pairs of pigeons, as the farm was a seigneurial one, and carried sole right to a dovecot.

When the harvest was complete, the barns held more than 8,200 sheaves, mostly of pure wheat, a tenth of which was almost enough to pay the rent, the harvesters, and the threshers. There were nearly 120 casks in the cellar, mostly waiting for the grapes to be pressed, but some ready for apples and pears. There were almost 200 fleeces in store, and presumably a comparable amount of hemp, peas, and beans.

This abundance was not simply due to the harvest: it also stemmed from the seigneurial function which Dumesnil rented from the Dames de Saint-Paul. In their name he collected two-thirds of the tithes (which were paid in kind, and amounted to 9 per cent of the gross harvest of the whole seigneurie), some lesser seigneurial dues, and a right over the wine-pressing at the unusual rate of a sixth (or one barrel out of every six). As a result of this, like many of his colleagues – about one or two in every village – he bore the great threefold title of '*laboureur*, tenant-farmer and collector for the seigneurie'; the first term was soon dropped, as conferring the least prestige, while the last came to be the most important as it linked Dumesnil firmly with seigneurial power and its accompanying reputation.

Unlike most of his fellow-farmers, who owned only their stock and equipment (as well as a fair amount of cash, probably, but that is always obscured by a veil of silence), Dumesnil kept a modest house and a few acres of land in the neighbouring village of Saint-Léger-en-Bray (where he was born in 1653), and this he rented out for just under 100 livres, a not inconsiderable sum.

Farming on this scale – which was not exceptional – produced income from a number of other sources as well as from land and seigneurial rights. Dumesnil hired out (in return for signed I.O.U.s) his horses, ploughs, and carts, and was also ready to lend seed, wood, and money. At his death, eighty pieces of paper, all I.O.U.s, were found, for sums ranging from as little as 6 livres to over 100, totalling almost 2,700 livres, the equivalent of the income of nine priests. In each case the reason for the debt was given: for ploughing, for carts, for general loans, or even (shockingly!) for money.

The people in his debt – mostly humble people from the village and surrounding area, labourers and vignerons – seem normally to have repaid him with labour, which of course increased the farmer-collector's power, giving him an almost modern role. At least he does not seem to have fallen to the level of money-lender.

It seems most unlikely that anybody in this sort of position was uneducated. Dumesnil indeed left a small library containing both Testaments and some travel books, as well as the usual Jansenist works of piety. Furthermore, the deputy guardian of the girls and the under-age children was also the chaplain of the local convent.

The total amount of movable goods left by Dumesnil at his death – which was far short of his total wealth – came to considerably over 15,000 livres, a sum equivalent to at least 100 plough-horses, or, if you prefer, to 5 kilograms of gold.

I have not described Dumesnil at such length out of a liking for facile erudition, or a desire for picturesque detail, but because men like him were to be found everywhere, two or three to each large village in the regions of Beauce, Brie, the Ile-de-France, Picardy, and the new northern provinces, where they were known as *censiers*. They farmed on a large scale, in an almost modern way, and wielded considerable power in their villages, especially as they paid by far the largest taxes, and were very closely connected with the seigneur-ial framework, tending to form a closed caste of their own. In the seventeenth century (even by the sixteenth, in Paris and the north) their children married only among themselves: the weddings them-selves were memorable, with perhaps as many as three or four canons present by virtue of being relatives. Some families were settled, others moved from one large seigneurial farm to another. Most of them, one might add, enriched themselves further during the eighteenth century, taking advantage of the sale of church lands during the Revolution, and of their ability to pay for them in *assignats* or paper money, so that by the nineteenth century they had taken their place among the provincial notables and in political assemblies, and often now boasted noble-sounding names, which there is no need to list here.

The farmers of Limousin and Bigorre

Historians have tried to find similar sorts of figures in the rest of the kingdom, but nothing strictly comparable has been found. The probable reason for this is that, away from the Paris basin, the large seigneuries were let out to wealthy town dwellers rather than to local country people, who were not on the whole rich enough to afford them. Nonetheless, there were well-off, and powerful, families in the country and on the fringes of that society, but they were of a different sort.

From the work of those more recent historians who have looked at life in the country, from the Loire to the Pyrenees and the Alps, we find, instead of a single 'cock' of the village, both powerful, non-rural 'masters' such as nobles, ecclesiastics, and townspeople, and also, in contrast, a small number of well-off country families. I shall try to sketch them both.

In the mountains of Limousin, there was nobody in the villages around Ussel, where the land and the climate were both harsh, who was even remotely comparable to Claude Dumesnil. The richest were known as farmers, *laboureurs*, but this simply meant that they were not share-croppers, and certainly not labourers, and that they owned their own land. But as to how much they owned, a land-survey carried out in the following century provides some late but valuable information: out of sixty or so 'farmers', no more than seven possessed two teams of two oxen (the others had only a single team, or else were forced – as the poorest were – to use cows to pull their swing-plough). These seven owned between 20 and 40 hectares of land, no more, although the quality of the land, and the purpose it was used for, were more important than the surface area. Thus the most highly-valued estate, which belonged to one of the many Moncouriers in this part of the country, only extended to 23 hectares, but was much more productive than the 45 hectares owned by his neighbour, Antoine Bouarde. The Ussel farmers grew rye (wheat was usually out of the question) to feed themselves and, when they could, to sell. They could only use a biennial system of rotation and so they had to leave half of the 40 per cent of the land that was cultivated to lie fallow each year, to 'rest'. The remainder of the land had to provide food for the livestock: there were good grass meadows, fair grazing, and poor heathland, all of which were valuable as the livestock was of fundamental importance, being almost the only source of money. Even so, they did not own very much – nobody is known to have had more than seven cows, although some did have as many as three dozen sheep – but that is still a very long way from the 2–300 owned by the rich farmers in the north. On the other hand, they had pigs which could feed freely on acorns; and pork, with rye and, to a lesser extent, chestnuts, provided their basic food and profit: often they also had hives of bees.

This arrangement, with livestock providing the essential foundation, created a reliable subsistence for the family, and paid their various expenses. Inside the houses of these farmers, there was little show of wealth, but there were good beds, chests with plenty of good linen, a few copper or pewter objects, and sometimes some faience in the richest households. Much later on, towards the end of the eighteenth century, the earliest cherry-wood wardrobes made their appearance. Such were the richest rural inhabitants of a fairly poor part of the country.

If we move south, to the area round Tarbes, to one of the plains of the Adour where they have the advantage of maize already established, vines, and extensive, good common land which is a boon for livestock, we find one parish, Azereix, consisting of between 120 and 140 'houses' (the local unit), which has sufficient documentation for us to get a very clear picture of life there in the seventeenth and – even more – eighteenth centuries.

About thirty men are referred to as 'farmers', and they owned and farmed more than 6 hectares. All the others, about 100 of them, were manual labourers, save for a few specialists such as the blacksmith, the tailor, the baker, the barber–surgeon, and the parish swine-herd. All the farmers had houses roofed with Pyrenean slate: the rest were thatched. The farmers held a number of municipal responsibilities – this being a part of the country where consulships were powerful – and assessed the taxes in their own way (and in accordance with their own surveys!). With very few exceptions, the children of these farmers married within the same group.

Although status, wealth, and power are clearly defined in Azereix, there is less an opposition between classes than a whole spectrum of positions. The most powerful farmers had more than 15 hectares, but nobody had as much as 20. There is only one exception to this, which stands out in the eighteenth century: the Dulong family far outstripped the richest farmer in wealth and allied itself to a family which was already partly established in the city. And although the Dulongs lived in the village and farmed there, they called themselves 'Monsieur' and even 'bourgeois' or townsmen.

But leaving that exception aside, all aspects of communal life continued to be dominated by the same households of rich (but not very rich) farmers, without, however, crushing the majority of average and poor households.

It is a vastly different position from that of the great farmer-collectors of the cereal-growing northern plains, however, with their links with large seigneuries into which they could integrate themselves, or else be swallowed up.

Money-lenders: from the notaries of Emblavès to the Arouets of Poitou

For our final example, we move to the basin of Emblavès, where the upper reaches of the Loire cross it, a little to the north of Puy, where we encounter another kind of society, controlled by very different individuals. Like everywhere else, there was a sub-stratum of poor peasants who did not own anything to speak of – at best half a hectare: here these were known as 'workers' or 'day-labourers', they gave and received dowries of a few livres, sometimes as much as 30, and paid minimal taxes, perhaps 20 sous. Others, called simply *mizerables*, lived in tumbledown hovels on the proceeds of a few days work a year, and begging.

Then there were the people known as *laboureurs*, who had less than 10 hectares, and were more small-scale tenant-farmers than landowners. Their dowries were over 100 livres, but often were never in fact paid. They paid their moderate taxes, belatedly: some rose in the social scale, some fell. Overall, they constituted a sort of social reservoir.

The people we are looking at, the ones with the real power in the rural area (though not the very rich, which would bring us to the Polignac class), fall into two very different categories, both of which are very typical of central southern France: the *ménagers*, or house-holders, and the notaries.

The term *ménager* was frequently used in the Languedoc and in part of the Midi. In Provence the slightly more lustrous title of *maître de mas* (master of the farm) seemed to carry much the same meaning. But in the corner of Velay we are looking at here, a *ménager* was a landowner farming on a fairly large scale, and theoretically never a tenant. He 'held' well over 500 *cartonnades*, a good 40 hectares, half of which would have been rich cornfields, a quarter various types of pasture, while the rest would have been vines and forest. The *ménagers* of the Emblavès basin, taken as a whole, paid 60 per cent of the total taxes, although they represented less than 25 per cent of the heads of family. They consistently brought the same size dowry when they married, 1,000 livres, a quarter of which was often paid in coin and currency. The richest among them were known respectfully (or perhaps mockingly) as *sieurs*, and these even occasionally married a younger daughter of the local minor aristocracy, although such lapses were uncommon.

The *ménagers* of Velay provide a good example of the highest level which could be reached by families farming their own land, an activity which it was quite uncommon to find pursued on its own in seventeenth-century France. While by no means negligible, a holding of 40 hectares and a dowry of 1,000 livres hardly represents untold wealth.

The real 'cocks' of the countryside in this part of Velay were not normally peasants, even rich ones, working the land themselves, and extracting its 'fruits'. The truly rich preferred to live in small towns, in substantial houses with gardens, stables, and a few fields – symbols of wealth and wise investment rather than more speculative financial investments. But these individuals, the 'royal notaries', speculated in a different way.

There were three different categories of 'scriveners and port-folios', as they were still called at the beginning of the century, two of which were falling into disuse. The 'pontifical notaries', linked to Rome, were primarily involved in ecclesiastical affairs, especially benefices: most of their responsibilities had disappeared, or been absorbed by others. The 'seigneurial notaries' still existed, but they mainly operated in the very large seigneuries like the comté of Dunois (Châteaudun), and they were naturally connected with the remnants of seigneurial law, as we shall see. Almost all notaries in the seventeenth century bore the title of 'royal notaries', which meant that, although they had a smattering of law, they had bought their practice or office, or had inherited it, while remaining strictly attached to the courts of justice (the Châtelet, in Paris, originally a straightforward royal bailliage, then 'presidial', which gave it a new importance). The basic task of these officers was to 'keep notes' (minutes, of which they could provide 'engrossments', authentic copies, paid for by the line and therefore written in a large hand) of an important number (though this varied from region to region) of deeds, both insignificant and of fundamental importance: gifts, small sales, a huge variety of leases, and, above all, marriage contracts and probate papers (documents which contain a wealth of information for historians, but which are very unevenly preserved and presented); the large part of a notary's job seems to have been the drafting and subsequent redraftings of what were usually known as 'settlements of revenue'. Beneath the off-putting jargon, these actually concerned loans at interest (which were in principle forbidden) simply disguised as contracts for the sale of a 'revenue' (the interest) in return for a certain 'principal' (the capital). These loans were not unsecured, either: there is plenty of evidence for the old adage about never lending except to the rich, or at least to people with guarantors. All these contracts, duly preserved in their original form (the 'minutes', sometimes with a bit left out), had an absolute value, and thenceforth provided evidence in law. There was an almost unbelievable number of notaries in France then (three or four times as many as there are now, at least), and the whole basis of their business consisted of dealings in money; the records we have of these transactions sometimes seem suspiciously fictional or incomplete, and a significant number of contracts seem to have been concluded 'by private agreement' (i.e. without seal or witnesses), and these include some quite important ones. But, outside Paris and a few other places, notaries in most parts of France do not seem to have risen to great material power, or to any great social standing; although this impression may be mistaken, and at all events they quickly did so in the next century, as we well know. An additional complicating factor is the presence in some smaller places of notaries of a sort, but who had neither the office nor the title, having merely had some basic legal training: village scriveners, or simply 'practitioners', poor relations of the *procureurs* (procurators), or the humblest officers of the law.

The royal notaries and scriveners of Emblavès, like most of their counterparts in central and southern France, were not content simply to 'take note'; they preferred to concentrate on one of the additional benefits of their office: lending money. In this region they lent mainly to country people, but not indiscriminately; particularly not to labourers or manual workers, but to those who owned a few fields and some livestock, which in Emblavès meant the *laboureurs*. These loans did not all take the form of 'settlement of revenue', which was a complicated contract, normally used only in the most exalted circles. There were also plain I.O.U.s, dated and signed (or 'marked') by the borrower, and known as promissory notes, notes of hand, or bonds – all legally binding debts. We have already encountered these kinds of notes, and they were indeed pervasive in the seventeenth century as they answered a need for money to buy wood, or seed, or a cow, or to pay royal or provincial taxes. The rate of interest is never stipulated: instead they either increased the sum due, or lent less than the stated amount. If the *laboureur* was able to pay the money back, then the notary had done him a good turn, though he had been paid for it; if he could not repay it his possessions became liable to distraint as no court would risk not declaring the mortgage invalid, even if it had not been precisely stipulated. The creditor thus had the opportunity of taking payment in kind, which often happened.

This pattern which we have frequently encountered and described is one of the keys to understanding this period of French history, and perhaps later periods as well. In Emblavès, it operated almost entirely to the advantage of the notaries, who came to control the countryside along with the richest *ménagers*, and who provided their children with dowries of over 3,000 livres, as well as furniture, linen, and sometimes jewels. In the more advanced and more fertile provinces, of course, one finds far greater sums; here, it was as high as one is likely to find. The power of the notaries continued to grow throughout the following century, as they lent more money and amassed more land – as the work carried out at Saint-Etienne, in what is now Haute-Loire, very clearly shows. Other historians have revealed similar situations in Poitou and the surrounding areas, and this may well have continued into the nineteenth – perhaps even the twentieth – centuries.

Within the sub-provincial framework, as far as we know it, these activities still possessed characteristics stemming from a legality that was used and exploited very cleverly. Money-lenders pure and simple, most of whom were to be found in the towns, are more difficult to track down as all their business was conducted by private documents and pledges, which they accumulated and rarely returned to their owners. However, with the help of some reliable inventories and account books, which were never intended for publication or public scrutiny, it is possible to unearth a few of these important – and, from this standpoint, unpleasant – individuals.

In Gâtine, in Poitou, for example, which was an area of large-scale share-cropping, where most of the farming was livestock farming, there was a certain amount of livestock leasing (as there was in other parts as well): the owner of a flock of sheep, of whatever size, gave them into the care of a share-cropper who had enough pasture for them, in exchange for their keep and half the profit (though he did not always share the losses). This was a sufficiently profitable form of speculation for some individuals, with interests in both small towns and the country, to make a speciality of it, involving perhaps hundreds of beasts. Thus the eminent historian, Dr Merle, discovered among the people he called 'livestock bankers' one Jean de Maignou, of Saint-Maixent, who had twenty-two separate claims on leased livestock, amounting to hundreds of sheep, in the care of people in the countryside round about (he died in 1646, and the existence of these arrangements is disclosed in the inventory of his possessions). There was another character who operated in a similar way, with involvements in some thirty farms, who is interesting for an additional reason: he was called Helenus Arouet, and was the great-grandfather of the man who called himself Monsieur de Voltaire (whose father was also a notary, but in Paris).

In the century before there was the unforgettable figure of Guillaume Masenx, immortalised by Le Roy Ladurie, who tracked down his account book, published in 1896. Masenx lived in the Gaillac region, and seemed to be able to make money out of everything, and particularly out of the small farmers and *bordiers*, or small-scale share-cropping farmers. He lent money and corn by the month, at rates of as much as 8 per cent a month, and even 14 per cent a fortnight. He also lent rye, and took his repayment in wheat. Much of what was owed came to him in the form of land, as we can see from the detailed itemisation of his cunning and malpractice (Ladurie calls him a 'shark'). Of course, this is the sixteenth century, and he is an exceptional character, so we may not wish to place much emphasis on him.

Thus, hard work and good luck of a few historians can help us to understand how, throughout most of the Midi and central western France, the position that was occupied in the north by the big farmer-collectors (and sometimes also by well-to-do townsmen, or convents) was held by notaries, practitioners, and money-lenders. They took advantage of a rudimentary legal education, and a deep knowledge of the community in which they found themselves, in order to dominate it completely and exploit it as far as they could. They do not fit the traditional idea of the 'cock of the village', but the role they played brought them comparable, even superior, benefits, even though they may have been less visible. They probably came from outside the community, and had hard lives, but they are as much a part of the past of the French countryside as the church tower, the manor house, the sickle, and the swing-plough.

10

Vine-growers

It is hard for us in the late twentieth century to imagine the position that the vine, and wine, occupied in the life of our ancestors.

The splendours of wine

Perhaps the most surprising fact is that vines were grown in almost the whole of the kingdom in 1600, and in earlier centuries as far north as Scotland and Denmark. Wine grown in those latitudes was probably not very good, but the people who drank it then, in those countries, may not have had the same tastes or the same palate as we do today. As far as France is concerned, we know that vines were grown well to the north of Nantes, and the last vinestocks of the Rhuys peninsula survived until quite recently, producing a wine of which it was popularly said that three people were needed to drink it, the extra two being to hold up the drinker. In the cereal-growing region of Picardy and the adjoining provinces, vines covered the slopes of the valleys of the Somme, the Oise, and their tributaries, or climbed up towards hilltop towns like Noyon and Laon; one historian, indeed, has called the latter a 'wine capital' in the Middle Ages. 'Capital' is an exaggeration, but it is true that in the market at Amiens, in the mid-seventeenth century, there were normally wines for sale from the Somme, Noyon, and Beauvais (where, apart from the few surviving vinestocks, you can find vines growing wild again in the hedgerows), and from 'France', i.e. the Ile-de-France. In fact this last region was the biggest wine-producing area in France until the mid-nineteenth century: the 'village' of Argenteuil, for example, was still cultivating 1,000 hectares of vines at the time of Napoleon III, with these yielding between 120 and 150 hectolitres per hectare. In Louis XIV's time, with all the 'French' vineyards developing very rapidly, there were certainly more than 20,000 hectares under cultivation (on the eve of the Revolution, the figure was 26,000). Thanks to the detailed records of the taxation authorities, we know that production was normally 200,000 hogsheads (a hogshead being 268 litres), and in the best years greatly exceeded 300,000 (in 1727 the figure was some 900,000 hectolitres). The vineyards of the Languedoc were not included at this period, except in local figures, with the exception of true *liqueurs*, or dessert wines, like Muscat and malmsey. There needed to be some serious impediment of soil, climate, or altitude to prevent every small area of France producing its own wine.

Were our distant forebears, then, particularly keen on what Rabelais and his hero Brother John of the Entommeures called the *bon piot* and to which they attributed hundreds of medicinal qualities? The answer has to be both yes and no. For a long time wine was considered to be a sacred drink, the beverage of the gods (although of course they also enjoyed mead); then, with the coming of christianity, wine became the symbol of the divine blood, just as bread was the symbol of the body. The communion wine was always drunk by the priest: the faithful, strangely, or perhaps sensibly, had to be content with bread – still unleavened, as among the Jews – in the consecrated host. On the occasions when a religious sect claimed the right to take communion 'in both kinds', as in the scriptures, the Holy Roman Church at once pronounced it heretical and called for its suppression. All the same, communion wine needed to be produced close to where it was going to be used, as what transport there was was insufficiently frequent, fast, or cheap, and some historians have taken this to be sufficient explanation for the scattered cultivation of vines, and their earlier prevalence in northern areas, without having recourse to explanations that involve climatic changes. There were changes in the climate, though, and it is now fairly well-accepted that there was a general fall in overall temperature between the mid-sixteenth and early eighteenth centuries over the small corner of Europe that contained the French kingdom, and this may explain the retreat or complete disappearance of vines from the more northern areas, like the upper Somme and Oise valleys.

So wine was used at mass, and, according to the anecdotes current at the time, it was seldom unpalatable, but there were of course many other occasions when it was drunk: at times of merrymaking, holidays, feasts, or just to welcome visitors; it was, as the erudite said, the 'liquor of sociability'. Tuns, barrels and casks consecrated to Bacchus, who was never forgotten and often personified, were to be found at carnivals (only in the towns, though), at most of the agrarian rituals, at all the patronal festivals, at weddings, and at the great 'entries' of kings or princes, when it was usual to see the fountains 'pissing wine', as writers of the time bluntly put it. However, it needs to be said quite clearly that festivities and drinking sessions of this sort were exceptional, despite the frequency with which they occur in folk tales and traditional stories, as there had to be a *fête* before drinking on a large scale could take place, and such holidays were *very* uncommon, occurring perhaps three or four times a year. So these doubtless memorable days must have made all the more of a contrast with the ordinary days when the liquid intake would have been water – not always clean – or pinkish, vinegary, or rancid *piquette* (poor quality wine).

It was customary for wine to be used, although only occasionally, as a medicine, and particularly as a tonic. It was an ingredient in dozens of apothecary's recipes, mixed with flowers, herbs, crushed entrails, dung, and spittle. On its own, wine – often good wine – was often given as a pick-me-up to convalescents in hospitals, even to the poor, as well as those in comfortable households. In the second quarter of the seventeenth century, everybody, even very humble households, believed – as some still do today – that a good glass of wine, preferably red wine, would 'give you back your strength' and 'improve the blood'. They therefore liked to keep a little 'bottled wine' or a small keg – preferably of the local wine – within reach, in case it was ever needed.

It could also be used for the almost sacred requirements of politeness or friendship, and would be brought out to welcome a relative, a wealthy neighbour, a 'master', or someone they wanted to honour. *Trinquer* (the word means something like to toast, or clink glasses) is a word which goes much further than *boire*, *trink*, or drink, and the act is more ritual and symbolic than a mere gratification of the palate; this ancient ceremony is one that has lasted over the years.

If we look at what was drunk on these occasions, then in addition to its sociable value, which tends to blur or relax normal distinctions, wine can be seen as an indicator of social divisions and gradations.

As we know, the poorest drank clean or polluted water, and a variety of drinks made out of fruits, berries, or leaves macerated in barrels. On Sundays or one of the rare holidays they might have some wine from the tavern for a change; it would be that year's wine, locally grown, and so was quite likely not to have travelled far, or grown stale; it might even be drunk out of clean 'vessels'. Indeed tavern-wine (or wine kept at home, where that was possible) was much the healthiest drink available at that time, the sole drawback being its expense.

The growers themselves were in a more advantageous position as, although the greater part of their harvest was sold, they were usually able to reserve a small barrel from the vintage to drink *en famille* or in company, on Sundays and feast days. But for everyday drinking they also had to make do with water and what, around Lyons, they called *buvande*, which was made from water that was added to the *rafles* that were left after the grapes had been pressed, producing a liquid which was considerably more drinkable than many others.

In the more comfortably-off households of the richer peasants, the average and petty bourgeoisie, and the lower to average ranks of the clergy, drinking wine with meals was a jealously guarded privilege – at least for the men, as women seldom drank it, and servants never did. If possible the wine had to be good, and ideally it should be home-grown. Drinking wine made from one's own grapes was a status symbol, something to be proud of: the vines would be grown on the outskirts of the town or else in the kitchen garden behind the house, and the cultivation would be carried out, under strict supervision, by day-labourers, by vine-growers paid at piecework rates, or by the nearest farmer who would keep the master supplied with wine as well as corn, capons, and firewood. This, along with the customers of the numerous small taverns, explains the large number of vines that were grown on the outskirts of towns, often in gardens, and almost always on slopes not far from a river. If there was a shortage of land in the immediate environs of the town, then its wealthier inhabitants encouraged the planting or enlargement of vineyards at some small distance away, near the indispensable transport route that the rivers provided. This was the origin of the vineyards of the Saône and the Rhône, including Beaujolais, which were developed to satisfy the thirsts of the rich towndwellers (and the ordinary people) of Chalon, Villefranche, Vienne, and of Lyons, where we know from statistics still available that each inhabitant (including infants) drank half a litre a day. In the reign of Louis XIV, Beaujolais even began to supersede Burgundy, which could not produce enough to supply the half-million inhabitants of Paris.

Above the level of the ordinary townsmen and the rich farmers, among the strata which were regarded in the kingdom as aristocracies (either of birth, or of the law, finance or the church), other demands soon began to make themselves felt. These men did not want anything to do with *piquette*, poor, unmatured wine, regarding it as a drink only fit for menials: they preferred wines of quality even if they had to be brought from as far away as Spain, and were not deterred by the high price of transportation, or the various taxes – seigneurial dues, city taxes, provincial taxes, and royal taxes – which the powerful could usually find ways of exempting themselves from. At the royal table and the table of all the most important people, they drank the great fortified wines of Spain (Malaga, sherry, and particularly Alicante and malmsey) – all transported by sea, mostly via the Breton ports – and the commoner and perhaps less highly valued wines of Burgundy and Champagne (though the latter were not yet, of course, champagnised) and those of Orléans, which were still enjoyed. Wines from Bordeaux were drunk increasingly both in the region and abroad: in England, the Netherlands, and Scandinavia, where they were sometimes 'strengthened' with eau-de-vie, precursors of aperitifs like pineau and ratafia which some connoisseurs still enjoy around Charente. The best wines, from the sixteenth century, came from Ay and Vertus, but also from Irancy (near Auxerre) and Beaune which were long regarded as the finest of all, until Louis XIV's patronage of champagne to some extent supplanted them. Some of these great wines (such as Hermitage, or Côte-Rôtie) had been produced since the time of the Romans, but the majority were the result of a gradual process of slow and careful creation, involving soils, vinestocks, the right dressings to give them, and of course the crucial vinification itself.

There is also a quite natural explanation why so many of the most highly regarded growths were developed in the neighbourhood of important religious centres such as cathedral cities, abbeys, colleges of canons, and hospices: namely that in those places there were people with enough time, skill, and precision of hand and eye, who also had a taste for the best things in life, and the good sense to allow the intermingling of sacred and profane. The other creators of fine wines were the opulent *parlement* families of Bordeaux, Dijon, and Paris, even families of almost ministerial rank, such as the Sillery family and others with land in Champagne who were in fact the real creators of champagnisation, rather than the Benedictine monk, Dom Pérignon, to whom legend traditionally ascribes the discovery.

It is most unlikely, however, that the exhausting work involved in keeping the vines free of weeds and in harvesting the grapes was actually carried out by canons or parlementaires. The (in both senses) interested masters may have watched the work on the vines from close quarters, but the work itself was done by the vine-growers.

The humble art of the vine-grower

A stereotyped image of the vine-grower, or vigneron, has developed over the years, depicting him as red-faced, independent, quarrelsome, strong, fond of drinking, and somewhat anticlerical. Such figures may have existed among vine-growers or anywhere else, but it must be said that most were certainly not of that type.

In the seventeenth century a vigneron was first and foremost somebody who knew how to grow vines. And this meant caring for them, going to look at them, in a manner of speaking 'feeling' them, every two or three days; it meant spending long hours digging, manuring, digging again, pruning – a job that required skill, intuition, and precision – breaking up the clods, pulling up grass, cleaning the stock, fixing the vine props in place, and tying the branches to them (not too tightly) with red osier collected from the ends of the rows, checking the ties, keeping an eye on the division of the 'limbs' (the future bunches), and taking off surplus ones where necessary; thinning out the leaves (taking off those leaves which might otherwise prevent the grapes from ripening); more weeding, by hand and with spades or hoes or whatever tool they used locally;

consulting with neighbouring growers so that a date could be set (often the seigneur) for the proclamation of the grape harvest, hiring harvesters, both 'pickers' and 'carriers', ordering baskets and panniers, made of wood or osier, for donkeys (usually) to carry the grapes to the vat and the press (which might be seigneurial or might not); then presiding over the complex, slow, very precise operations that followed the pressing. In addition to all that, the vine-grower also had to make provision for replacing vines by layering them at the right time, and preparing a site for the new plants, as the cuttings or slips or *provins* have to be left for three years before they can produce harvestable grapes. The list of responsibilities is almost endless, even leaving aside the work that had to be done in the cellar or storeroom, and all the regional variations, even in matters such as the height of the vine. But even a brief synopsis like this is enough to demonstrate three characteristics of the vine-grower's work.

The first is the large number of working days it requires. With the exception of a short respite in the winter, the work had to be done daily, and was often exhausting, being entirely done by hand (and foot). Vine-growers needed to work two and a half times harder than ordinary cereal-growers, let alone livestock farmers: the ratio has been worked out several times, particularly for the Beaujolais region. Vines therefore represented a considerable investment of labour, and 2 hectares, or 3 at most, were enough to keep one vigneron fully occupied.

It was also work that needed special skills. Strength and stamina were obviously important, too, but they were no good without the right sense of approach, of movement, and the precision of hand and eye involved in dressing or cutting the vines. In fact, it has always been recognised, even by the few agronomists writing in the sixteenth and seventeenth centuries, that successful vine-growers needed to have a particular aptitude; this is shown, for example, in the care with which the great seigneurs, the clergy, and the rich towndwellers selected men for the job. With hard work, determination, routine, and experience it was possible to grow cereals, raise livestock, or do both. A vine-grower needed intelligence as well. It was this additional quality which enabled men who could work successfully with vines to take the title – for it was a title – of 'vigneron', and to ensure they always used it.

As a title it was all the more distinguished as, without any need to acquire a pair of oxen, or horses, or the equipment they pulled, its owners achieved the sort of social status normally accorded to those rich enough to be called 'farmers'. Vine-growers did not possess any working animals (they worked with their hands), nor any draught animals. In precipitous countryside pack-animals such as donkeys or mules could be used to carry baskets of grapes, or manure, or new soil: or sometimes the work could be done by men.

This specialised work required a large investment of time, muscle, and grey matter and this meant that the area of ground on which it could be employed was small. Even with the help of a wife and one or two children (in the unskilled tasks) a vine-grower could not manage more than 3 hectares: less than that if the vineyard produced better quality wine, and therefore needed additional attention, and harvesting grape by grape. Then again, like every peasant in France and Europe, he had to cultivate his kitchen garden, where he grew quantities of the indispensable peas and beans, and a couple of small patches of corn; and he would also have the use of a scrap of pasture, or common, where his cow or sheep could graze. Much of this not very exciting work was done by his wife and children, but digging, ploughing, and harvesting still had to be done by him. Consequently, although vignerons were obviously specialists, or at least skilled workers, they were not, and could not be, monoculturists: at that time, the very idea of complete specialisation was non-existent on the land.

The French vine-grower is often taken to be the prototypical smallholder, farming his own land, economically and spiritually independent. This was sometimes the case, in particular localities, as we shall see. But normally the title of 'vigneron' designated an aptitude, a skill, and nothing more.

In fact many of the seventeenth-century vignerons were 'vignerons by the year', servants of a kind who were more specialised and more skilled than the others. They were paid by the year, and often by the acre, sometimes for each job they finished (there were always at least eight), and although they were often smallholders on a very small scale themselves, they were regularly employed by rich towndwellers, or the extremely rich hospitals, abbeys, and other chapters of canons in the cities and on their periphery to work in their vineyards. They had to haggle over the number of props, or the number of *provins*, and they got paid in dribs and drabs, sou by sou. Nonetheless, children followed in their fathers' footsteps, and took over the 'management' of many of the vines, which suggests that the arrangement suited both masters and servants well enough.

The vineyard smallholders of Anjou were for the most part involved in share-cropping agreements. This was in the less wooded area of Anjou, along the Loire and the Layon, and the slopes above them, and which then included Bourgueil, where as well as the main crop of vines, 5- to 8-hectare holdings were polycultures, and provided the master's house with choice produce, fowl, espalier fruit, and with good fish, like shad, which have now all but vanished from the rivers.

The Beaujolais peasants were also share-croppers, but they were treated less kindly, and given less freedom. They had often come down from the hills, or changed over from a vague mixture of planting and livestock-raising to growing the heavy, productive vines that the bourgeois of Villefranche and then Lyons (and eventually those of Paris, at the end of the century) needed to drink themselves and, more importantly, to sell. They were subject to harsh contracts of *vigneronnage*, similar to share-cropping, but which bound the vine-grower to vines that were not his own, and forced him to sell almost half the vintage if he wanted to feed his family. Hence the vignerons' houses with unstocked cellars and storerooms, apart from a few 'vessels' that only contained *piquette*. It is quite clear that most of the profits from their hard work went to the masters, the big merchants who exported the wine down the Saône and the Loire, and provided stocks for (among other places) the huge taverns of Lyons (the Charité tavern, in the following century, sold nearly 50,000 litres a year, retail, at a profit of between 55 and 123 per cent, according to the always reliable historian Georges Durand). It also explains why the vine-growers in the early years of the Beaujolais region, in the seventeenth century, normally drank *piquette*, the local drink, although this fact is still somewhat surprising, and seems not to take account of the existence of taverns, Sundays, and holidays. Yet these people were, like vine-growers who owned their own land, very exceptional: most of those we have looked at so far have been share-croppers or (skilled) day-labourers.

All, however, were passionately obsessed with the desire one day to own their own vines, to harvest and make their own wine, to sell and to keep for drinking themselves sometimes.

And evidently it was a desire which was often realised. Of all the kinds of cultivation to which arable land was normally given over (basically gardens, fields, meadows, woodland, and vines) by far the highest percentage of peasant-owned land was *always* vineyards (and probably gardens), even if it was a dense collection of tiny plots. Very little of the 40–50 per cent of land owned by peasants in the seventeenth century was meadowland – which remained the fief of the rich – relatively little was wooded, and only a moderate amount was fields. It was, however, rare for less than 60 per cent of the vineyards to be owned by them, and in some localities the figure rose as high as 80 per cent. These would consist only of two or three rows of vines, *microfundia* as they are sometimes technically called, lovingly tended, with a few small cover crops when the plants were young, a few fruit trees dotted around, with some plums, cherries, red peaches, and a *bouillée* (a local Loire word) of osier at each end. The main motivation for the attention bestowed on this small plot of land was the stake the peasant held in it, for it produced two or three times the value of the same quantity even of good land put under the plough, although it took three or four times as much labour to achieve; but nobody in the seventeenth century could seriously have considered costing their labour-time. The vintages were certainly extremely varied – some years as much as five times the harvest of others, or even more – but at least the product, satisfactorily sold, was a useful source of money (particularly if the growers had succeeded in cheating the extortionate excisemen – the *gabelous* (cellar-rats) or *maltôtiers* – of the Royal Excise Farm (*Ferme royale des Aides*)) and one which enabled them to pay the tax collector, to think about providing a dowry for a child, and best of all to buy a few extra vines.

In at least one region – the area along the banks of the Seine and its adjacent slopes that extends to the borders of Normandy and forms the district of the Ile-de-France, the largest vine-growing area in the kingdom – a kind of small-scale democracy (or para- or pseudo-democracy) operated among the vine-growers, covering more than 20,000 hectares which had once produced excellent white wine, but which had now descended to a coarse red which the more cunning innkeepers enhanced with colouring or elderberries. This vast vine-growing region supplied Normandy and Picardy with quality wines, and Parisian bourgeois or church owners of suburban vineyards, but their main customers were all the *guinguettes* (taverns) 'outside the walls', and thus outside the jurisdiction of the town, where a jug of wine was a third the price, and where at Belleville, for example (though this was in the eighteenth century), a certain Ramponneau sold an average of 400 litres a day, and probably three times that on Sundays.

Unusually, only some 15 per cent of the 20,000 or 25,000 hectares of that Parisian vine-growing region belonged to bourgeois owners and the church. All the rest belonged entirely to the peasants of the Ile-de-France, with the exception, here as elsewhere, of the rights of the seigneur (and the tithe-owner), which in this area were very light. This means that practically all the vine-growers owned and worked their own land, except for a few poor devils who had to work on the vines of the 'Parisians' and who still found time to tend a row or two of their own, although not enough to provide them with a living. Apart from a few cases, there was no share-cropping, or *vigneronnage*, and no leases that required a half-share of the produce. With 1 hectare of vines, or occasionally 2 (seldom more), and an equivalent amount of land devoted to corn and dry legumes, the vine-growers of the Ile-de-France had enough to occupy themselves all year, and to provide a comfortable living. They were, so to speak, skilled workers and smallholders and thus different from labourers (who were not specialists, or landowners, or thriving), but they also had nothing in common with the large farmers of the corn plateau, who were ten times richer and, not surprisingly, paid ten times as much tax. Apart from his land (and his house, with its typical tiled roof, which always belonged to him too), the vine-grower's wealth consisted of a small horse, or a donkey, sometimes a cow, less often a pig (though strangely enough, there was always some fat pork in the salting tub), a few fowls, no rabbits, as a rule, and in addition a reserve stock of a few bushels of beans, lentils, or dried peas, some bundles or sacks of rye but never any wheat, which was all reserved for the gourmets in Paris. He was fiercely attached to his house and land, and practically never left his village to take a wife from elsewhere (except in the immediate neighbourhood). The requirements of commerce, and the chicanery of the *gabelous*, who supervised the production, consumption, and sale of the wine, had long obliged the vine-growers to learn to read, and even to write (they had always been able to count); the literacy rate among the men was high, well before the accession of Louis XIV, but almost all of the women were illiterate, and were visibly kept away from the vines, the wine-press, and the rats, and confined to working in the garden and the back field. At one time it was thought that around 1760–70 the thriving democracies of vine-growers had shown France, and the world, the first effective methods of contraception – a clear indication of their independence; but this was too neat an explanation, and had to be abandoned. In reality, this was a movement that was widespread in all the areas round Paris, and anyway nobody thought about it, or dared to think about it, or had the right to think about it during the period the Great King ruled over the vine-growers in his direct subinfeudation, although he was visibly more concerned with the conduct of great ladies, their servants, and prostitutes. But that is another story. We are dealing here with vines and vine-growers.

The wine itself, which was made in the areas around Paris and Lyons, played very little part in the exchange economy of the kingdom as a whole, as practically all of it was consumed where it was made.

Wine produced for export – it was the largest or second largest export, depending on the year – left from the 'Atlantic rivers' (as they called them) for the northern regions where people wanted drinks which were fresh, potent, and fortifying. In an earlier period the trade had been dominated by the English, and they never gave up their interest in it, but in the seventeenth century the Dutch carried it on almost alone. Each year after the vintage, their ships sailed up the rivers in the vine-growing areas to the market towns which at that time had large colonies of their compatriots; they sailed up the Dordogne, the Loire, the Charente, and the Adour, or else waited at the estuary ports. They paid cash for what best suited their clients, who extended as far as Belgium: this included wines from Touraine, Anjou (but not Nantes), from the whole of Charente, Bergerac and Bordeaux, and Cahors, which was then much prized; the wines from the Charente and the Adour, which did not travel so well, were either fortified with spirits or simply distilled, and indeed there is a good case for maintaining that the Dutch were responsible for the development of Cognac and Armagnac, at least in their coarser early stages. In these other, very different, areas the status of the vine-growers, who were often share-croppers, sometimes smallholders or servants, could not have differed very much from those we have already seen, although the technical aspects could vary considerably (particularly in the case of the great Bordeaux growths). Or at least we may take that to be the case: there is little work specifically devoted to the seventeenth century, although as usual the eighteenth century has fared better, especially in matters of trade.

At this point, where commerce enters the picture, we move out of the realm of the peasantry, who merely provide the raw materials, and into the world of shipping and big business, with its many subtleties and broad horizons.

II

Peasants-plus: or from the semi-artisan to the semi-shopkeeper, via the schoolmaster and various other figures

Seventeenth-century peasants cannot really be adequately described in terms of cabbages, corn, cows, vines and poaching, any more than the peasants of other centuries. They could all use their hands, their bodies, and their energy to work with wood, not only cutting and splitting it, but making or mending implements, yokes, furniture, and seats; the women stitched and knitted, but many of the men were also well able to make things out of wool and hemp, and even linen. Every peasant was something of an artisan and odd-job man, even a bit of a merchant when he had to negotiate the sale of a calf or some lambs or – in the case of women – butter, cheese, and eggs. It was a period when people showed no interest in the specialisation of tasks that we set so much store by.

That said, there was a handful of men, and sometimes women too, in each village of any size who were essentially different from the others. These were the tavern-keeper, the miller, the school-master and, where they had them, the cooper, the cartwright, and sometimes the saddler. But there were no 'shops' in the ordinary sense: for those they had to go to the local market town, or else wait for the pedlar.

The tavern-keeper

The French church, particularly after its reform around the middle of the seventeenth century, fulminated constantly against tavern-keepers; its denunciations grew even more violent in the eighteenth century, doubtless because it saw these places of perdition becoming the source of propaganda about 'lamentable errors'. The main objective of the bishops' attack (it was from the bishops, and their 'council', the theoretically annual synod, that the attack came) was Sunday-observance, especially attendance at mass. The tavern had to be closed during the holy office, including the back door which was sometimes used by early-morning drinkers. This is quite understandable, particularly as attendance at mass was compulsory, and as some priests, not so long before, had sometimes set a bad example.

All the places where it was possible to drink, eat, or rest were subject to unbelievably complex and restrictive legislation. This was not so much the work of the Holy Roman and Apostolic Catholic Church (to give it its full title), although it was far from disinterested, as of the most admirable of the fiscal administrations which the Ancien Régime entrusted – in fact, sold – to groups of wealthy men of great ability and competence, in this case the General Excise Farm (*Ferme-générale des Aides*), which later became the department of Indirect Taxation. A host of often highly competent employees, who were also armed, supervised the very complicated dues which they had to collect 'in the King's name' on wine, when it was harvested, stored, drunk, drunk to excess, sold wholesale, sold retail, sent by water or otherwise, and when it came in or went out anywhere. All this activity can provide us with detailed information about the world of taverns, *cabarets*, inns, and other drinking places (the word *café* is a relatively recent one to come into popular use), and this particularly in the towns, where their numbers were extremely large: one for every hundred inhabitants, including children.

What went on in the countryside is less well-known, and less knowable, but some facts are nevertheless clear enough. First, there was at least one *cabaret* in each village of any size, which sold that year's local, usually red, wine from the barrel, by the jug, or by the pint. The customers were local, or people who were travelling through. Some establishments were larger or were better situated on main roads or in small market towns, and these also had the right to serve snacks or bowls of soup. The proprietor (or proprietress) was not generally a 'specialist', but was often also a vine-grower, or a cooper, for whom the extra work was a comprehensible and commonplace diversification. The only exceptions to this were the tavern-keepers, who provided food and sometimes sleeping accommodation. The ordinary *cabarets* were usually small places, with a few tables and benches, a few jugs and only a small number of customers at any time; these drinking rooms were closely watched on Sundays by the *maréchaussée* (the constabulary), the landlord, if there was one, and sometimes by the priest, to try to ensure that there was no gambling or drunkenness. It must be said, however, that the police registers often record Sunday night brawls, sometimes fatal ones, which followed quarrels between country louts 'affected by wine' or 'full of wine', depending on the writer's style. Women are seldom found in these sordid fights.

The other people who kept *cabarets* under observation were the agents of the Farm. These 'cellar-rats' supervised the deliveries, and subsequent fate, of the wine, to check that none of the taxes due had been evaded. They had a more difficult time with what we might call part-time *cabarets*, which vine-growers were able to open, or half-open, in their own houses, ostensibly to taste their own vintage (after the seigneur, in accordance with the right known as *banvin*, had first sold his – at retail, and sometimes wholesale). After the whole vintage had been rigorously checked, it too could be sold wholesale or retail; and in the latter case a 'bush' (commonly a fir branch) was fixed above the door of the vendor, who was then only allowed to sell the wine a pint at a time, and only out of barrels which had been marked in advance. All sorts of fraudulent practices must have been possible in this situation, but the feared 'cellar-rats' would keep a watch on the place, sometimes arriving before the customers and the jugs had disappeared, in which case the customers had to claim to be 'friends' of the vine-grower. It is easy to understand how the indefatigable tradition of the tax-evasion came to grow up and thrive in France, particularly in the rural areas, which were then taxed very harshly.

The main *cabaret* was almost always in the village square, not far from the church, well placed to receive parishioners as they came out of mass. They also came in after the end of the games which sometimes took place in the afternoons – games of quoits, ninepins, football, *tamis* (a sort of tennis), and the like. Set further back than the church, it constituted a second centre to the village; some people, indeed, may have looked upon it as the more important. It also sometimes served as a meeting-room for what was later to be called the municipal council (of which we shall have more to say below), and even as the setting for the seigneurial court, which sometimes held its 'days', or sessions, there. Worst of all it was the centre for payment of royal taxes (or their provincial substitutes) as it was there that the unfortunate individuals whose turn it was to collect them installed themselves and carried out their unenjoyable and virtually unpaid task. When they were in the neighbourhood, the recruiting sergeants for the king's army installed themselves there, too, and stood people a 'mug', a 'glass', a 'half-bottle' or a 'pint' in return for having some well-built simpleton pointed out to them, who would be lured by a drink and gold Louis or two, and then would wake up sober the next morning and find himself a member of some illustrious regiment or other.

The miller

A sort of kinship existed between the tavern-keeper and the miller, despite the obvious differences in their jobs and their location in the village. Both had a reputation for hard-headedness, though certainly not for honesty (the measures they gave being unreliable), and the parish priest frequently complained about both of them.

There must, on average, have been one miller in each village: some had more than one, and others none at all, probably as a consequence of demand for their services and the availability of the two main energy-sources, water and wind.

Almost all grains and fruits have always been ground to obtain flour or oil (from olives, nuts, and rapeseed). All that was necessary was a heavy movable wheel which could be rotated on its axis against another fixed wheel fitted with grooves or channels, according to skill or custom. The long, hard, stultifying task of grinding was done first by slaves, then by animals (often with their eyes blinkered, like the mules of the Midi). At the period we are speaking of, it must have been thought that the traditional use of wind- or water-power was the eternal method. The only exception was in Brittany, and perhaps in some mountain-regions, where hand-mills were used to grind black corn (buckwheat). Old plans and maps, including those of urban areas, and thousands of paintings, especially Flemish ones, contain countless windmills, surmounting the hills with their four, broad, canvas-coloured sails, which revolve around a horizontal axis; down at a lower level, water temporarily leaves the river and runs faster through the millrace, where it falls on to the blades of the wheel, turning it and, with it, the heavy millstones. These old mills are now back in fashion again, and lovingly or clumsily (or sometimes absurdly) restored they are once more part of the landscape. Indeed in Anjou and the Vendée, some have actually been brought back into operation.

But the attractive folklore should not be allowed to obscure one obvious fact, namely that the construction, and maintenance, of a mill was very expensive, and only the rich and powerful were able to undertake it. This meant that it was the responsibility of the seigneurs, most of whom were ecclesiastical landowners. Hardly any mills were owned by the peasantry, except for a few cases where seigneurs through absence or indifference had let them at a pepper-corn rent 'for long years' to well-established rural communities, usually in the Midi, on condition that they took responsibility for their upkeep; and this was sometimes a poor bargain. In most provinces, though not universally, milling was therefore the mon-opoly of the seigneur, who had the power to choose the miller himself. The terms of his lease meant that he had to maintain all parts of the mill, which were very complex, and keep it working as much of the time as possible. If necessary, this involved forcing the peasants who were (in the Breton phrase) *soumis au destroit* (which meant they were obliged to get their grain ground there) to fulfil their obligations. As well as the mill itself, the lease included the adjacent cottage (or sometimes it was just part of the mill itself), some cow-sheds, a good-sized garden, a few strips of meadow (or sometimes cultivated land), and fishing rights if there was a river. Millers were therefore always true peasants, cultivating their garden, raising stock (particularly near water, where there was an abundance of grass), and needing to have some beast to carry packs or pull a cart; and the mill could not operate every day of the year, as it needed wind, or water (but not too much, or too little, and not frozen), and of course it also needed grain to grind. On the whole water-millers were the more powerful as they could exploit the possibilities of the water and the waterside, and in some cases charge tolls. There must no doubt have been some poor millers, like Daudet's Maître Corneille two centuries later, but they seem to have been rare. Their reputation is quite different; most of them were regarded as rogues, because they normally managed to take more than their customary or agreed due of the grain that passed through the mill. Despite an enormous number of detailed regulations, it is probably true to say that millers habitually took one sixth of the grain given to them to grind, and often much more. The interminable wrangles that followed usually concerned the ownership of the 'middlings', the bran, the quality of flour that came out of the grindstones and, more than anything else, the measures of corn. In the Beauvaisis region, where the cathedral chapter and a few others owned about fifteen mills in the town (though some of those were for fulling cloth), and more than twenty along the small Thérain river, which flows into the Oise near Creil, the millers – who were formidable characters – seem systematically to have used measures that had a false bottom, which could be moved up or down depending on whether they were measuring grain that was being taken in or flour that was being delivered.

There is another interesting aspect of the millers' reputation: apart from the automatic accusation of crookedness, the relatively technical nature of their job and the fact that they lived at some distance from the rest of the villagers up on the hill, or down by the river, may have aroused a sense of suspicion, particularly when the mill was working at night. Perhaps they were thought to be casting spells and practising fearful (and absurd) magical rites; but for whatever reason it was by no means uncommon, towards the end of the century, for parish priests to speak ill of them, accuse them of being too fond of the drink, and of spending more time in the tavern than at mass. It is not possible to say how much of this was the truth, how much imagination, and how much just habit. But the miller continued to occupy an important place in village life.

A small schoolmaster

The same cannot be said for schoolmasters, although they later became one of the rural characters of the Third Republic. We have already come across them when we looked at the different stages of childhood among the poor peasantry in the seventeenth century. At first, not every village had a schoolmaster, and they must have seemed less useful members of the community than the miller or the tavern-keeper. Often they had the reputation of being weak or deformed, and therefore ill-suited to the heavy work of the countryside.

Schoolmasters were almost never clergymen. The priest was fully occupied, at least in theory, with 'holier' tasks, and the great 'restorers' of catholic education for the poor (the deserving poor, of course), like Demia in Lyons and Jean-Baptiste de la Salle in Rheims and Paris, had not yet had time to train and send out their 'good masters'; and anyway, even in the next century, these people were almost exclusively involved in the towns. So while he may not always have conformed to the popular caricature of the odd-jobman, working as sacristan and cantor, digging graves, sweeping the church (a rare occurrence), doing some work in his garden, and, in what time there was between the vintage and the renewed labours of spring, working as *magister*, it is quite clear that the schoolmaster, who would have had no education except for what he may have had from his family, or taught himself in the evenings, carried on several jobs at the same time, as most peasants did. He might have been a joiner, a shoemaker, or a roofer, as well as a gardener and a vine-grower.

The village community, as we already know, and as we shall see again, guaranteed the schoolmaster some sort of minimum wage, to which were added a few livres from the fabric (church possessions, usually) and, in the east of the country, from tithes, plus *écolages* or school fees which were paid in proportion to the schoolmaster's work (whether he taught just reading, or more than that) and what the parents could afford. The *magister* was usually given somewhere to live, often in a kind of communal building, the 'hall' of which (sparsely furnished with benches, and sometimes tables) was used as the classroom, where the children stumblingly recited the alphabet, or a prayer, in unison, or (if they were lucky enough to have one) spelled their way through an elementary reader. There was no objection to the schoolmaster being married, as his wife could take the little girls (separately, of course) until they were old enough to work in the house, so they would at least learn a few prayers: there hardly seemed any need to go further than that.

These seventeenth-century schoolmaster–odd-jobmen never enjoyed very much esteem; but at least people were not afraid of them in the way they were of some solitary shepherds or black-faced charcoal-burners.

Shepherds

The figure of the shepherd has always been shrouded in mystery and legend, as can be seen from the old almanacks: the earliest of these dates from 1510, went through countless editions, and was called the *Grant Kalendrier et Compost des Bergiers avec leur astrologie et plusieurs autre choses*. This did contain a few appearances by shepherds with their cloaks and crooks, long knives, and brave dogs (though not many sheep); but their main function was to provide a background for a kind of calendar, a set of vague predictions (this is Nostradamus' century), and more importantly the astrology which for 5,000 or 6,000 years has continued to epitomise the erratic vaticinations of feeble humanity. The seventeenth-century shepherd still preserved some of the mythical characteristics of the ancient biblical figure because he still often lived for weeks on end among his sheep, feeding them, caring for them, lambing them, while they in return provided him with milk, cheese, and a kind of simple fidelity. In the few areas where transhumance persisted, shepherds continued to live like this until the present century.

But each rural community almost always had somebody they called a shepherd, and quite often more than one. They all had in common the fact that they had been chosen by the local forerunner of our municipal councils, who paid them in various ways (in proportion to their *taille* or the animals entrusted to them). The reason is very simple: the animals had to be fed, and the fields grazed, while the sheep also had to be kept away from the fields where crops were growing, the 'closed' pastures, or the reserved woodland, which might seem more enticing to the sheep. The easiest course was for one man (or two when the sheep were kept separately from the 'red beasts', or *aumailles*, as the cattle were known) to collect everybody's sheep into a single flock, and bring them back each evening, or else to take charge of them for several days or weeks at a time. Hence the early morning blasts on the horn calling the beasts together so that they could set off, in as orderly a way as possible, driven by one or two dogs, along the special paths called 'green roads' or 'cattle tracks' towards one or other of the communal pastures, or on to fallow land that was not yet ready for the next sowing.

It was quite usual for full-time shepherds to have some knowledge of veterinary medicine, so they were able to deal with a damaged hoof, a scraped foot, or a few common diseases, and to help with lambing and calving; they probably also had some acquaintance with the herbs and flowers of the woods and meadows, and their imagined and actual properties. Their knowledge of 'simples' and animals, and their habitual solitude and familiarity with the sky and the stars often led people to attribute to them abilities as healers, and bonesetters, if not thaumaturgic or magical powers. People were also often afraid of them precisely because they were so much at home in the wild and among animals, which were always seen as somewhat mysterious or frequented by mysterious beings both beneficent and evil. There are records of several trials, and some legends of uncertain date, which roughly confirm this.

But sometimes the shepherd was just a poor labourer happy to earn 4 *sols* per day by taking the village sheep out to the fallow fields for the few weeks between the last gleaning and the first ploughing, and he would be made use of, and despised, rather than feared. In the extensive woodland stock-raising areas, quickset hedges and ditches were an effective substitute for cowherds; but in the acorn season the pigs were still collected together and the swineherd and his stick prevented them from scattering in different directions. The job of swineherd was generally, though, a temporary one.

In fact where people were employed to look after livestock, they tended to be extremely prosaic individuals, smelling of grease or dung, and often were not very bright.

Semi-artisans

Others were more intelligent, notably those peasants who were semi-specialists, more like artisans. Wherever the clay was workable, there would be a potter. Coopering, which needed meticulously precise workmanship, flourished wherever there were vine-growers, and indeed coopers were sometimes vignerons themselves. Farriers, apart from those employed in the great royal and seigneurial stables, operated where there were enough horses to shoe, which in practice meant only in the northern provinces. Clog-making was another skilled job that was done wherever there was plenty of suitable wood, and where the peasants were no longer prepared to leave their leathery feet unshod in all weathers (and as long as they could pay for them). There do not seem to have been any grocers; the small clientele were able to buy what they needed from the neighbouring market town or, more usually, from the pedlar. Similarly, smiths, cartwrights, and saddlers only operated in the market towns, where they often combined their trade with running a tavern or an inn. In the provinces where there was no cottage textile industry (at that time called *manufacture*, but always carried out by families), a weaver – who sometimes did some tailoring as well – offered his services when the time came round to weave the wool or hemp which each family had washed, spun, spooled, and dressed. He too was one of these 'peasants-plus', as I have called them: people who cultivated the land but who in their spare time, or when necessary, practised a separate, possibly artisanal occupation, for which they presumably had some aptitude.

Everybody who lived in the villages, even if their work was apparently specialised (as in the quasi-industrial weaving industry), was thus basically a peasant, attentive to the beasts, plants, and things of the land; and this even included the parish priest, whom we shall be discussing in the next chapter.

The marginal figures

There were two kinds of figures who were marginal to this tightly structured pattern of rural life: the permanent and the transient. To what extent did they belong in it?

The permanent ones included the village idiot, the infirm, the unmarried mother, who was also the local prostitute, and small groups of old widows and crones.

The two latter categories were found universally. The old women were impoverished, and lived alone in tumble-down hovels with a bit of garden, a couple of hens, and an insufferable goat that nibbled everything but provided milk and cheese. Some were resigned to being single because of poverty and ugliness; others were widows whose children had gone away and either died or forgotten them: all are in the registers, marked down on the tax rolls for one sol, one *liard*, an *obole*, or 'as a reminder'. Sometimes they became sedentary beggars, passive rather than aggressive, and the priest and a few other good souls (who, being good christians, knew that almsgiving was a good investment for eternity) gave them enough to keep themselves alive. They topped up the alms with a bit of pilfering here and there, or by selling a few spells (against blight), and teas or philtres, which were meant to be aphrodisiac, abortifacient, cleansing to the blood, or tonic – and which sometimes may have been. Then one winter morning they were found dead on their straw mattress.

The village idiot, the *imbecille*, is another classic figure, and sadly not an uncommon one. Like the infirm, village idiots were given simple tasks to do, such as collecting dead wood, or gathering berries or leaves. For the rest, they should have been able to rely upon family and christian charity; but the truth is that few of them seem to have lived for very long. Either a *hospice* was found for them in the neighbouring town, or it was so arranged that they did not prolong unnecessarily an existence which was both useless and a burden on others.

There were generally one or two unmarried mothers, with several children, in each rural community. Even in the seventeenth century these women seem to have been tolerated. They were usually robust and energetic, doing labouring work or sometimes working as potters or weavers. The fact that figures like these so regularly appear in the villages prompts the question whether they fulfilled a social function, by helping genuinely married women not to have children too often. This is a simple hypothesis, and one which ethnologists could confirm: there were still vestiges of that kind of specialisation in similar rural communities in the late nineteenth century, although that proves nothing about the seventeenth. All the same, the existence of these women continued, even if it is not possible to say just what their real function was.

No such certainty surrounds the other marginal figures, who to all intents and purposes lived outside the village structure.

In most places there were people who installed themselves on the edge of the village land; in some places these were called *logistes*, and they were reminiscent of the English 'squatters'. Their numbers grew greatly in the following century. Beside a marsh, or some wasteland, or a poor common, or at the edges of a wood, an almost ruined hovel would suddenly be re-roofed and re-inhabited, or a rudimentary shack would appear. In it would be a group of strangers – often from some place not far away – dirty and famished-looking. They would try to offer themselves for manual work, or small jobs like basket-making, mole-catching, simple repairs, fruit picking, and so on; they tended to be regarded with suspicion, looked at askance, and sometimes they were chased away; but sometimes, if they proved energetic, useful, and good christians, they were accorded respect. In some places they lived in abandoned caves or old underground refuges – Picardy is full of them, and in some parts they constituted complete underground cities, which were used during the invasions of the Thirty Years War – out of which smoke would suddenly start to appear, and then, from an entry half-choked with brambles, would emerge a few human beings who had been chased away from their previous place, or looking, as they said, for their 'bread': a beggars' camp, in short.

In Brittany and the south-west in the seventeenth century, there were still hamlets and places set apart for a type of pariah of the rural community. Called *cagots* in Béarn, and *caquins* or *cacous* in the celtic areas, these people were believed to be descended from the old families of lepers (although leprosy disappeared almost everywhere in the fifteenth and sixteenth centuries, for reasons which are not entirely clear). They were still regarded as dangerous and con-tagious, and they had to be easily identifiable, for example by wearing a pointed hat, or by carrying a white stick. They were not allowed to marry outside the group, nor to go into church until after everybody else. They had to keep away from other people (in some countries, such as Norway, they had their own door and a special enclosed precinct) and above all they had to be buried separately. In addition, at least in Brittany, they all automatically became rope-makers, and provided the ropes for hangings as well as bell-ropes and ropes for wells. The hostility towards them seems to have begun to wane towards the middle of the seventeenth century, or at least the Parlements (at Rennes and Pau, for example) gave orders from time to time that they were no longer to be treated as outcasts or plague-carriers. But it appears that the country people were much slower at changing their attitudes than the judicial elite; and the memory of the 'outcasts', the rope-makers, and *cacous* was still alive in Brittany and Béarn at the beginning of this century.

The other marginal figures were not really marginal so much as itinerant. The pedlar was always welcomed, particularly by the women, and he came regularly with his tray or his mule to sell ribbons, lace, kerchieves 'for the breast' (only later were they used for noses – at this stage they still used their fingers), chaplets, needles, brooches, pictures both pious and profane, and little blue-covered booklets, mostly printed at Troyes, out of which we may be sure the people who could read, and their audience, enjoyed tales, predictions, oracles, recipes, and anecdotes. Potters often passed through, too, and sellers of cooking pots and cauldrons made of iron or copper, with their mules or carts. Barbers, tooth-pullers, and purveyors of wonder-working medicines tended to frequent the small towns on market days, and some of the peasants would encounter them there. They sometimes went as far as the bigger villages, but never risked going to small ones.

On the land, though, one did see beggars and semi-beggars, too often for the taste of women, who were often at home on their own with young children in the afternoons. These would be soldiers who had deserted or been dismissed, vagabond preachers or healers, pilgrims with their staff, flask, and cockleshell (Saint James of Compostella was still often visited), or petty pilferers who led a vagabond existence, looking for some apples here, a few eggs there, perhaps a hen, or some linen left out to dry. The general attitude to all these itinerants was a mixture of scornful pity and total hostility, and neighbours would often be called to the rescue, armed with sticks and forks. In fact, after all the horrific stories, it is surprising to discover how few misdemeanours, let alone serious crimes, there were in the country at this time. The only exception was when, in wartime, soldiers arrived in the rural areas, and made for the barnyards, the livestock, the trees, the houses, and the girls: but these events tended to happen in the first half of the century: and we shall have more to say about them below.

There is a sense in which the parish priest, and sometimes his curate, too, belong in the mixed group of 'peasants-plus'. But priests technically belonged to a different 'order', the first in the kingdom, and after all they were 'men of God', or they tried to be.

The peasant and his parish priest

The many functions of the village church

Pictures in French children's books, at least at the time when history was taught in primary schools, always represented the church and the château together at the centre of the village, towering over it somewhat; both would be old buildings, constructed of fine stone, with slate roofs, surrounded by tall trees, symbolising the dual domination of temporal and spiritual power, the seigneur and the priest. This familiar picture is not entirely unfounded, but it is far from being universal.

Whether it was romanesque and dark, gothic and light, Italianate and elegant, small or large, the village church was much more than the 'house of God'. It stood at the heart of the village, and represented the village and its inhabitants in all their human complexity, not just the religious aspects of their lives. Each new-born child was taken there to be baptised, often with unseemly haste. At the age of twelve or so children made their first communion, at which point they entered, to some extent, the group of full christians: sometimes they would be confirmed, if the bishop decided to visit, which he did more frequently towards the end of the century. Once grown up, at the age of about twenty-five, each administered the sacrament of marriage to their betrothed, while the priest simply said 'In the sight of the Holy Church' (in the sense of the community of christians) and then added a blessing. At some later date (except for the rich and the powerful, who were buried inside the church at a distance from the altar proportionate to their social prestige) they were buried rapidly in the churchyard, in the presence of a few people. As a general rule, the churchyard surrounded the church, and with it formed a sacred place, which was often called the 'parish garden' although, as it was seldom enclosed outside Brittany, the name was only symbolically appropriate. In reality, as so often, sacred and profane were closely entwined, and the 'garden' was used by lovers as a meeting-place, and by itinerant merchants for the stalls they set up at the patronal festival; it also provided rich pasturage for animals, which had either escaped, or were there with their master's tacit approval, and even dogs and pigs used it as a source of food, having discovered that they could find a kind of nourishment if they dug down a bit.

As well as the activities which the early sociologists of religion (Boulard and Le Bras) called 'seasonal' – after the four main seasons, from baptism to the last rites – the church became the focus of parish life every Sunday. With the fields and houses at rest (no spinning or sewing was allowed on the Sabbath), all the inhabitants of the parish except those seriously ill (and occasionally some strong-willed individual who was at loggerheads with the priest) went together to mass, where they all stood in their places, men in front and women behind; and, in accordance with some synodic regulations, refrained from spitting on the floor or taking their dogs in with them. Their faith was deep-rooted, no doubt, but this was also a communal, social ritual. Yet there was no choice involved: resting from work and attendance at mass were both compulsory, particularly at the height of the reform of catholicism at the end of the century. Woe betide anyone who tried to ignore it, as he risked being denounced from the pulpit, and even (though this happened seldom) being prosecuted by the local petty judge. So everybody went to church on Sunday mornings, as it was a time for meeting people, for contemplation, for young people (and not so young people) to make eyes at each other, for comparing aprons and bodices, and hearing the news either during the sermon or after the *Ite missa est*, when the latest decisions of the king or the magistrate were pinned up, or announced, along with notices of land for sale and share-cropping leases available. After church, the tavern, the second centre of Sunday life, would open. It was not unusual, especially at the beginning of the century, for the local priest to be found there too, although theoretically he was forbidden to go. After dinner (taken at midday) the rest of the day was devoted to conversation, and games for different age-groups (such as quoits, ninepins, and versions of football and tennis which would look very primitive today), while the youngest bathed or danced – activities the strict priests and rigorous bishops of the latter decades of the century would not put up with, after the much-sobered Louis XIV and the pious Mme Maintenon had granted them their new power. If there was a threat of rain or a storm, the adults could obtain special permission to fetch in hay or corn from the fields: occasionally they dispensed with it, which could theoretically lead to punishment; but one has the impression that such sanctions were rarely employed.

By the time the evening came, especially if it had been a fine day, half the village might (and not only in the vine-growing areas either) be fairly merry, even slightly drunk: though probably not 'full of wine' as they put it – a state which often ended in fights with fists or sticks and nasty wounds, which we know about from numerous 'police' records (the seigneurial authorities, of whom more later). The next day, after a sleepless night, work began again; the villages ignored St Monday, which was the prerogative of some of the urban trade guilds. And so ended the Lord's day, in which the parish church had indeed played a central part.

The village church had other uses, too, some of which were a legacy of the distant past. They were very solidly built, and in the frontier zones like Thiérache, Provence, and Aquitaine – where there was the threat of invasion – they were often fortified and so could provide a refuge in the absence of any other stronghold, and sometimes a centre of resistance against the soldiers, whoever they happened to be serving. When the nearest fortified town was too far away, and the village did not have an extensive network of underground dwellings like the ones which doubled the size of some villages in Picardy, giving them almost complete security, as soon as the danger was known, or merely feared, or when there was a panic, all the peasants crowded into the church with their carts, linen, and sometimes their flocks as well, hurrying to take refuge under the protection of the Lord and the thick walls. On these occasions, the house of God became very much the house of man, and re-discovered one of its most ancient functions.

Its role as an administrative centre was much less unusual. The parish priest may have been 'the shepherd of souls' but he was less, or less uniformly, in control of the material aspects of church life. There was a sort of parish council, sometimes called the 'fabric', made up of the richest and best-qualified men (usually the two were conterminous), which met approximately once a month to decide what needed to be bought in the way of lighting (candles and oil for lamps) and 'holy linen', and to deal with the upkeep of the interior, the siting of benches (where there were any), perhaps the choice of a preacher in Lent, the acceptance of pious bequests of land or income and their appropriation, and the location of the land belonging to the church or the fabric, which might be several acres or more. They offered advice when it became necessary to nominate a wise-woman, or a schoolmaster–verger–sacristan–cantor–gravedigger–bell-ringer, or a new churchwarden or parish councillor; the most important post in the richer parishes was that of a kind of secretary-cum-treasurer, who kept annual accounts which were sometimes presented at a special banquet (some of the rather lavish menus of which have survived in provinces such as lower Brittany), and, naturally, they advised on this post, too. These accounts were particularly full and burdensome when the parish dutifully contributed to the repair or reconstruction of the part of the church building that was assigned to them, usually the nave.

These meetings about matters religious and material (there was no opposition between the two terms in those days) were held either in the church itself or in a sort of annexe, a sacristy or upper-storey room, where the archives were normally kept (and indeed still are in some churches in the Pays de Léon). In Brittany the parish council was unusual in that it also functioned as the municipal council, and its secretary–treasurer, who bore the odd title of 'the fabric' played an essential part on it, though as the holder was replaced every year, or almost as frequently, it was necessarily a transitory one.

The municipal council proper, an assembly or community of inhabitants of which I shall have more to say later, was more often a separate entity, or was at least in theory as the men with administrative ability tended to circulate from one group to the other. Sometimes, in the Midi or in the far north of the country, it sat in a special municipal building: sometimes in the 'auditory', the seigneurial court of justice, if there was one; sometimes in the tavern; and sometimes in the church or the sacristy, especially when the normal group needed to be expanded from the usual dozen or so members to include all the resident heads of family.

It is quite clear from this that the village church in the seventeenth century, and earlier, had a great many more functions than it has had in the twentieth. Similarly that semi-mythical character, the country priest, was not only (or indeed completely) each parish's man of God.

The priest, or curé

The clergyman in question, although naturally an ordained priest, was rarely entitled to be called a *curé* in strict legal or canonic terms, as this was a title reserved for the *curé primitif* – an institution, community, or person descended from the original creator of the parish, the person who once had it in his charge, in his care, the *cura animarum* of which he was the 'curate', 'the one who cared for', which popular consciousness understood and expressed very well. Most of those, therefore, whom we call *curés*, or priests, were technically only permanent *vicaires en chef*, or curates, or *desservants* (priests in charge of chapels of ease) – although these legal niceties did not usually disturb their congregations. In Brittany, however, there were no *curés*, only *recteurs*, as is still the case today. A *recteur* was somebody who directed not only the parishioners but also the numbers of priests who increased greatly in the truces and the chapels of the numerous villages and other scattered locations which made up the extensive parishes; he normally lived in the main village of the parish, and was a powerful figure, sometimes one to be afraid of, and always very comfortably provided for. Outside this far-away, populous, and rich province, every parish without exception, it seems, had at least one priest. In the largest there were also one or two curates, half-starved creatures at the beck and call of their spiritual and temporal masters (it was the priest who paid them). In very pious or old-fashioned provinces (such as Auvergne, Limousin, or Quercy) there still survived not only the unbeneficed priests (who celebrated mass now and then during holidays, or when the need arose), who were to be found in most places, but strange 'brotherhoods' of priests – half-a-dozen, a dozen, at one time as many as forty – all from the locality and sometimes called 'godsons' (of their church), who lived together (sometimes quite well, depending on their location), often in communal households, and used ancient and slender allowances or the more substantial income from lands to celebrate masses 'founded' by pious souls decades before.

But apart from these provincial or localised exceptions, the *curés*, the ordinary parish priests as they were known to their parishioners, were able to carry out a great variety of functions if they wanted to, not all religious.

First, let us look at where they came from and the sort of training they received.

Nowadays, a priest studies at a seminary, is appointed by a bishop, who is his direct superior, and is paid – rather badly – through the intermediary of the bishop and his diocesan council. His ministry is restricted almost always to the religious sphere. The great majority of priests, even very recently, still came from the country, particularly the most devoutly catholic provinces in the west of France.

In the seventeenth century the situation was entirely different.

As far as we know, and we know a lot about quite a number of dioceses, only a small minority of priests came from rural backgrounds, no more than one in five, and even then their parents were fairly well-off, large farmers or tenant-farmers, or country merchants, dealing in cloth or wood. The great majority came from the towns, but almost never from the populous groups like tradesmen, shop assistants, or labourers. The children of the nobility and the upper strata of the bourgeoisie only went into rich monasteries and convents and well-endowed canonries (not counting the episcopate, which was almost always a noble preserve), and so parish priests came from a middle class comprising medium to large businessmen, the less important legal officers, and the best craftsmen in the most highly regarded crafts.

It may come as a surprise to some that the poor and humble were thus excluded, but it must be remembered that those classes were largely illiterate, and priests absolutely had to be able to read and write. It is further explained by the conditions under which access to the priesthood was possible.

Nobody could be ordained priest unless they already had a 'benefice' (or to put it more simply, the certainty of obtaining an ecclesiastical office, and therefore its always considerable income), or unless they could produce a legally drawn-up document, called a 'patrimonial title' or 'clerical title' (documents which were always carefully preserved) to show that they had an annual income of over 50 livres-tournois in 1660, or 100 by the end of the century, an income which had to be given by the parents or sometimes by a friend or 'protector'. An income of this size, normally guaranteed by land, represented a capital of 1,000 livres or more, which was not something often encountered among the needy peasants and ordinary village people, nor, by definition, among the poor. This, therefore, is one reason why seventeenth-century priests are *never* poor, contrary to long-standing belief (although the image may have been applicable to some curates and unbeneficed clergy). It is also the reason why, quite apart from the sacred function which they discharged with variable commitment, they were normally accorded a certain social consideration.

This was all the more noticeable when they, or their family, had already been known in the parish for a long time; and it is perhaps a surprising fact that three-quarters of country priests were born within the diocese, usually in the neighbouring town or market town, or at any rate within the *pays*, in the original basic meaning of the word. Of course there were exceptions, but in all but a few special cases the others came from neighbouring dioceses, or occasionally from more distant dioceses who had too many priests for their own needs. Parish priests therefore shared an understanding of the locality, the customary laws, the rural ways, customs and behaviour, and most important the dialect with their parishioners, and this made sympathetic contact much easier; indeed, given that France was less a unity than a collection of very separate regions, this was sometimes the *sine qua non* of pastoral success.

As for how a priest arrived in his parish, it was unthinkable that his future parishioners could have chosen him. Nor were most priests appointed by their bishop, except in the diocese of Bordeaux and one or two others. The 'patrons' or 'founders' of a village church, or their descendants, the *curés primitifs*, retained the absolute right to 'present' livings; all the bishops could do was give the chosen priest a canonic appointment, after verifying that he met the required conditions and that he was a member of the priesthood. The appointing patrons were frequently from well-established ecclesiastical institutions, chapters of canons, often of the cathedral, and long-founded and customarily prosperous abbeys, also episcopal; but sometimes the patrons were laymen – there were nine such cases in Paris in the seventeenth century – even on rare occasions protestants, though by then that situation almost never arose. Bending the procedure slightly, old priests were allowed to 'resign' in favour of younger ones, often nephews or godsons, a move which could bring perhaps a third of livings into the same family; in the diocese of Paris, it was almost a half.

The priest as the village jack-of-all-trades

Priests who were thus sent out to parishes in a country region which they knew fairly well had to fulfil a number of functions, not all of which seemed to have a religious significance.

To take the religious ones first. He had to dispense all the sacraments except confirmation (performed by the bishop when he was in the neighbourhood) to the souls who within their bodily forms constituted his parish. He had to celebrate mass, hear confessions, take communion, preach the Sunday sermon, hear the catechisms of children between the ages of seven and twelve (when they came, or when he remembered), all of which were an integral part of his holy ministry. At the same time the priest, like any other cleric, was strictly bound to remain celibate and chaste, to behave in a dignified manner, wear his hair short and his (preferably) dark coats long, and never to take part in public, or even private diversions, such as hunting; he was forbidden to use a sword, pistol, or musket, and he was forbidden to play any sort of game, even ninepins or quoits; and of course he was forbidden to use the tavern. He was not allowed to engage in business, to become a lawyer (with a few exceptions in the towns), or even act as a tutor. These legally binding interdictions were gradually augmented by additional obligations.

Since the fifteenth century in upper Brittany, and the sixteenth century in most other places, first the more serious-minded bishops and then royal legislation required priests to keep a register of the baptisms they conducted; this was soon followed by a register of marriages solemnised by them, and somewhat later by a register of burials at which they officiated, although the details of this latter register are less clear. They could also be asked to draw up lists of their parishioners, *status animarum*, from time to time, but this was almost never done in France (although it could happen elsewhere). In this way they became 'officials of the civil state', (though civil was the least suitable word to use) and were almost made official census enumerators. But in practice they kept the catholic, so-called parish, registers very unevenly, as historians, demographers, and genealogists have discovered as the use of these records has increased.

Although they were very thoroughly kept in Brittany and the north of France, the documents do not achieve credibility in all places until after 1736, and even then not for burials, and only rarely in the Midi, where the clergy were either less diligent or more independent. After the 'Code Louis' of 1667, though, they were often better drafted.

The priests occupied a privileged position, as the ability to read and write (and some slight knowledge of Latin as well) were rare accomplishments in the villages; also they were the only people who had the power to bring all the able-bodied adults in the parish together once a week, and who had some knowledge of the families, and some of their secrets. Therefore, at a time when what we would call the municipal authorities often (though not always) had very little power, and the seigneur was frequently absent or some distance away, they naturally came to be used, (always without being paid for their services) by the various civil, judicial, financial, and administrative authorities.

When the king, and his council, felt a need to communicate to 'his people' the content of the edicts, ordinances, and proclamations which he promulgated with increasing frequency, he could have them proclaimed in the major urban centres by his bailiff or some other official, announced by a trumpet or a drum, or he could have them posted at crossroads. In the countryside, however, it was the priest, whether he liked it or not, who posted information and made announcements, by giving a short account after his sermon of the royal decisions as he understood them, and making them comprehensible by couching them in the language of the village.

In the same way he sometimes had to act as an auxiliary to the judicial authorities. Whenever a crime or serious misdemeanour was committed in the region, and the criminal was unknown or a fugitive, he read out what was called a 'monitory' proclamation from the pulpit, enjoining anybody with information about the events or those responsible to inform the competent legal authorities immediately. He was frequently called to testify in court as a character witness, as he theoretically knew all his 'flock', and was thought of as professionally trustworthy and reliable.

He was called upon to act in a similar role when disputes arose over issues of taxation. When peasants believed that the collectors had imposed too much *taille* (roughly equivalent to the modern income tax, and paid by more than half the kingdom) they could bring an 'action for over-assessment' before the fiscal tribunal of the local *pays* (whose members, known as *esleus* (elect), were officers of the crown who had purchased their office); and, as in many other tricky cases, the priest was frequently called to give evidence about the plaintiff, as well as the experts summoned for their knowledge and ability – usually rich farmers. Towards the end of the century, and in the following one, they were also often interrogated by the resident administrator of the province, then by his subordinates or subdelegates, though no reasons were given, and no consequences ensued.

It is clear, therefore, that the role of the priest went considerably beyond his strictly parochial ministry. Priests were able to discharge these additional duties more easily when they kept a moral eye on the bearing, conduct, and behaviour of all their parishioners, whether children, adolescents or adults, whether in matters concerning the school (if there was one), Sunday observance, games and enjoyment, going to the tavern, or the 'uncovered breasts', often denounced from the pulpit. They were, in theory at least, the mentors of the rural population, even though some of their activities brought them into close contact with their parishioners, particularly those to do with the land.

For most parish presbyteries were surrounded by large gardens, often extending to a couple of fields, a vineyard and a meadow, which were frequently the result of old bequests which over the years had become church or presbytery lands, sometimes hardly distinguishable from those belonging to the fabric. This land would generally amount to several hectares, perhaps as much as ten; this was certainly so in the Maine, where the matter has been closely studied. But, coming from an urban middle class which had never lost contact with the countryside (indeed, in areas like this where town and country interpenetrated to such an extent, the idea of separating the two would have appeared absurd), they could very well be used to owning land themselves, or inheriting it, or even buying it, and farming it or having it farmed by servants, day-labourers, share-croppers or small tenant-farmers, although in actual fact such instances were fairly uncommon. Every parish priest, though, like all the peasants round about, could also appear in the normal and comforting guise of a man who pruned his trees, tended his vines, kept a few animals – perhaps even a cow, but often a horse or a mule – and harvested and threshed his own corn.

Sometimes he sold some of his produce, and almost always he sold what he received in tithes (and occasionally in 'firstlings' (*prémices*), as in the Léon), as we shall see. Not all devoted so much of their time to the material cares of farming and their rural income: some merely looked after their gardens, their espaliers, and their fowls; but in any event they seem normally to have been well integrated into their country surroundings.

This was not, however, the main aim of their ministry, and we must turn back to their fundamental purpose, in the service of God, the sacraments, leading their flock, and the parochial tasks: how were they prepared, and how were they received, as priests?

The emergence of the shock-priests

The answer to the first part of the question, for more than 200 years, has been simple: they were prepared by the seminaries. But as most of the French seminaries were not founded until after 1650 (Rouen in 1660, Bordeaux in 1682, Paris in 1696) this does not apply to most of the seventeenth century. And even then, the small numbers of young priests coming out of them could not have taken up appointments in the countryside before the end of Louis XIV's reign, only gradually replacing the older priests who obviously had not had a seminary training.

In this particular respect, the seventeenth century was not just a transition period (like so many others) but a time of harsh change, almost of rupture. It has to be said, after all the customary precautions and an awareness of the nuances of regions, individuals, and dates involved have been taken into account, that for the often unsuitable and sometimes unworthy priests of the sixteenth century, the seventeenth slowly substituted generations of completely worthy, very well-trained, and competent priests who became, with a few exceptions, an honour to the eighteenth century.

The mediocrity of the rural clergy around 1650, and sometimes later, was not something that was only pointed out by protestants, libertines, and the rabelaisian authors of satires and spicy stories. It is much more seriously revealed by two sets of documentation, both largely indisputable as they issue from the Church of France itself. The first are the pastoral visits, tours of inspection, which every bishop had to carry out among his parishes at regular intervals, and these are the more important. Some of these irregular reports were kept, published, and studied. The other reliable sources are the papers of the ecclesiastical tribunal *par excellence*, the officiality (which was juridically controlled by the cathedral chapter, and by one dignitary in particular: the 'official') whose prime function outside marital law was to examine the conduct of the diocesan priests; and these archives, although they have been unevenly preserved, contain an enormous wealth of information.

The main impression that emerges for the first two-thirds of the century is of a clergy which has been very badly prepared for its task, which is unsurprising, given that the only training was that provided by family or friends; catechisms were not heard often, or with regularity, the sacraments were administered somewhat haphazardly, mass was not always celebrated with the proper strictness and amidst some disorder in the 'holy place', and sermons were either said very little, or were incomprehensible, or were over-familiar. When they were questioned by the investigator, too many priests showed only an approximate knowledge of theology, and Latin, and even of some ordinary prayers. From the material point of view, churches were badly maintained, and the lighting and vestments were inadequate. Not enough was done to combat, or at least distance the church from, devotions, rituals, and popular festivals of uncertain orthodoxy. There were too many relics – most of them of dubious worth – and the cemetery was badly maintained. Parish registers were irregularly kept or neglected or sometimes mislaid altogether. Situations of this sort were quite common, figuring in at least half the cases and, it must be confessed, occurring most often in the centre and the south-west. And although cases like the following were doubtless less common, they are certainly not exceptional.

As far as the private conduct of the priests was concerned, those who lived at the time of Louis XIII and Mazarin do not seem to have liked short hair or long coats. They frequently appear with swords at their side, particularly when they come from noble, recently ennobled, or would-be noble families. Quite a number appear to have enjoyed hunting as much as the gentler pleasures of the ministry. When they shared the life of the peasants, their cares and their joys, they were not above a game of ninepins or a visit to the tavern. It was in connection with strong drink, indeed, that many of their weaknesses appear, and while it seems likely that in some cases the peasants tricked their pastors into drinking, many succumbed without any great resistance. This could have very grave consequences, leading to evening quarrels that ended in blows, often serious ones. It was not a period noted for gentleness; from records of court evidence, the rural areas were probably as violent as our own time, and violence was probably more common, although the weapons were usually the more natural ones of fist and cudgel. But the most frequently noted of the priests' transgressions concerned their obligatory chastity, confessions of which were backed up by superficial and insincere penitence; they concerned visits to the debauched women of the village, keeping servants who were obviously well below what was called the canonic age (later set at forty-five) or who behaved with insufficient gravity, or keeping a nephew or niece as a pupil in the presbytery and thus risking gossip. The peasants may not have minded these suspected or actual sins, they may even have joked about them; and the episcopal authorities, who were not always beyond reproach themselves, may sometimes have preferred to turn a blind eye. But when a supercilious, or devout, or simply more serious prelate was appointed, anybody suspected of licentiousness was brought before the court of officiality. Between 1650 and 1679, for example, the Jansenist bishop of Beauvais, Choart de Buzenval, had more than 400 priests before the court, out of a diocese that only had 438 parishes; more than 300 of them were too fond of the ladies, or the tavern, or both. Things improved rapidly after that.

By the first decades of the eighteenth century the picture is very different, with serious, trustworthy, diligent, and sober priests, dressed all in black, long resident in the parish where they reintroduced order in the church, took steps against doubtful devotions and processions, weeded out the uncertain saints and relics, kept their parish registers admirably (with the exception of some places in the centre and in the Midi), and were respectful of the bishop and his entourage, and the administration, the judges, and the *maréchaussée*. What had happened to bring about this transformation?

It was simply that, a century after the Council of Trent decided on the reform of the church, between 1545 and 1563, the consequences of the decision were finally being seen. The process of the implementation had to pass from the 'head' of the church to its 'members', moving out from Italy to France, and from the Midi, from Paris and the provincial capitals out to the regions, under the influence of the various bourgeoisies, and pious orders and societies; eventually the seminaries were established and their teaching laid down (it was formal, sober, and fundamentally intolerant) and a new style of priest was produced who gradually replaced the old, slack, and sometimes ignorant ones. At the same time the episcopate was improving, and in 1695, by a relatively little-known decision, Louis XIV strengthened the bishops' authority over the priests and parishes, and put his courts at their disposal.

A series of changes on that scale cannot all take place at the same time nor at the same pace; it seems that priests were still maintaining the old tradition of neglecting their duties and doing as they pleased, for example, in Rouergue and Quercy, when Louis XIV was on the throne. It should also be said that it is evident from legal records that in a few places, though normally in the towns where they were less subject to scrutiny, there were blaspheming, drunken, promiscuous, and even sodomitic priests. But these do seem to have been the exceptions; and every profession, even the priesthood, will always have a few unreliable or atypical members, a few disreputable fringe elements. They doubtless provided a useful contrast to the sober and unbending virtue of the great majority of the rest.

Far from a poor man

The parish priest, although a man of God, was not of course a purely spiritual being, and needed a material income. The situation was entirely different from that obtaining in the late twentieth century, except for the fact that he received payment for certain of his pastoral tasks, such as masses, baptisms, marriages, and burials, in accordance with a usually diocesan scale of payments; these fees were called *casuel* partly because payment was made separately in each *cas* or instance, but also because income of that sort was necessarily variable and uncertain, and because it was in fact (as was often remarked) an almost insignificant amount. But in all other ways the seventeenth-century priest had nothing resembling a salary whether from the diocese, the state, or any other body.

In fact canon law regulating the maintenance of the clergy had been laid down long before, along with the upkeep of the parish church and the relief of the poor. Tithes, or tenths, were originally a tenth part of the chief fruits (i.e. produce) of the land, and they obliged peasants universally to give the requisite fraction to the priest as soon as the crop was harvested, who in most places received a considerable quantity. Before continuing with the peasant aspects of this, it must be plainly said that, over the centuries, most priests were partially dispossessed. In a good three-quarters of villages, the bishops, the chapters of canons, the wealthy abbeys, and even lay seigneurs had confiscated most of the tithes for themselves, in particular the so-called 'gross' tithes which consisted of essential products such as corn, wine, and sometimes oil. These great churchmen in effect stole most of the income of the poor, the small sums intended for the upkeep of the house of God, and the pittance of its priest. Doubtless they let him have some of the rich income they got from the land, under the (quite serious) title of *le gros de curé*. They left to him the more difficult task of extracting what were often very small or contested tithes, such as fleeces, cloth, the 'increase' of some animals, or the tithes due on land that had been newly ploughed or whose crop had changed. Such was the rapacity of the tithe-owners that royal legislation had to be passed by Louis XIII, and later as well, to lay down a 'vital minimum' for parish priests, consisting most often of a portion of the tithes deemed to be 'sufficient', or expedient, the value of which was fairly quickly set at 300 livres (and increased in the eighteenth century).

The important thing is what that sum represented: it was roughly three times the salary of a 'town labourer' with a family to support, and much higher in relation to a 'country labourer's' wage, although he would have other sources of income, even if only his garden and few livestock. Everywhere except in a few backward or obviously impoverished dioceses in central and central-southern France, all priests received this minimum, and the majority received much more.

For there was always the *casuel* to add to the *gros*, which amounted to about 50 livres, twice that in a large parish; there was the portion of tithes which the priest kept, which was also about 50 livres (when it was a large amount it was included in the 'sufficient' sum), the produce of the garden and fields, which probably accounts for another 50 or 100 livres, and finally that strange, often forgotten, resource known as *obits* or *fondations*. These were capital sums, annuities, or lands left by pious individuals to endow regular masses in perpetuity: the practice grew up in the fourteenth century, became enormously widespread in the fifteenth and sixteenth, continued into the seventeenth (but began to die out in the eighteenth); the capital was administered by the parish fabric, who paid the income to the priest, and the total amount he earned from these 'foundation masses' was generally more than 100 livres, and could sometimes be a great deal more.

This, then, is the picture: apart from in a few underprivileged localities, the income of the religious leader of the parish was generally more than 400 livres, often 500 and could be as high as 1,000 livres a year. The thorough studies which have been carried out for most places for the period before the Revolution give figures which are almost twice as high: in Anjou, for example, the *average* income under Louis XVI was almost 2,000 livres. Even in the less prosperous reign of Louis XIV, priests could always be assured of a modest degree of comfort. The commonplace tale of the poverty of the parish priest which was so widespread, even in the seventeenth century, became pure legend – or in some cases not so pure. The priests who were less well-off – although none was poor – were the curates, the unbeneficed clergy, or those who were more or less voluntarily itinerant.

What attitude the peasants had towards their priest remains an enigma to historians, or at least to those historians who have decided not to put forward an idea or a statement without examining proper sources, sources that are dateable, direct, sufficiently numerous, and always used critically. Evidence that stems from the peasants themselves is extremely rare and often tells us little. Most of the information comes either from legal documentation of trials and indictments, which affect such a small minority of instances that they cannot necessarily be seen as 'significant'; or from synodic ordinances (which come from the bishop's entourage) which are often repetitions or versions of earlier pronouncements, from manuals of good conduct for the faithful, endlessly reprinted (and which may have shown what 'evil' should be avoided), and guides for priests and confessors, which mainly tell us about the latter and those who write for them. So-called peasant art usually comes from towns, and can seldom be dated, except where there is reliable documentation. The work of the chroniclers or even worse the old folklorists (with one or two exceptions) are either highly subjective or else recount legends or miracle-stories without indicating their origin, later versions, or their date (something which some social scientists conveniently despise). A great deal of what has been spoken and written about habits of thought (*mentalités*), cultures, the presence or absence of piety, respect and disrespect, and a sense of the sacred or the demonic are based on uncertainties or mere possibilities, or at worst on little more than unfounded guesswork.

It seems certain that most peasants must have held a kind of elementary faith, reduced to a rudimentary form, and that this faith also contained the residual traces of paganism, nature cults, astrology, and demonolatry as well as authentically christian elements. It is practically impossible to determine the proportions of each, and involves interminable discussions which often seem to have more to do with bad faith than faith. But it is the priest who concerns us here.

As far as the priest's role as collector of tithes was concerned, the country people had the same distrust and the same genius for fraud as they have always had towards all tax collectors. But one correction needs to be added, one which appears in numerous lists of complaints a century later, namely that the great tithe-owners were infinitely more to blame for having divested from its rightful purpose the tithable produce which was intended for the maintenance (which they do not argue with in principle) of the church, its priest, its pastor and the poor; for the eighteenth-century priests were adept at taking the bitterness of the taxpayers who had found endless demands on their income, and redirecting it against the higher ranks of the clergy.

Most peasants probably did not feel particularly hostile to the human weaknesses of the pre-seminarian priests, such as a fondness for wine, women, or a fight, as long as these did not go too far. As the one who administered baptism, communion, and above all the last rites, the priest seems generally to have enjoyed the respect and fear that attend the sacred and helped sustain the great hope of paradise (often the only thing to hope for in a life which could be harsh at best), which provided a consoling vision, and even if a time had to be spent in purgatory, that period could be shortened by prayers and masses. But how strong these feelings were could depend a great deal on the character of the priest. As long as he tolerated or pretended to ignore the veneration of some miraculous tree or spring, and accepted the traditional processions, agrarian rites, festivals, or simple games by resourcefully sanctifying them, and did not remove too many saints or relics of dubious authenticity from the niches where they were enshrined; and as long as he allowed some familiarity in church, some walking about and talking, then, always provided the priest retained a degree of dignity and reserve, everything would be all right.

Things seem to have gone less well, however, when the serious-minded, austere, strict, imperious priests arrived from the seminaries and starting putting down cults, customs, and images, and trying to institute order and discipline during mass (and these comments are made on the strength of the protests and even attacks against these exacting, unbending priests and their discipline). When the first manifestations of catholic reform finally reached village level, in the last part of the seventeenth century, the villagers can hardly have been happy about accepting them, with their prohibitions and dessications and priests who ruled by severity and by instilling a fear of damnation for the least sin. Some of their sensitivity and imagination, a degree of pious disrespect, and perhaps some forms of devotion must have become indistinct or vanished altogether, alienating for a while at least some of the more forceful characters, and perhaps encouraging them to lampoon the church, or leave it altogether. This was certainly said to be the case in the mid-eighteenth century in some provinces which quickly became alienated, in part at least: future 'mission areas' for the church on the defensive in the late twentieth century. On the other hand, though, generations of worthy, well-trained, and domineering priests certainly brought an increased degree of obedience to a flock which, particularly before 1675, had descended to quite violent revolt. By sacrificing one part of their former audience, the church, in the country as in the towns, prepared the 'depths' of France for order, discipline, perhaps for servitude, and certainly for submission.

Which demonstrates, once again, how different the end of the century was from its beginning.

13

The peasant and his seigneur

There are two or three traditional images which go some way towards describing the links between the peasant and his seigneur. First, there is the Third Republic state-school propaganda lithograph of serfs stamping on frogs in the château moat so that the village tyrant can sleep undisturbed; this sort of thing may well have happened in a few places, in the distant past. The opposite side of the coin is represented by the sensitive portrayal of the kind seigneur and his gentle, charitable wife, presiding at mass, at marriages, and at village festivals, distributing presents, and succouring widows and orphans, both of them surrounded by respect and universal veneration. There must have been a few instances like this, though there were probably more imaginary cases than real ones. The most common image, and perhaps the most justified one, is of a haughty seigneur, contemptuous of the peasantry, exacting every one of his honorific and material dues, and hunting deer and partridge over cultivated and fallow land with complete impunity (which 100 years later became the most frequent complaint in the lists of grievances, the *cahiers de doléances*).

All these pictures have some truth in them. They also all assume only one seigneur to a village, living in a château and definitely of noble rank. Not all seigneurs were noble, however; many, especially in the north and the east, were ecclesiastics and some were ordinary – rich – bourgeois; and the king himself, who was above all these distinctions, was the seigneur of a large number of villages.

Nor was there always a château in each village, nor necessarily one single seigneur, and the seigneur anyway tended less and less to live there himself. Reality always turns out to be more complicated and subtle than the neat versions of it current at different times.

The seigneur as the 'first' man in the village

But first of all, what exactly was a seigneur in relation to the seventeenth-century peasants. Leaving aside the enormously complex local variations, the seigneur was essentially the most important and most pre-eminent of their superiors, and was unchallenged in this position save for a few local incidents, some of them serious. As far as the peasants were concerned the origins of his superiority were lost in the mists of time, which made his position the more secure, almost sacred, and made him seem a part of the natural order of things in the area.

In the natural and social orders of things, the seigneur always came first. He was the head of the village, the first 'inhabitant' as it was sometimes expressed, and this provided a justification for some of his rights, and brought him all sorts of honours which were duly accorded him with more or less good grace. He was the most important figure in church where he had his own bench and sometimes his own doorway; he was always the first layman to receive communion, and sometimes the priest had to burn incense before him as if he was some kind of living demi-god; he was also first when it came to tombs, having a special place reserved for his burial inside the church, a tomb which in the west of France was called his *enfeu*.

In some parts of the country he had a right of patronage, which meant it was he who chose the priests. His arms were often painted all along the walls inside the church, half-way up, and sometimes outside as well: this was called the *droit de litre*.

He was first in the material life of the village, too. Normally, he was the biggest landowner and had the largest flock of sheep, which would be the first to graze the meadows and fallow fields when they became available; he alone had the right to a dovecot, with 100 or 200 pigeons, which were a constant annoyance to the peasants. He or his spokesman announced the *ban*, the start of the harvest, particularly the grape harvest; his grapes were always picked and pressed first and his wine sold first, from a position of monopoly (the right of *banvin*). He frequently owned the wine-press, and often the oven and the mill, all of which might be seigneurial rights, which meant that the peasants could be forced to use them (and to pay for the privilege). In the seigneur's absence all his material privileges could be exercised by his tenant, who thus acquired some of the dignity attached to them. Having said that, it was very rare for one seigneur to exercise all the rights listed above, or to claim all the signs of superiority. Whole provinces, for example, ignored the seigneurial ownership of wine-press, oven, and mill, and often they became 'common', the property of the community, and came into private hands. But although there were some exceptions, the list of material and spiritual precedences corresponds to what the reality would have been like in most villages and localities in seventeenth-century France.

The seigneurie, the area of seigneurial authority, could be very extensive indeed – hundreds of hectares – or it could be no more than a few acres. In most cases it was divided into two quite distinct zones: the first comprised the manor and everything directly dependent on it (including the garden, orchard, mill, dovecot, park, and the adjacent land which was often called the 'farmyard land'); and the second (which was given a variety of local names) consisted of all the various farms and fields which belonged to the seigneur and whose tenants paid the seigneurie a small recognitive fee in respect of that fact. The exact extent of it was usually carefully defined and often kept within boundaries (which sometimes date back a long way). Within his territory the seigneur, no matter who he was, had judicial authority, and this had always constituted, and still constituted, one of the most solid and tangible bases of his power.

Seigneurial justice

In theory this right extended to cover criminal justice, but the king's courts gradually took over this function from the seigneur, who relinquished it willingly, as the upkeep of a prison and the sustenance of prisoners seemed a pointless expense.

Disused gibbets and pillories continued to feature visibly in most places despite this, functioning as honorary rather than terrifying symbols of the local seigneur's 'high' justice. The places where these once stood are often still called 'the justice' or 'the mound', as symbolic scaffolds of that sort were always set up on a natural or man-made hill.

Although the seigneurial court rarely dealt with crime (apart perhaps from some preliminary findings), it heard a large variety of smaller misdemeanours and conflicts and its 'gracious jurisdiction' was especially active.

It was extremely uncommon for the seigneur himself to preside over the court (although he might have done in earlier centuries) either because he was usually unfamiliar with the law, especially local law, or because he was never, or seldom, in residence, or because he regarded the task as below his status. Except in the large princely or ducal seigneuries, the job was left in the hands of a less exalted individual, who purchased the right to it and thereby became the seigneur's officer from whom he received a small salary which he generally supplemented in ways that were not always strictly proper. A petty judge like this would usually hold some royal office in the neighbouring town, or he might be a lawyer or simply a *gradué* or 'practitioner' of law: from that position he might collect several appointments as a seigneurial judge – in Brittany which was full of small seigneuries he could easily accumulate ten or more – which does not seem entirely legal. As in all courts of this sort the seigneurial judge was flanked by a 'procurator fiscal' who acted as a sort of public prosecutor and spoke in the name of regional or local custom, or royal law, or for the seigneur himself. A clerk and sometimes an usher completed the personnel of the court, which sat once a week, once a month, or once a quarter in a room of the château or in the seigneurial farmhouse, or sometimes in the tavern.

It is easy to dismiss these courts as unimportant, and certainly the self-important justices of the towns regarded them with considerable scorn, but they were an integral part of peasant life, and sometimes performed a very useful service, even if at other times their proceedings were of arguable value.

The cases they heard and tried to settle involved the small-scale disputes that always arise between neighbours, over rights of way, walls (and whose responsibility they are), overhanging trees, ploughs which eat into a neighbour's land, a cow or a couple of sheep wandering where they should not, or the donkey of Chicaneau who crossed 'one of my fields' and cropped a strip 'the width of its tongue' as it went, as Racine wrote. There were also more serious quarrels which came to blows with fists or sticks, if not with distaffs or spindles, after a day spent drinking at the market or on the road. The seigneurial judge also sometimes made decisions about work in the community, and these were sometimes taken in agreement with the local inhabitants or experts who had been called in: these decisions concerned, for example, the date on which to open, or close, the meadows or the common, when to get in the harvest, and most importantly when to begin harvesting the grapes. In exercising its right to decide the latter, the *ban* (which was effectively a command within the seigneurie), the courts operated simply as the seigneur's intermediary, but, as the judges were often small landowners themselves, they could sometimes inject a degree of common sense and a first-hand knowledge of the facts of rural life into what might otherwise be mere authoritarianism. And occasionally, too, the peasant community made the decision on its own.

The court also had to be familiar with custom and usage in order to settle the numerous problems of all kinds which were raised by inheritances. The seigneurial petty court, the forerunner of the old justices of the peace, was called upon to assist families in settling the difficulties created by the obligation to provide tutelage and guardianship for minors. The same court required inventories to be compiled after the death of the father or mother to safeguard the interests of the minors involved, superintended the process, and sometimes instituted and oversaw the division of an estate. It is because of these seigneurial justices rather than the notaries (except in Paris) that we have such a detailed knowledge of the interiors of peasants' houses, how they were arranged, what furniture and other goods they contained: utensils, tools, linen, stores of food, animals, what seeds had been sown, what was going to be harvested, as well as various papers, and title-deeds, when there were any, and coin of the realm on the very rare occasions when it was declared. These inventories were not drawn up free of charge, but the price paid was in proportion to the correctly estimated sum of the listed goods, and was in any event low by comparison with modern charges as there were practically no death duties in the seventeenth century, at least as far as the royal exchequer was concerned (although Louis XIV became interested in the idea later).

In all these useful or helpful activities, which made seigneurial justice an integral part of country life, the courts seem to have been well regarded by those who had to use them. They were looked upon in a very different light, however, when it came to another aspect of their work: when they passed judgement in conflicts between peasants and the seigneur, usually over matters of money, they showed a very visible and pronounced bias.

For the seigneur was more than just the most important man in the parish, theoretically the most highly honoured and respected, and the local arbitrator. He was also sometimes a tyrannical master, and at all times the principal collector of taxes, a fact which is not always mentioned.

The principal collector of taxes

By almost universal juridical consensus, although some of the peasants were loth to accept it, the seigneur was principal and sole proprietor of land and water, and would remain so in perpetuity. All the peasants who had arrived and built homes and made use of land or water or forest had been able to do so because one of the seigneur's forebears had granted them a right of use or usufruct, in return for payment. By recognisance and duty, the villages (known as *manants* from the Latin *maneo*, to live or reside) had to pay dues (or *cens*) to the seigneur, as we have already seen, (which made them copyholders or *censitaires*, and their lands *censives*) and also some supplementary payments in money, kind, or labour (these were the remnants of the *corvées* which were still sometimes operative in the seventeenth century, but often redeemed in other ways); there were so many variations in these dues that to list them would require a book to itself, which would soon exhaust the reader's patience. The most widespread, after the *cens*, which were always very small if they were made in cash (as monetary units constantly become devalued), were the *lods et ventes* we have already encountered (death duties due to the seigneur, amounting to between 10 and 20 per cent), champarts, *agriers*, and *rentes*, which were a great burden as they had to be paid in kind and at rates which might be exorbitant (as much as a third on occasion), but which fortunately only operated in some regions, notably the west and mid-west. Mill, oven, and wine-press charges varied from light to heavy, but none was universal. This greatly simplified account of the major part of the seigneurial dues (which were sometimes incorrectly called feudal dues in the seventeenth century) helps to explain, to some extent at least, why historians and essayists have reached such widely differing conclusions about them. It seems to be the case that the seigneurie made fairly light demands in the area around Paris, where farming patterns that one might call 'pre-capitalist' were already dominant. We are told that they were also light in the Midi, and it certainly is true that the many areas owned by the crown in Gascony were kindly treated. But in the north, east, and above all the west, the burden of *lods et ventes* and champarts was crushing, the latter being set at between 10 and 25 per cent of the harvest in Poitou, Aunis, and Saintonge. Most rural communities complained of an increase in the seigneurial burden during Louis XIV's reign, but this was not really justified, as what took place in some provinces was just a return to the old order after the havoc and neglect caused by foreign and civil (the Fronde), and even, under Louis XIII, religious wars. And besides, those who have to pay usually complain to some extent, even if only in the hope of some slight alleviation.

Overall, however, and given the inconceivable variations that existed (the notion of a 'unified' France still seems very inappropriate), seigneurial payments were definitely less demanding than ecclesiastical tithes, and, after Richelieu had tripled the royal taxes, were much more bearable than them, especially as the latter had to be paid in coin.

The peasants in the seventeenth century did not feel any systematic or frequent hostility towards their seigneurs, but naturally they used all the means at their disposal to avoid paying more than was absolutely necessary. The commonest method was stubborn passivity or more or less affected ignorance. They would claim not to know from which seigneur a field was held, or try to pay nothing for thirty years until the fixed limit was reached, or claim that a particular champart was not due as the owner of the neighbouring field was not paying it, that it was not part of the *detroit*, the area subject to, for example, the seigneurial mill. The seigneur needed vigilance, well-kept documentation, or a good administrator in order to receive what he estimated as his due.

The areas of confrontation

Issues did emerge, all the same, around which peasant resistance began increasingly to crystallise, such as hunting, ownership of ponds and rivers, fishing, forests, and waste and common land. The arguments basically concerned the notion that all the land in the seigneur's territory belonged to him, including the water (except for the major rivers, which belonged to the crown), the woods, and wastelands; according to that principle, it was only out of the seigneur's generosity (which usually had to be paid for) that he allowed any of his 'vassals' to use water from the river to irrigate the meadows, or take a bit of wood from a few limited areas, or put their livestock into the 'common' pastures at certain times of the year. The peasants' view, on the contrary, was that wastelands, woods, and water were all in some way at their disposal, and that they could take what they liked, at the times they deemed best and in reasonable quantities. The various disturbances which some provinces suffered between 1560 and 1659 allowed a degree of laxity to develop, which was doubtless the reason for the increase in the depredations, particularly of the forests, which strengthened the general, disingenuously naive attitudes of the country people. After 1660 things became more clear-cut.

The seigneur never compromised on fishing or hunting, and royal legislation now moved in the same direction. The monarchy, encouraged by Colbert and excellent foresters, acted in concert with the seigneurs, who knew the price of wood, the ease with which it could be sold, and the constant demand for it, and they took what were sometimes very harsh measures against the general use of common land and the uncontrolled use of the forests for cutting wood, pasturage, gathering fruit, and snaring or trapping animals. Armed gamekeepers and forest-wardens stepped up their rounds, and fines were imposed as often as reports were submitted. In addition, there were edicts of 'confinement' which were complex, but in effect confined the peasants' right to pick and gather fruit to a few clearly defined sections and a few specific periods of the year. On the whole, the legislation and jurisprudence gave the right to the seigneur against the peasants, who had to provide written proofs which they obviously did not have. So although some of the finest forests and some of the common pastures were safeguarded, this was largely at the expense of the peasants, who did not, for the most part, accept the new regulations. Misdemeanours involving waters or forests, such as poaching, continued, as the agents of enforcement could not be in every place at once, not to mention those who turned a blind eye, or participated themselves. Veritable local conspiracies, of a sort which became much more common in the eighteenth century, began to appear, as, for example, when an entire village dismembered a wild boar or a deer outside the gamekeeper's house, or when another village, led by the priest, went every night to empty the seigneur's fish-pond. These were all sensitive issues, and the peasants expressed their feelings about them very clearly just before, and in the first few weeks of, the Revolution, which began for them with legendary hunting parties.

In the seventeenth century, though, apart from a few exceptions (notably in Brittany) which we shall look at in the chapter on revolts, the peasants appear to have tolerated the seigneurial regime without too many complaints, just cheating as much as they could and paying as little as they could; the commons, forests, and hunting remained sensitive issues. The peasants do not seem to have imagined that the principle of seigneurial power could be challenged, or that it might one day disappear. It was what their fathers had always known, and as they saw it they could not live in any other way.

Seigneurial variation

As there were different types of peasant depending on whether they lived in Picardy or in the south, and whether they were rich or poor, so there were different types of seigneur and different kinds of seigneurie.

One sometimes imagines the seigneurie as following the dimensions and boundaries of the parish in the way the parish boundaries follow the farming land, one mini-*échevinage*, one priest, and one seigneur in one château or manor. And indeed this was sometimes the case, though probably not, so far as we know, in the majority of instances. Some villages' lands were divided into two, three, four, or even ten smaller seigneuries (of unequal size), which encouraged fraud as each peasant pretended not to know which seigneurie each of their fields belonged to. In a fairly large diocese such as Beauvais, with over 400 parishes, this subdivision occurred in about 50 per cent of them. In the provinces which had long traditions of habitation and seigneurial rule, it sometimes happened that a house belonged to one seigneur and the garden to another, or that a single plot belonged to two seigneurs, either because of an earlier division or because smaller pieces were now all one, or for some reason lost in the mists of time. This was by no means uncommon, and in the heart of upper Brittany it was quite usual; the great advantage of this situation for the peasant was that all the seigneurs could not be present everywhere, nor any judges or agents they might employ, especially when their part of a seigneurie was reduced to tiny fractions.

Some seigneuries on the other hand were large enough to encompass several parishes or parts of parishes; or, the commonest pattern, one person would hold several seigneuries, sometimes a great number of them, spread over a relatively small region, as was the case with great nobles, important members of the *parlements*, the most important religious communities, and the king himself. These seigneurs did almost no administrative work themselves (except for the canons and the convents), delegating it to administrators or agents who were energetic and experienced, and therefore effective and harsh on the peasants.

It is thus quite clear that the seigneur was not necessarily a good (or bad) nobleman, living in his country seat. The crown held seigneuries as far away as Gascony and Béarn. The seigneur might be a lady, or a collectivity (such as the Abbey of Saint-Denis) rather than an individual man. If he were a man, he might be a great gentleman or just a townsman, judge, or merchant, for seigneuries were sold like calves or houses; but whenever an ordinary man became a seigneur he lost no time in using the title (a handle to one's name has always impressed foolish people, even when it means nothing) and if need be buying nobility for himself (a title which Louis XIV sold for 6,000 livres in his old age). It is still not sufficiently well-known that the clergy, who were often extremely rich, held a great number of seigneuries either in their individual capacity as bishops or abbots, or as regular or secular collectivities, especially in the north and east of France, and that these were usually among the largest, wealthiest, and best managed of estates. The Abbey of Saint-Denis, the chapter of Chartres Cathedral, the bishop of Beauvais and the bishop of Strasbourg were all, for example, seigneurs as many as thirty times over, sometimes more. And despite their piety, the peasant populations of these seigneuries do not seem to have relished their dependence on the clergy. Partly this was because these holy individuals were better at collecting their feudal and seigneurial dues than anybody else; and partly because as they were normally also the tithe-holders they already took something like 7 or 8 per cent of the principal harvests and sometimes livestock from their tenants in kind, as well as collecting rent in money for the fields, vineyards, and pastures which they leased out: in this way, they exacted a threefold tax on those who lived in their seigneuries. The peasants were well aware of this, and the pious seigneurs were to be forced to realise it in the course of the decades that followed.

This sort of situation was uncommon, though, and characterised the north-eastern third of the kingdom particularly; although some of Le Roy Ladurie's chapters in Languedoc, like the bishops of Armagnac, found themselves in situations which were not all that different.

During Louis XIV's reign, these great seigneurs, laymen as well as clerics, started to use the services of the largest tenant-farmers, who might be of rich peasant origin or descended from bourgeois in the town, in the administration of the income from their lands. These men worked very hard, for their own benefit as well, so the peasants were never glad to see characters of that sort arrive. Most of them came from big farms, or had had close contact with them, and knew the peasant tricks and the range of their excuses much better than a merely competent seigneur who lived some distance away. But these were really an eighteenth-century phenomenon, even if some were established earlier than that in the better areas and seigneuries to 'collect the money', as they put it.

What one found more often in the time of Louis XIII or his son were gentlemen of modest means who had chosen to live in their small manor house, or who returned after serving in the army for some decades. Some would be pleasant and on good terms with the peasants, others, perhaps, would be worn out or senile, with a weak or foolish wife and children who quickly left home to do their 'service' in the army. The peasants often despised them and tried to cheat them out of their dues and champarts. As Fléchier's admirable account of the Grands Jours d'Auvergne in 1665 clearly shows, there were still some very unpleasant tyrants in the country, ruffians and crooks, some of whom were severely punished, indeed decapitated, if and when they were caught.

Basically seigneuries and seigneurs were like the provinces and the peasants of the kingdom: large and small, powerful and indifferent, rich and badly-off, tyrants and victims – but they were less often victims than tyrants, and more often rich than not. They do not get swallowed up in averages or uniformity: variety is the rule everywhere, but variety of seigneurie. It took the night of 4 August 1789 and the shock of revolution to shake the foundations of this secular institution, which could appear in such different guises without jeopardising its solid framework.

Yet a form of peasant power was sometimes arrayed against it, not always well armed, but courageous; and, in the long run, it was that which survived.

I4

Peasant power

If the contemporary records are to be believed, the fiercely independent peasant of the twentieth century was not a familiar figure in the
seventeenth. From the time of King Henry (and earlier), rather than
at the onset of Louis XV's reign, the peasants of the kingdom were
powerfully grouped in 'rural communities', and these groups possessed a degree of strength almost inconceivable in these days of
ubiquitous, self-important bureaucracy and red tape. There were so
few officials then – the regional administrator, the *intendant*, had a
staff of ten – that the country people had to group together in order
to get anything done at all: and such groups had existed 'since the
beginning of time'; certainly since 1500, and perhaps earlier.

The forerunner of the municipal council

It is therefore legitimate to use the expression 'peasant power' to a
certain extent, as taking the place of other sorts of power which
either did not exist, or were too far away, or did not offer any
insuperable opposition. In addition to this, but without any need to
go to the extreme lengths of hypothesising some kind of 'primitive
communism' (although it has been done), it has to be recognised
that the very existence of a village or large hamlets and their land,
within one or more seigneuries, and the existence of a parish,
entailed a certain minimum number of habits, customs, and rules,
and meant that there were simple decisions that had to be taken – and

could only be taken – by the people involved. This was the origin of the modern municipal council, although it is a very different proposition, practically run and controlled by the prefectures, if not by the ministry, both happily non-existent 300 years ago. The old rustic assemblies had lovely names: *échevinage* in the north, *général de la paroisse* (parish general) in Brittany, *jurade* in Bordeaux, and the splendid Roman title *consulats* (consulates) throughout the Midi. In the more ordinary provinces they were called *la communauté villageoise* (village community), *la communauté des habitants* (community of residents), or simply *le commun*. Whatever their name, they were fully recognised by local and provincial customary law, which were the real laws in the localities, and by the crown authorities, who were also pleased to find a locally based organisation to collect their taxes which they would otherwise have been unable to do without a more modern system of tax collection.

It is not difficult to see why institutions of this sort achieved particular power in places where the dwellings were grouped together in one agglomeration or in a small number of large hamlets, even though each hamlet sometimes, as in Limousin, had its own small community. One forgets that everybody in the locality owned or leased or share-cropped a certain number of fields or plots of land which they farmed and which might be both out in the country and next to their neighbours'; and the same was true of the vineyards and sometimes the pastures. It was therefore no more than good sense that the various tasks, especially harvests and haymaking and grape-picking, should take place or at least begin everywhere at the same time, or nearly, so that the gleaners (who had a few days leeway), the scavengers, and the livestock did not get in and damage what had not yet been gathered. So compulsory dates were fixed after general discussion and mature consideration of the state of the future harvest: the seigneur's representative was often involved in these discussions, as we have seen, but not always. In addition, it was thought sensible to take steps to protect the crops, the rows of vines, and sometimes the pastures from the attentions of some scavenging urchin or an old woman trying to do a bit of early gleaning, or an animal that preferred young corn, fruit, or rich grass, to the over-grazed or short grass of the roads or the heath. The assembly therefore, after due consideration, appointed individuals to act as guards over the harvest and the vintage (the latter still exist in Alsace) and decided not to destroy the barriers and walls (which were sometimes no more than moral impediments) which kept the meadows 'out of bounds'. Once the harvest was in, a 'communal' shepherd (such as we have already encountered) was needed to watch the sheep as they grazed the fields which had been 'emptied' and gleaned, and he was paid by each peasant in relation to the number of beasts entrusted to him, except in those cases where he was (poorly) paid by the community as a whole. If there were common lands, heath or scrub, the community might engage other shepherds – after discussions with the seigneur – to keep an eye on the animals and stop them wandering into the prohibited areas, or to keep pigs within the areas designated for acorn gathering.

The tracks between the parcels of land, around the houses, and out to the pastures needed repairing from time to time, which meant laying down large stones, clumps of earth and grass, and bundles of faggots so that carts could travel down them without the risk of turning over, breaking, or getting stuck in the mud. Work of this sort had to be agreed and carried out communally, as did the maintenance of the well, or the washing place, in the middle of the village, or where there was one, the communal oven. The wage of the schoolmaster, if there was one, also had to be agreed, although as we have seen he was not solely dependent on the peasants for his income.

Matters became more complicated when all the inhabitants, or those of a separate hamlet, owned one or more commons for 'time immemorial' (a useful phrase), to which the seigneur also laid claim. In these situations there tended to be not only a certain amount of fraud, but also harsh and sometimes violent conflicts, of the sort described earlier, which were almost always won by the seigneur.

The usual practice was for the 'community of residents' (which did not include those who were not actually domiciled there) to meet to discuss and agree such matters after Sunday mass from time to time; they were summoned by the ringing of the church bell, or sometimes by name, and they met in the 'accustomed place'. In the north, and in most of the Midi, this meant the municipal building; in Brittany, a room next to the sacristy; they had doubtless met in the church itself at some earlier date, which was something the seventeenth-century clergy vigorously opposed, and they continued to meet in the porch or the narthex, where the wooden or stone benches on which they sat can still be seen; in good weather they met beneath the lime trees in the square; and sometimes in the large room at the tavern where many discussions must have taken place.

Records of their deliberations and the decisions they reached have survived better in some areas than in others; there are many more in the so-called peripheral provinces (Brittany, the north and the whole of the Midi) than in the old Capetian centre. Records took the form of registers or loose sheets of accounts, appointments of crop-watchers or syndics recorded with a notary and, fortunately for historians, a mass of conflicts and trials. Before turning to these, there are a number of seemingly simple questions that need to be asked, about who attended the meetings, who really called them, and who, if anybody, presided over them.

In the Aquitainian Midi, where the unit was the 'household' rather than the conjugal family, it was the heads of households who met together: there seems to have been no question of involving the humbler share-croppers, however. In Provence there is very precise documentation which shows that only the richest, those whose land was estimated as the most valuable, met together. In the old Capetian areas, in both town and country alike, those eligible were referred to in Latin as the *sanior pars*, which meant the soundest, best, and therefore richest section of the community. It was not so much that the poorer people were forbidden to come as that they realised it was not their business, or else they were made to realise it. So the meetings would consist of farmers, householders, *pages*, heads of household and large tenant-farmers, with perhaps an energetic woman of substance, recently widowed. Depending on what issues were to be discussed (some assemblies, particularly in Burgundy where things tended to be done rigorously, had agendas), ten or twenty people were called together, sometimes many more, who all signed the deliberations as best they could, with their name, initials, a professional mark or a cross. The discussions were sometimes enjoyable and often very serious, and thousands of them – especially for the eighteenth century – have come down to us.

In some cases, in Burgundy again and in Champagne and the frontier regions and the Ile-de-France, which had already been laid waste during the Fronde, really tragic problems were raised, usually in connection with the arrival of soldiers; it did not make much difference whose army they belonged to, even if it was the king's. Peasants in the seventeenth century detested soldiers (and refused to enlist despite two attempts to force them into the militia). They feared them even more than the plague, which the soldiers some-times brought with them along with other epidemic diseases. The soldiers were badly paid, it is true, but they pillaged, burned, beat, and raped. When they were seen approaching a village, the commu-nity either tried to defend themselves (sometimes the villages were fortified) or else blocked the way with carts, tree-trunks, barrels, and piles of earth; sometimes they went out and negotiated with the captains and leaders of the groups so that, in return for a sum of hard cash, they agreed to take their soldiers on to 'do damage' (the current term) somewhere further away. These negotiations could be expensive (even more so when they failed), and the villagers often had to borrow the money they needed and for that they naturally turned to bourgeois in the neighbouring town, to officials, notaries, or ordinary money-lenders. Many communities, especially in Bur-gundy and Franche-Comté, had been burdened with these debts since the time of the wars of religion, and more recent wars had made them worse. They had to pay them back, or at least pay the interest on them. Colbert and his regional administrators settled these matters and benefited by imposing new taxes on them. But there was no opportunity for debts of that sort to mount up again as Louis XIV's army, apart from a few harsh but short-lived episodes, thenceforth protected the interior of the kingdom, and his regiments behaved a little less badly.

When community bodies were faced with these different sorts of questions, ranging from the occasional to the everyday, and from the ordinary to the most serious, they seem to have reached their decisions collectively, despite the existence of individuals with impressive-sounding titles who were nominally in control of these lively and sometimes very entertaining assemblies (as for example the detailed arguments about bells or the schoolmaster). These leaders were variously known as mayors in the north, consuls (usually in pairs) in the Midi, and syndics elsewhere. They seldom had any official finery or splendour, and it was their job to represent the community in person in any representations it might have to make or any proceedings it undertook. If there was nobody among them who had sufficient time or knowledge, they happily engaged the services of some petty official or a semi-notable with a smatter-ing of legal knowledge, who was then given the title and functions of 'procurator-syndic'. This too had to be paid for, and was another reason why the community needed resources, which could either be raised by its members clubbing together, or by having at their disposal common land (particularly forest land) which was unencumbered with *rentes*, and which produced a good income or could be sold. That, of course, was only possible in the strong peasant communities of the north, Burgundy, the mountains, Brittany, and the Midi.

When a community instituted proceedings, this might be against the neighbouring community, the seigneur, the tithe-holders, or a creditor who would normally live in the town. These proceedings could sometimes take a very long time and cost a great deal of money, such as the ones Racine described in *Les Plaideurs*, but fortunately they were not all like that.

Peasant power embattled

So far, I have tried to describe the assembly of leading inhabitants in terms of its basic functions of developing, organising, and protecting the locality on which the community was based and over which it exercised its rights.

As we already know, it was not the only body to lay claim to rights. The seigneur or seigneurs had theirs and, as they saw themselves as the 'first residents' of the locality, in both senses of the word, they were often antagonistic, and conflicts could arise, as we have seen.

On some matters submission or agreement posed no problems. If there was a disagreement over champarts or the mill, the correct dues were laid down. It often happened that the seigneur or his representative called a meeting of the common assembly, and presided over it. This seems only to have happened in certain regions, like Burgundy, and does not appear to have aroused serious conflict. Similarly, when it came to the proclamation of the *ban*, particularly the date of the vintage, sober-minded people always succeeded in reaching agreement. In Burgundy, where the seigneurs were powerful, the residents sometimes even met in the seigneurial court, on the orders of the judge, and they seem to have accepted this practice. No comparable docility was to be found in the Midi.

The most serious complaints regularly concerned commons – wasteland, heath, thin pasture, or poor woodland – whose ownership and use was in dispute between the seigneur and the body of residents; and that other perennial cause of high feelings, hunting and fishing. Royal legislation customarily gave right to the seigneurs, but left some 'uses' and a few acres to the rural community. Such arguments were, however, meaningless in the great corn-growing plains, where many localities had no common land at all (hence the frequent dullness of their assemblies). It was the same, for opposite reasons, in the mountainous and heavily forested regions, which had often only lately been incorporated into the kingdom, like Franche-Comté and, a century after it, Lorraine; there the peasants' ownership of extensive and magnificent forests was never open to question, and they were able to clear their own pastures and cut enough wood to meet their construction and firewood needs, with some over to sell at the market. This wood was shared out among households in accordance with long-standing and variable norms, and the right to cut it, known as *affouage* (similar to the English 'common of estovers') still contributes towards the unacknowledged wealth of a good number of villages in those parts of eastern France, even today.

The community of residents thus often found itself in opposition to the seigneur, but not necessarily violently so; relations with the church were more complicated. In most provinces the priest seems not to have participated in the deliberations, except in relation to material questions which concerned him directly, or which concerned the schoolmaster, the presbytery, the cemetery, or the maintenance of the buildings. Usually these last issues were the province of the 'fabric', which it will be remembered was the assembly of church-wardens which dealt with matters affecting the material fabric of the church and its dependent buildings. But for one thing, there were not always enough competent men in a small rural locality to constitute two separate assemblies dealing to some extent with common issues; and in other places, at least in a large province like Brittany, one single assembly, known as the 'fabric', had the power to deal with both realms, which in other places were kept separate.

Apart from a few cases involving money or personal incompatibility, there were not many conflicts with the priest himself, what few there were being about relatively insignificant matters such as the time of mass, bell-ringing, or choosing a new schoolmaster or wise-woman; but the issue of important repairs provided matter on a different scale. In these cases the two assemblies of residents and parishioners were both utterly opposed to the tithe-owners in the argument over who paid, although there was no doubt that both parties had responsibilities. A belated edict of 1695 attempted to make the nave (and the cemetery wall, and the presbytery) the responsibility of the residents, and the chancel (and the tower if it happened to be above it) the responsibility of the tithe-owners. When there were also local traditions, and a number of separate tithe-owners, and the sums at stake were not small, the multiplication of difficulties and proceedings can be imagined. In the eighteenth century the regional administrators had to become involved. Whatever the result, the peasants always ended up by drafting a tax-roll for their own contributions.

The rural community, under its various titles, already had extensive experience of this kind of task. For a long time the auxiliary tax-farmers of the crown had used them – as there were no trained book-keepers among the peasants – to assess the peasants for the various denominations of tax which were imperiously demanded. Even in the oldest provinces where the assembly seemed weak or inactive it could count, without much pleasure, on the regular task of assessing and collecting what were still occasionally called 'contributions'.

The fiscal mechanism was established well before 1600. First in Paris, then in each provincial capital, and after that in the market towns which were the seat of bailliage and usually also of 'elections' (these were areas of jurisdiction and taxation sectors which had nothing to do with voting), the amount of contribution to the royal (or provincial) taxes would be set, after often lively discussions, for each fiscal unit or parish. At the end of every summer, the rural community received its notice of assessment, and they then had to busy themselves finding it. The syndics, *asséeurs*, collectors, and leading members of the community were made responsible for the payment of the sum required, against their own property. As we shall soon see, in the Midi where land registers or *compoix* had been in existence for a long time, and where all the land belonging to ordinary people had been measured and its value estimated (some belonged to 'nobles' and was therefore exempted), this was a simple operation. In other places assessment (or *égaillement*, or *assiette*) was calculated on the basis of each person's resources. Of course the privileged (the nobility, the clergy, and most royal officials) paid no taxes, and neither did the really poor. They tried to distribute the taxes among those remaining in a way which could not be really unjust, partly because everybody knew how much everybody else had, and also because a labourer with three hens and a garden could not provide the cash that the large tenant-farmer nearby obviously could. Two, four, or six men in each community were designated responsible for the annual collection, an honour which nobody would have chosen themselves as it meant taking personal responsibility for the whole amount, a responsibility which extended to all his possessions. Sometimes the peasants appointed insolvent collectors from whom the most persistent authorities would never be able to extract any money. But the tax officials soon realised that a close eye had to be kept on these appointments, and they forced the richest members of the community to make themselves available and then to take turns at the job. This 'tourniquet' was an eighteenth-century development, though; there was nothing of that kind under the great cardinal, and extreme reluctance of the communities of residents to settle the taxes, which were much increased, not infrequently forced them to despatch bailiffs, accompanied by soldiers, to try at some risk to themselves to persuade them to pay at least a part of what they owed.

During the first part of the century, civil, religious, and foreign wars forced many communities directly or indirectly to borrow to settle their taxes. This prepared the way for the next weakening blow they suffered. The restoration of peace after the Treaty of the Pyrenees was signed with Spain in 1659 and the advent of a period of peace more conducive to the re-establishment of order and the powerful administrative abilities of Colbert signalled the start of their decline, at least in those parts of the kingdom closest to Paris. The new minister, who had had a great deal of varied experience under Mazarin of administration, business, and state affairs – some of them fairly shady – was perfectly aware that most 'communities of residents' and those in the towns were deeply in debt, and that many of their creditors were not conspicuous for their honesty. He therefore conceived the laudable plan of auditing their accounts, and making them settle their debts after he had had them carefully scrutinised. It took some years, but gradually he achieved the result he wanted: to pay the debts many communities sold their property, or assessed themselves once again, under the strict supervision of judges, tax officers, and *commissaires* delegated by Colbert himself, indeed often his own relations. In short, they impoverished themselves, and most of them came under the clearly meddlesome authority of the network of administrators and his own men which Colbert gradually established in the kingdom. Thus the administrative and financial role of what in France are nowadays called *communes* began to take form. It was only a beginning, however, as thirty or so regional administrators and their clerks and accountants (about 1,000 in all) could not exercise a great deal of supervision over so many small communities. Also, in the outlying provinces which although part of the royal domain still retained numerous 'liberties' – Brittany, Gascony, and Languedoc in particular, but others as well – the institutions and traditions were strong and active enough effectively to resist the instructions of what later came to be called central power. At the end of Louis XIV's reign the time had not yet arrived when the administrator's authorisation had to be sought in writing before the sacristy wall could be strengthened or the presbytery have a new roof: but arrive it certainly did, and the process began in the old Capetian realm.

In addition, the period of peasant revolts against taxation also stopped, and the rural communities seemed to be drowsing, in obedience or resignation.

15

The peasants and taxation

Peasants have always paid taxes to a variety of persons and institutions, whether they were measured in labour, produce, or pence, and although these have fluctuated in amount there has nearly always been some degree of reluctance and trickery involved in paying them. In the seventeenth century there were three principal beneficiaries of this taxation: the church, which had been supported thus for 1,000 years or so; the seigneur, who had been receiving them for about half that time; and the king (nobody ever talked about 'the State'), who had been receiving taxes for less than 200 years. There was sometimes a fourth body levying contributions, namely the community of residents itself who just raised what was necessary for the communal aspects of peasant life, as we saw above: but this fourth collector was always the least demanding and everybody knew more or less what the small sums collected were spent on.

The real distinguishing characteristic of the seventeenth century was that for the first time royal taxes became heavier than the others, and more particularly that they now had to be paid in money, whereas the church and the seigneur took most of theirs in grain, wine, chickens, and other forms of produce. And peasants found money very hard to get, and even harder to part with.

We have already come across these three types of taxation (leaving aside the fourth, which was not universal) but only from the point of view of those who collected them: now we need to look at them in the other perspective.

But before doing that, we must try to reconstruct what might be called the fiscal atmosphere of the period. The first and perhaps surprising fact is that French peasants have never to my knowledge paid as much in tax as they did in the seventeenth century, except perhaps in the eighteenth, but then, at least as a whole, they were better-off. Then we have to understand the non-system which, so to speak, reigned in the countryside at that time.

It was a non-system because there was practically no comparability between one place and the next. In one place the seigneur's dues were light, and in another they were heavy. Church tithes might be 12 per cent in one village and only 3 per cent in another nearby. Salt cost almost nothing in Brittany, while in Anjou it cost thirty times as much (which may have been the original reason for butter being produced with and without salt). The heaviest customs duties were more often levied between provinces (at Ingrands on the Loire and Valence on the Rhône) than between nations. In some provinces there were taxes on wine (*aides*), and in others there were none. The basic form of direct taxation, the *taille*, meant one thing in Normandy but something quite different in Languedoc (where they also paid less). The old Capetian provinces from the Somme to the Cher, and from the Couesnon (which was foolish enough to put Saint-Michel in Normandy) to the Meuse had always paid heavy taxes, whereas the most recently annexed provinces, notably Brittany and Provence, were always treated very kindly, although this did not prevent them from mutinying as much as the others, and sometimes more. Everywhere the towns were less taxed (per head) than the country, often paying less than half as much: this was called 'privilege' (a private law, which only applied to a person, a group of persons or an institution).

The classic, or more classic, privileges appear again in the definitions of taxable objects. It will come as no surprise that in a population of which 80 per cent or more were peasants, it was they – 'the donkey of the state', as Richelieu is meant to have called them – who provided the basis. But the great cardinal's words take on additional meaning when one remembers that non-peasants and practically all the rich paid nothing or almost nothing at all. It seemed to be quite accepted by all except a few eccentrics that the richest landowner in the kingdom, the church, whose revenues were almost as great as the king's, should 'serve by prayer' alone and not by taxation which was in some way alien to its deepest nature. In fact the clergy did pay a small amount, but of their own free will, one might almost say as a favour. Such payments were called *don gratuit* or 'benevolences' in addition to which there were a few supplements and, more importantly, security for part of the state debts, which were considerable: but that is not a problem we need be concerned with here, although it does crop up indirectly. The nobility, later to be called the 'second privileged order' (as if there were only two!) paid a few taxes here and there, particularly for some of their lands in the Midi, as we shall see; Louis XIV, when he was short of money, tried twice to tax them, by 'capitation' in 1695 and by a 'tenth' (of their incomes, in theory) in 1710; the nobility paid very little, and not for long. Less well-known, and sometimes surprising, is a whole host of mostly fiscal privileges enjoyed by almost all the 'officers' of the crown (officers of justice, officers of finance, and so on) and also by others: most, for example, were 'exempt' from tax (as Paris was) or *abonnées* so they received a discount, or benefited from special statutes, or 'liberties' which was another form of privilege. People in the country were aware of all this; when it benefited the people in the towns and cities they did not approve of it, and a good number of peasant revolts were in part directed against the towns (and later against what was called the Vendée).

Taxes for the church

The oldest of the taxes that had to be paid by all those who cultivated the land was originally placed on the statute book at the time of Charlemagne. In the mid-seventeenth century, the law was still theoretically derived from a capitulary of 801. It had what might be called a gospel simplicity about it, if the Gospels could bear the slightest responsibility for this institution (some theologians none-theless worked very hard to show they did). The principle was that all men 'who gathered the fruits of the earth' should give some of them to the church, in theory a tenth or 'tithe': the church was then meant to use the amount received 'for the support of pastors, the maintenance of places of worship, and the relief of the poor'.

As we already know, it was the allocation of these sums which had changed most since the time of Charlemagne: almost none went to the poor, only very little to the church buildings and that after a great deal of wrangling, and the priest was frequently deprived of the share that was rightfully his. The bulk of it went to high-ranking, rich clerics.

What had changed least over the years was the universality of the tithe. Only a few of the oldest religious orders, like Cluny and Cîteaux, succeeded in doing without it. Even the nobles paid tithes, though at a lower rate than ordinary people; and so did the protestants, who had to subsidise the 'papists' under Article 25 of the Edict of Nantes (1598). In reality, however, the most noble and the richest paid nothing directly, as they neither cultivated the earth 'with their hands', nor materially 'enjoyed' the fruits of the earth: their tithes had to be paid by their tenants or share-croppers.

The tithe was assessed on the basis of the 'main fruits', by which they did not mean apples and the like but the principal produce of the province or area. In most places this meant corn, and usually vines; also oil – olive, nut, or rapeseed, depending on the region; 'increase of livestock' (the young animals born during the year) was also subject to tithes, as were the hides of beasts, particularly fleeces; where enough of it grew, flax was included, otherwise and more commonly it was hemp. In fact it would be easier to list the things that were not tithable: woods (except for some coppices), mines and quarries, game and fish (with some exceptions); natural meadows were untithed, but artificial meadows, created by sowing clover, lucerne, or sainfoin – still very unusual outside the Paris region – were tithable, which certainly did nothing to encourage their development; and the fruits of trees which grew on tithable land were not themselves liable, on the strength of the customary principle (which was not always upheld) of 'not tithing the upper and the lower', which helps to explain why so many pear, apple, nut, cherry, and olive trees were set among the vines in cornfields. Working animals were also exempt, which may perhaps account for the large number of working cows (there were still some in Périgord at the beginning of the twentieth century). The most important exemption covered gardens and closes, as long as they were less than a certain size and did not contain too much 'tithable produce' such as barley, or vines that were not growing up trees. In some places there was no tithe levied on what were called 'unusual' crops, but on the other hand all 'new' crops (which, by definition, were unlikely to be usual) were subject, as were even changes or interchanges of crops on the same piece of land. This extremely simplified account of how tithes operated reveals enough of the complexities they involved to show why the tithe became the source of so many conflicts and court-hearings.

Strangely, perhaps, there was less argument about the rate of tithe, despite the fact that this varied from 3 per cent in lower Brittany to 12 per cent in Armagnac, and sometimes from one canton to the next, although it was normally around 7 or 8 per cent. But then people were used to it, and the rate often seemed to them to have been fixed (although in the long term it appears to have diminished somewhat), and peasants were not very well informed about what was happening in other places, although this began to change towards the end of the eighteenth century and provoked some disturbances, notably in the south-west.

In practice, the most significant element was the tithe on grain. Each year when the harvest was finished the sheaves had to be stacked in bundles and the peasants had to wait patiently for the tithe-owner's cart to come round, as this was a *quérable* tithe, one which had to be collected in person, and it was also the first to be collected (although this was never specifically stated). Unless there was some earlier arrangement to take so much per acre, which was uncommon, the tithe-owner, or more often his tenant, took one sheaf from each bundle: one from a bundle of nine if the tithe was one ninth, or from a bundle of thirteen if it was one thirteenth, and so on. Only when this had been done could the grain be gathered in. Arrangements in respect of other produce varied, but were seldom characterised by simplicity.

There had been a large number of peasant revolts against tithes in the previous century, following the example of the protestants, who naturally refused to pay them, and, huguenot or not, nearly one third of the provinces and of course all the Midi, including Poitou, had withheld them. The problem was settled by Henry IV with the Edict of Nantes, and in the seventeenth century the peasants merely quibbled, cheated, and sometimes complained. They made the most of the difficulties that arose in the normal course of events, such as paying tithes of perhaps one twentieth on fleeces, when a peasant only had three sheep (this would be settled by some other transaction, sometimes in money), or arguing over whether certain nut trees were actually in a field or merely at its edge. Other frequent bones of contention included the exact number of piglets born in a year, whether or not some crop was 'new', and then whether it attracted a smaller tithe, or the usual one, or indeed was exempt. It also sometimes happened that sheaves disappeared overnight, or that vats of grapes got covered up or that the bundles of tithable sheaves were carefully put together with the main bulk hidden right in the middle. A more serious source of conflict was the straw, which unlike the grain was not tithable, but which the tithe-owner habitually kept for himself, if he did not try to sell it back to the peasants. Complaints were even louder when as often happened the tithes were collected by the rich local (and therefore well-known) agent of a tithe-owner who lived some distance away.

Despite all these ruses and resistances, the collection of tithes would finally be completed, and the peasants' harvests and other revenues would be reduced at the outset by something between 5 and 10 per cent, which was not inconsiderable and assured the church of an enormous income amounting to several tens of millions in gold, little of which went to the minor clergy, the 'shepherds of souls'.

Taxes for the seigneur

The less ancient deductions made by the seigneurs are generally thought to have been less burdensome, at least by most modern historians, yet some of their conclusions may perhaps have been a little premature. Not many people have done the slow, painstaking work of examining the question in the closest detail, and the task is made even more difficult by the extraordinary diversity that existed in seigneurial dues and the way the right to them was exercised. This plethora of different practices has meant that, by choosing the right examples to support their argument (which is an old and not very honest rhetorical trick), historians have been able to sustain the above opinion as effectively as its opposite. We do know, though, that the fiscal burden of the seigneurie was light in the area around Paris and in most of the Midi, very heavy in the west, particularly the mid-west, and the same in the east, and part of northern France. We have also, in a previous chapter, seen the peasants in confront-ation with their seigneur (or seigneurs), at the broadest level. In order to assess the weight of seigneurial dues, therefore, let us, for once, take some examples from a single region, north Burgundy, which provided the basis for a recent excellent study by the late Pierre de Saint-Jacob.

All the peasants in Burgundy paid fixed dues on a fixed date each year. Usually these were known as *cens*; in addition there were sometimes small extra payments or *surcens*. In money terms these were light, as the original sum had become substantially devalued in the course of four or five centuries, but where they were expressed in some other form they were often more burdensome. For houses and gardens the peasants paid a certain sum of money or so many measures of grain, often oats (which in fact were often re-valued in money terms according to the rate in this or that market: the average price over the year, or the price at Martinmas, for example); then they paid a similar amount for the use of commons, pastures, and coppices. Their land cost them so many sous or so many measures of grain per unit of surface area, a sum which could vary from 1 livre to 30 or 40 livres. In some places there was also a seigneurial tax or *taille*, which was older than the royal tax, and therefore amounted to less, but which nonetheless reached something like 200 livres in some localities such as Savoisy and Bussy-le-Grand. Rights of banality were commonplace in these areas, but were relatively cheap, except oddly enough for the oven, for the use of which the seigneurs charged 5 per cent of what was cooked, or the equivalent amount of money. *Corvées*, days of obligatory, unpaid labour (which the peasants fulfilled either with their horses or with their hands) were still the norm, although they were reduced to three or five days each year; this usually meant one day at haymaking, one at harvest, and one at the vintage, chosen when the work was most demanding, of course, as the seigneur himself decided when they should be. Another fairly widespread imposition was the unpopular *tierce*, a kind of seigneurial tithe in kind which often exceeded 10 per cent, and could be as high as 20 per cent, and did not prevent other tithes from being extracted as well. It should be said here that this kind of due was also found outside Burgundy, under different names such as champart, *agrier*, and (in Provence) *tasque*, sometimes on smaller areas which had only recently been brought into cultivation, and sometimes over much larger ones, as in Poitou and the Charentes, where they could be as high as a third.

Apart from these normal but uneven dues, the peasant in northern Burgundy usually had to join in maintenance work on the château and its moats, and sometimes its park as well, to give a present to the seigneur when he got married, and pay *lods* on a scale between 8 and 16 per cent *ad valorem* on every land transaction he made (whereas the crown took nothing in the seventeenth century, and even later only took the 'hundredth *denier*' or 1 per cent).

All these seigneurial dues in Burgundy have been established as a result of serious and well-founded work on the region; and they do not seem to represent an extreme case, given that, as has already been mentioned, apart from Poitou and Saintonge, there were places in the Jura where mortmain, a lightly improved version of medieval serfdom, still held undiminished sway. Seigneurial demands have also been shown to have been light in other places, such as the Ile-de-France. There are many other provinces about which our knowledge is incomplete, or about which we know very little. In any event, the nineteenth-century peasantry long feared the successful re-establishment of what they exaggeratedly called 'feudalism', from which the Revolution, reviled for some of its aspects, had liberated them. And surely no twentieth-century peasant could envisage taxes of this sort on the crops they harvest, or on the sheaves of corn (if there are any still), or on the wine they make, and their livestock, and their stores, still less the return of all those ancient dues, which were the cause of anger and resentment whether they were heavy or not. Whenever the 'good old days' might have been, which we nostalgically project back into the past, they certainly were not in the seventeenth century.

Yet there was very little peasant resistance to these seigneurial levies, less than there had been in earlier generations, and less than that put up a few generations later, when they managed to deflect demands for reform into a full-blown Revolution. They never missed an opportunity to cheat, or pretend ignorance, and they made the most out of the weaknesses of some seigneurs, or their absence. But the seigneurs usually came back in the end, or employed somebody who had the shrewdness they lacked, and set about regaining their traditional and only temporarily forgotten dues. That was when rumbles of anger were heard. These only really became serious, though, in 1675 in Brittany (and there were other reasons involved as well) and that was because some owners had attempted to exercise or extend rights – notably champarts – which the peasants thought went against sacrosanct Breton custom. More of those later. Across most of the country, apart from a few local incidents and the recurrent grumbling complaints, the peasants treated the seigneurs fairly well between 1600 and 1715; but that was largely because their hostility was directed against the dangerous encroachments of the crown taxes.

The lion's share: the royal taxes

For us in the twentieth century, the revenue is synonymous with the state. But the word 'state' meant nothing in the seventeenth century (except for 'the Estates' in a few provinces). Where we speak of the state, they spoke of the king. And the word *fisc*, or revenue, although it existed, referred rather to a seigneurial domain and its laws. The word used instead was *impositions*.

The three main forms these took – *aides*, *gabelles*, and finally *tailles* – were cleverly and gradually introduced during the fourteenth and fifteenth centuries, and to begin with applied throughout the old Capetian kingdom which spoke the northern dialect, and encompassed the country round the Loire and the Seine and their tributaries. The other provinces managed to preserve some of their privileges and their own laws (and lower taxes) as long as they were associated with the old nucleus of the kingdom rather than absorbed into it. This is why the royal taxes are neither universal nor uniform, and why they take such different forms in the north and the Midi, and in Brittany and Alsace.

The peasants were basically affected by two or three kinds of tax which slowly attracted further accretions: the *gabelle* and the *taille* were levied almost everywhere, and the *aide* in the many vine-growing regions. However, they were levied very unevenly. The effects of this can be seen more clearly by looking at a number of individual instances and some surprising complications. We shall look first at a classic village of the old kingdom, somewhere in the Paris basin. Then we shall turn to a village deep in the Midi where everything was different.

The taille *in the north*

In the previous chapter we saw the 'community of residents', the forerunner of our municipal council, at work, and learned that each year it delegated two or four or six of its number to draw up the 'roll of *tailles* and other taxes included therein', which was the roll of direct taxation; this handful of men who were thus both assessors and collectors had to ensure that the money was collected and then sent (in coin, of course) to what later came to be called the 'Public Treasury'.

At the end of each summer, after a long period of 'arbitration' first at governmental, then at provincial (in financial terms called a *generalité*), then at sub-provincial level (known as the *élection* – corresponding to the old *arrondissements*), the amount that had to be paid was notified to each of the basic fiscal units generally called parishes, or *collectes*. After that, the collectors just had to get on and sort it out themselves (a phrase which is probably apt for what was a thankless task).

There were general rules which were universally familiar: nobles, clergy, officers of the crown, and non-residents (a category which gave rise to many disputes) did not pay anything. Nor was it possible to extract anything from the truly poor, from beggars, nor from many of the widows, so these were all entered as 'reminders' and put down symbolically for a quarter of a sou. This left a *taille* of say 3,000 livres to be raised from the non-privileged and non-impoverished residents of a village of some 200 'fires' (or about the same number of families, which would work out at about 1,000 'souls').

It is not difficult to imagine the hesitations, arguments, the complaints and disputes which the drawing up of the roll gave rise to. Each year's collectors tended to look after their own family and friends (their own assessment could not be put up, which was one of the few advantages of the job), but they knew very well that others would get their own back in subsequent years. The seigneur used his influence on behalf of his tenant, and the priest tried to obtain leniency for those connected with the church. From time to time peasants who believed themselves to have been taxed too highly initiated proceedings (before the tax tribunal of the *élection*) against the community, or the collectors, or one or two neighbours. The time came, after the harvests, in about October, when the roll was written (or scrawled), and countersigned by the local tax officers, thus signalling its acceptance.

Having examined a large number of these documents in regions which are well-known, I can say that, given the legislation of the period, I was not as shocked by them as some historians have been. The poor and the labourers always paid very little (3 or 4 livres, and often less), vine-growers and small-scale, unsuccessful farmers (or *haricotiers*) paid a little more (about 20 livres), and the rich – which here basically means the rich tenant-farmers – paid a great deal of money. Sometimes, one, two, or three 'cocks of the village' (to tell the truth, I have never come across that expression in the contemporary sources, even though it is meant to be very common) had to pay between 100 and 300 livres, or more, providing more than half the village *taille* themselves, and certainly paying a great deal more than a well-established merchant in the nearby town. It was a rough but effective system (money had to be raised where it could be found) and does not seem any more unjust than many other systems, including recent ones.

This does not mean that the unfortunate collectors had an easy task, but they were at least allowed a 1 per cent discount on the bill. The peasants generally paid sou by sou, in poor bronze coins, Sunday after Sunday, and only then after delays, promises, and excuses. Some months later the petty finance officials responsible for collecting the annual receipts would arrive with mules or carts to gather in what had been paid, but this was never the full sum, and indeed they would be fortunate if there were not still arrears owing from the year before. Forced to come back two or three times, the receivers would finally return with some poor bailiff and perhaps a few soldiers to intimidate the peasants, ransack their chests, threaten them with seizure of goods, and sometimes take one or two of the unfortunate collectors off to prison. Sometimes the situation turned nasty, as furious villagers roused the neighbourhood and forced the judicial authorities to turn back, pelted with stones or beaten with sticks, or at the least threatened. But in the long run, most of the money was paid, particularly after Colbert had taken charge and introduced severer measures, although the peasants always asked for rebates because of storms, hail, and epidemics. Then the next year it would all begin again.

It was not always exactly the same, however. There were a few short-lived moments when the death of the king or the announcement of peace gave new impetus to the eternal hope that taxes might disappear (as if they ought to die with the king) or that there might be a reduction of those contributions which were always called 'extraordinary' because they were only asked for in times of war. In reality, the return of peace sometimes reduced or transformed some war-time tax, but rarely ended it altogether, although that did happen in the case of the 1695 capitation, after a period of delay, and the signing of the peace of Ryswick in 1697. As the monarchy became more invasive, more expansionary, and above all more warlike, its growing needs gave rise to a series of unpleasant and unforeseen demands: there were increases (in *taille*) and a variety of supplementary taxes to pay for the *maréchaussée*, bridges and highways, and regimental provisions; and sometimes a second *brevet* was imposed on the *taille*, another heavy supplement. As always in this century the pressure of both basic and additional, sometimes brutally heavy, taxation was due to war. Seen in this perspective the responsibility is not so much that of the *Grand Roi* as of the great cardinal. When, with Louis XIII's full agreement, he decided to embark on the huge international conflict called the Thirty Years War, in 1635, he was forced not only to subsidise valued allies like Sweden, but also to create almost from nothing an army that by the standards of the period was vast, to equip it, provision it, provide it with munitions and artillery, and also to consider building a navy. The result was that Frenchmen's taxation doubled, then trebled, in a matter of years. This was a heavy burden, and it was imposed very hastily. To extract that quantity of money called for bailiffs, sergeants, and in the end the army. This sparked off the most serious sequence of revolts of the century. For the first time for many years these revolts were not against tithes, or feudal or seigneurial dues, but openly against the administration of the royal finances. They were severe, and they continued until 1675, as we shall see later.

Of all the taxes imposed by the *élection* areas, including the *taille* described above (all of which increased), there was one infamous tax which affected everybody in the countryside, and to some extent people in the towns as well. This was the tax on salt, the *gabelle*.

Gabelles

The word itself derives from the Italian, perhaps originally from Arabic, and had been used for a number of different taxes, but it came to refer exclusively to one important product: salt, both sea salt and rock salt. Wherever it could – away from the coast and where there were no salt-mines, and taking account of the provinces of Aquitaine which took up arms to reject the idea in the sixteenth century – the crown secured a monopoly over the sale of salt, which was not only an indispensable nutrient but also the sole means of conserving fats, meat, and fish. In all the so-called high-*gabelle* areas around the Paris basin, salt could only be bought from royal finance officials (or the agents of the General Excise Farm who gradually replaced them) who sold it at twenty times the price it cost them. As usual the high price did not affect the privileged who frequently enjoyed free salt or paid some very low token price for it. The price of salt infuriated the peasants, especially those who lived just inside the borders of the high-*gabelle* area. This primarily meant those in Maine and Anjou; but in Berry, Bourbonnais, and Champagne, too, they could buy contraband salt at a fifth or a sixth of the official price. The dealers in this contraband salt were keenly hunted by the authorities, but despite this they were very active and very popular, and very adept at disappearing, helped by the fact that they enjoyed widespread, complicit support. The finance authorities and the administrators countered this by organising compulsory sales from their stores at the rate of 7 kilos for each person over the age of eight per year, just 'for the pot and the salt box'; any salt needed for preserving food had to be bought over and above the prescribed minimum. Near the frontiers of the *gabelle* area, the regime was even harsher. In each village, collectors – similar to those who dealt with the *tailles* – were made to draw up careful lists of *gabellans* (often called *sextés*), who went four times a year to buy salt on behalf of their fellow-citizens, and to pay for it within six weeks. This created more accounting, more difficulties, more conflicts, and fraud on a huge scale, which was punished with great severity. This tax on salt, which is what it amounted to, remained the prerogative of the old France around the Seine and Loire, areas which always tended to be harshly treated, but the people were probably sufficiently prosperous, despite all the setbacks they encountered, to be able to bear it.

None of this affected the Midi, let alone Brittany, where they paid neither *gabelle* nor *taille* and only had a light system of provincial contributions.

Tailles *and land registers in the Midi*

All the Midi paid *taille* to the crown, but it differed in everything but name from the *taille* applied in the north. There it was 'personal' and aimed to tap the 'appearance' or probability of income, but in the Midi it was assessed on the basis of property, principally land, and was therefore called 'real' (from the Latin *res*, meaning 'thing'). These impositions were generally set and raised by the *Estats*, the traditional provincial assemblies, as these were the nearest authorities, and were deemed the best for the purpose; some of them were remarkably well-organised for the period, the Languedoc enjoying a particularly high reputation for the quality of its work. But besides the 'real' *taille* and the provincial *Estats*, the Midi was characterised by its *cadastres* or land registers, also known as *compoix*.

The rural communities of southern France (and of nearby Italy, which included Savoy) had long possessed these land registers. The first dated from the fifteenth century, and by the seventeenth most places had them, long before Napoleon's similar scheme, although the old registers hardly ever included a plan or map (these began to appear in the papers of the best-run seigneuries after about 1670). The *cadastre* consisted of one (or several) large registers written on heavy rag paper and often nicely bound, containing a list of *all* the land with houses, gardens, ploughland, vines, orchards, meadows, heaths, bracken, coppices, wasteland, rocks, and so on, amounting to several thousand entries at least, all designated by place-names and *confronts* (the adjacent parts) and duly measured (according to the system of measurement in use locally, which does not simplify matters), described in terms of its crops, and carefully assessed in livres, *sols*, *deniers*, and fractions of *deniers*. The 'consuls', the two leaders of the municipality, would call for a register to be drawn up; then the work would be carried out by professional surveyors, who provided the physical measurements, and sworn valuers, who carried out the assessments; these were often two rich peasants and a notary, and a draft of the register would be made by one or two clerks, which would then be countersigned by another notary or a judge 'of the place' (or by several) and 'verified' by the nearest court of *aides*, which had important financial jurisdiction. The registers also detailed the 'holder' of each piece of land at the time the document was drawn up, a list of them often being appended at the beginning or the end of the registry, with a reference to the relevant folios (which is a blessing for historians). Finally all the assessments of each piece of land (the *allivrements*) were added together to obtain the general *allivrement* of the *collecte*, of which each parcel of land contained a tiny but precise fraction. The origins of this typically southern procedure are still not certain (although the registers are similar to ones kept in densely populated

Roman societies); and of course it provoked disputes here and there from people who thought they had been charged too much, or *surallivré*. The main weakness of the system was the difficulty of finding out about sales and inheritances, which were liable to surcharges, the *compoix* rarely being corrected as that involved so much work and expense. It did, however, have one great advantage, which was that it provided a well-established basis for the division of the royal *taille*, provincial and local taxes (and sometimes seigneurial ones too). Once the total sum payable was known, then everybody's share could be fixed almost automatically (a simple rule of three would have been enough) in relation to the *allivrements* on their land. In fact the system seemed such a good one, and relatively equitable, that Colbert dreamed of extending it to cover the whole kingdom: but this did not happen until the nineteenth century.

There was another aspect of the cadastral system which is less often mentioned. It resulted, as we know, in a tax on land rather than directly on people (the other side of the coin was that the small number of people who did not own any land were not included, and had to be traced in other ways); because of this, the large land-owners, even absentees, paid taxes the same as everybody else – in fact usually more – even if they were officials, or bourgeois from the towns, or nobles. The third of France where these registers were operative, the Midi, was the only region in which the nobility were taxed, and were not ashamed of it. They were taxed because of their lands, and their lands were extensive. There was one restriction, though: some land was 'noble' (nobility being a category that could encompass land as well as people) and was in theory untaxed. But it was the responsibility of the people who held the land, even if they were ordinary peasants, to prove its nobility; and anyway there were not many of these noble estates, only a few per cent of the total, and they gradually declined in number under pressure from the holders of ordinary land. Although there are some criticisms to be made, the system was administratively superb; and when the peasants of the Midi revolted, as they did sometimes, it was not because of the cadastral registers but, as always, because of increasing demands made by the royal administration, which was always sending interfering people down from the north who did not speak Provençal.

The weight of taxation

It would be easy to criticise both the peasants' taxes, and the reluctance with which they paid them even when they were able to. But it might be more interesting, although not so easy, to assess how much of their income was taken in crown taxes, and indeed by all the charges levied on it.

Vauban, who had travelled over the whole of the kingdom and knew it very well indeed, has a simple example: a country labourer, around 1700, earned something like 90 livres in a year from his various jobs; *taille* and *gabelle* cost him nearly 15 livres, or one sixth of his money earnings. Having nothing except a house and a garden he paid very little to the seigneur, and similarly had no tithable crops. The 90 livres only represent his wages: he also had the produce of his garden and poultry, possibly a cow or a pig (although that is unlikely), and occasional work at home, which probably brought in the equivalent of another 40 livres; taking that into account, his tax is only 12 or 13 per cent of his probable income. But all the same that is a high proportion, and probably more than somebody in a roughly equivalent position would pay today.

Using cases analysed (in different ways) by well-established historians, let us now try to reconstruct the situation of the average peasant who farmed 5 or 6 hectares of good corn-producing land, and owned a cow, a pig, five sheep, and a few hens. Including *gabelle*, he paid about 40 livres in royal taxes, which was the equivalent of one or two good cows, or ten sheep, or ten hectolitres of corn in a good year (less in a bad year, because it was more expensive); corn did not usually yield more than 10 hectolitres per hectare, and no more than 4 hectares at the most would have been sown with cereals: so can one say that the royal taxes took a quarter of his income from the land? No, because he would also have sold a calf, some piglets and lambs, and some fleeces, cheese, and eggs. On the other hand, he had to pay tithes on the corn and livestock, and dues of various kinds to the seigneur (we may hope for his sake that he did not have to pay champarts on his land). However one looks at the facts, his taxes cannot have been less than 12 or 15 per cent at best. And if he was a tenant or a share-cropper, he had to pay his master in kind or in cash. On top of which, everybody had to put aside 15 or 20 per cent of their grain harvest as seed for the next year.

These figures come as close to the facts as is possible, certainly the facts as they apply to the north and centre of France. To go any further would involve juggling with the figures of pure hypothesis. The weight of all the taxes together meant that most peasants hoped for nothing more than to be able to support their families and put by a few provisions for bad times; and when the bad times came, they just tried to keep their debts as small as possible, so that they could eventually get their heads above water again. All in all the three kinds of taxation – ecclesiastical, seigneurial, and most of all royal – took at least 20 per cent of gross income, a rate which was never repeated after the end of the Ancien Régime.

And yet the real dangers did not lie in the burdensome system of taxation. It was illness which the peasants feared most, as that reduced or annihilated the strength of the father or mother, and there was no real help available, either medical (except for the bonesetters and healers, who were seldom any use) or social. The only charity in the country was private, and that could only help a small number of individuals. The other great dangers, as we have seen, were a series of bad harvests, the loss of a vintage, or the death of a cow (or even worse, a horse which was worth four or five times as much), because in those cases only the tithes were reduced; all other dues remained the same, and debt and distraint threatened. The unfair distribution of taxes and their continual increases played a major part in such misfortunes, even in the richest areas of the country.

For most of the time the French peasants bowed beneath the pressure of taxation, resigned or passive. But sometimes they revolted, and the time has come to look at them in action.

16

Peasants in the revolts of the seventeenth century

Under Louis XIII and Richelieu, Renaudot's *Gazette de France* and the *Mercure*, which were fairly regular semi-official publications, regularly carried reports of provincial revolts, including the long, harsh insurrection of the 'Nu-Pieds' in Normandy in 1639. After that, however, historians bent on praising Louis XIV and the *Grand Siècle*, for reasons of their own, glossed over all the episodes which did not seem to them to bring glory to their subject. So effective were they, that it is really only in the last twenty-five years that the revolts have been rediscovered, or so it seems; at any rate we have learned about things that have been forgotten, and analysed them in more detail, as, for example, in the whole of the south-west.

Between Henry IV and the death of Louis XIV historians have counted between 450 and 500 revolts in the huge area then covered by Aquitaine (which stretched from the Loire to the Pyrenees); some were small, some large, but all were marked by violence on at least the village scale, and lasted for at least a whole day. The most serious – a dozen here, half a dozen elsewhere – involved whole provinces and lasted three months or more, and had to be put down by troops. Aquitaine was the scene of a particularly large number of these angry uprisings, and they have been especially well studied too. But they occurred throughout the kingdom, and the total number of these *émotions* (as they were sometimes called) must be over 1,000, which puts a clearer perspective on the 'order' which reigned in the seventeenth century.

Country and town united in revolt: the successes

Some of these revolts took place in the towns, and did not involve the peasants at all. Conversely, in a number of instances, the peasants were not alone in their actions; occasionally the seigneur, minor nobles, even some priests helped them or prompted them for a while, though not always out of purely generous motives (royal taxes were in competition with their own dues). But for the short-lived riots, and some of the longer ones, the peasants had to rely on their own resources. And, when the end came, it was usually only the peasants who suffered from the inevitable repression that followed.

Despite their differences, these hundreds of revolts do have certain characteristics in common; some are predictable, others more surprising.

It is not, for example, surprising to find that almost all were directed against taxation – usually royal taxation, although some revolts in Brittany were against seigneurial dues – as throughout the century taxes increased and their demands were sometimes harsh in the extreme. What is more striking is that the peasants' anger – and the anger of the townsfolk – was aroused by new taxes, which the authorities tried to levy in new ways, with new officials or clerks who often came from far away and did not speak the language of the province. Any 'novelty' was therefore taken as an outrage, almost a sacrilege, against the customs, privileges, and the whole 'civilisation' of the place. It also seems that everybody thought that the best period was always somewhere in the past – before the wars, or in the time of 'Good King Henry', a sort of golden age accessible to everybody. With the exception of Paradise, nobody looked forward to the future, Everything that altered the solidly anchored ideal of the past was seen as criminal and almost heretical.

These feelings of nostalgia corresponded to a deep and exclusive love of their country, in the proper sense of the word: the land of their ancestors, described by a group of villages dominated by a larger village or a small market town – their *pays*. On a slightly larger scale, it included the province, as a group of several *pays*. Above that there was simply the king. All the provinces except those in the old monarchical centre between the Seine and the Loire had been joined to France one after another by force, treachery, or negotiation, but always with the condition that they could retain their own laws and customs, their own form of administration, their old assemblies, and their *Estats*. Unless this is borne in mind, it is not possible to understand the France of the Ancien Régime, particularly in the seventeenth century when the crown was stubbornly pressing on with its attempts at unification, standardisation, etatism, and absolutism. It was in opposition to this growing desire for unification that revolts started happening in the so-called peripheral provinces (which were the majority) in both town and country, and among some of the old nobility and the bourgeoisie as well as the ordinary people. Let me give some examples to support these assertions, which, although they are scarcely contestable, are not often mentioned.

The first major revolt of modern times, and one which was never forgotten even in the king's entourage, involved three of the provinces of Aquitaine – Angoumois, Saintonge, and Guyenne – in 1548. It was originally caused by the attempt, which began in 1541, to establish a 'northern' regime of *gabelle* in those provinces, with salt stores under the control of the tax-farmers and their clerks, who became renowned under the name of *gabelous*. They spread through the south-west, attempting to make everybody deal with them in future, which meant paying a very inflated price for salt which could be bought for a few sous at the Bay of Bourgneuf and the neighbouring salt marshes. To add insult to injury, these *gabelous* also came from the north. So when they realised that, contrary to legend, the accession of a new king (Henry II in 1547) would not change anything, the peasant communities, the *communes* as they called them, rose up one after another, sometimes several at one time, in the spring of 1548. All the able-bodied men in the village assembled at the sound of the tocsin, armed themselves (with sticks, pitchforks, pikes, and sometimes arquebuses), chose a captain, joined up with neighbouring villages and met up with other, similar bands, often in clearings in the forests. There they were joined by priests, who supported their flocks, and gentlemen adventurers (who also knew that the more their peasants paid to the crown, the less they would receive themselves). 'Colonels' were elected, and some who could write and had some understanding of the law drew up catalogues of complaints to be sent to the king, whom they still regarded with respect, believing that he had been misled and robbed by those who served him. The rebels then set out in pursuit of men they believed – rightly or wrongly – to be *gabelle* collectors or *gabelous*. As soon as they caught any, they punished them: their houses were burned, and they themselves were beaten, tortured, mutilated, killed, and sometimes cut into pieces. The armies of each province tried to have the gates of the towns opened, with some success (towns like Barbezieux, Pons, Libourne, and even Bordeaux). They seem to have numbered several tens of thousands of men in all. The greatest difficulty was in uniting the different groups, so that for example the 'Pitauds' of Saintonge had considerable difficulty in entering Bordeaux in August. And when the time for harvest or the vintage arrived they tended to go back home; the crown shrewdly chose that moment to send in their troops. At the beginning of the autumn these were under the command of Montmorency, the High Constable, and they showed even more savagery than the rebels. But this bloody repression failed to solve the problem, and the following year the royal government resigned itself to 'redeeming' all the provinces of Aquitaine, which meant withdrawing the tax-farmers and the detested storehouse clerks. From then until the Revolution the 'redeemed areas' bought their salt at a price that was five or six times lower than in the neighbouring provinces, though still two or three times more than that paid by the hyper-privileged Bretons. On this occasion the revolt was successful.

Similar outcomes were achieved a few times in the following century. In 1630, for instance, Louis XIII and Richelieu, always a bit short of money, wanted to impose the jurisdiction and powers of the *Elus*, their finance officers, on several provinces which had always been *pays d'Estats* and therefore partially independent and not subject to heavy taxes, as the *Etats* discussed the amount of taxation and normally raised it themselves. The first attempt was made in 1629 in Burgundy, at which there was an outcry in Dijon. The vine-growers in the areas round the city went further and burned the cardinal and even the king himself in effigy; and those two then decided it would be more sensible to drop the *Elus*.

The same sort of scenario occurred in a more developed form in Provence the following year. It began at Aix, where everybody from the *parlement* to the ordinary people and artisans protested. Some rebellious members of the higher echelons decided to arm the province to 'safeguard their liberties' and 'defend their country' (by which of course they meant Provence). The peasants thus gave their support to what began as an urban, anti-taxation, and 'provincialist' revolt. As usual, the troops arrived, under the command of the elder Condé, and had several of the rebels executed, none of them, of course, men of standing. After that the king wisely abandoned the plan to install the *Elus*, in return for a large sum of money in compensation.

There were comparable events in Languedoc at the same period, and there matters were made worse by the large protestant minority. There, too, the peasants joined in a revolt which appears to have been fomented by Languedoc bishops in the *Etats*, and by seigneurs and local potentates. After a series of complicated events, the king gave up the idea of the *Elus*, as he had in Burgundy and Provence.

In these three cases, the peasants joined in the struggle between 'free' provinces and a central government that was deemed to be taking that freedom away, but they were not the leaders. They did the same thing again and again under Louis XIV but he was not a king to give in at any cost. The time when the provinces could win was past, and would not return for a while.

The different types of peasant revolts

The genuine and purely peasant revolts usually began in spring, on a much smaller scale – in one village or one canton – and quickly reached their culmination and then died down in time for the main labours of the summer. Three main reasons can be adduced for these revolts: the price of bread; the quartering of soldiers; and the collection of taxes and the exactions of the clerks of the Farms, all of which we have come across in some degree.

Against the high price of bread

It is generally thought that revolts caused by the high price of bread only affected the towns, and it is true that the concentrations of ordinary people in the markets in towns or outside the bakers' shops tended to foster recrimination, anger, and violence, which could lead to bread being snatched and taken away: and in these women played a fairly large part. But parts of the countryside also experienced these demonstrations of anger, for as we know not all peasants were able to produce enough to feed themselves, and grain was subject to what they regarded as unacceptable speculation. As soon as a bad harvest was announced, prices started to rise, and panic and hoarders aggravated the situation. It was then that riots of one sort or another were liable to break out.

Peasants took part in them in a number of different ways. First, they attacked those whom they accused, often rightly, of creating scarcity in order to drive up the price of corn: the large tenant-farmers, tithe collectors, and above all the millers, who were always disliked. At other times the most severely hit of the peasants entered the towns searching for flour or bread and lent enthusiastic support to the housewives who were rioting and looting. But the violence most typical of these hard times occurred on the roads and rivers. Each small canton, afraid of running short, refused to allow grain to be taken out of the area to supply the towns or the neighbouring provinces. Any stranger who looked in the least like a corn-chandler was automatically suspect, and met with hostility, usually openly expressed. Rivers that were used by boats were watched, as were the highroads and the tracks. Merchants who knew the dangers of transportation normally loaded their carts, boats, or beasts at night. But they were still sometimes spotted by the peasants who often attacked them with staves, pitchforks, and arquebuses. When the merchants had been beaten and the grain recovered, the peasants carried away as much as they could, the women carrying it in their large aprons if need be. If the merchants sought the protection of an armed escort it sometimes happened, as in Angoumois in 1643, and in Anjou in 1693 and 1694 – which were terrible years – that the tocsin was sounded for some hours and whole bands of armed villagers set up ambushes. These were usually about thirty strong, although there were several hundred at Saint-Georges-sur-Loire and around Candé (in Anjou), and in June 1699 around Châtellerault. Other years of high prices – 1662, 1709, 1710 – provoked uprisings of this sort. Sometimes the authorities sent out the *maréchaussée* or some soldiers; usually they waited patiently for better times to return, so deeply were disturbances of this sort a part of the fabric of ordinary events, almost, indeed, of everyday life.

Against the soldiers

For some centuries, including the seventeenth, the peasants of France were openly hostile to the army and to soldiers. Any notion of 'national' defence seemed foreign to them, although they were totally prepared to defend the part of the country that was their home when it was under threat from land or sea. It may be that they thought of wars as the business of the king and great nobles. And it must also be said that, particularly before 1661, soldiers were often adventurers of variable and uncertain nationality who were employed in a regiment (which was the property of its colonel) in return for cash and the promise of an easy life and rich pickings. They served whoever paid them best, whether that was the prince of Germany, Sweden, the Netherlands, Savoy, or Spain. And some of these leaders paid as little as possible as it was easy to live off the land. It was customary at that period for war to cease during the bad weather, and for the army to occupy its winter quarters between October and March; and the armies did likewise. And as there were no barracks (except for a few elite troops attached to the king's person) the army had to be lodged and fed somewhere. The same was true when it set off again to resume operations, when again the soldiers had to rely on the people for shelter and provisions. The winter quarters were known as *logements* (quartering) and when they were on the move they were called *étapes* (or overnight stops). A whole body of legislation theoretically governed the conditions of both. In principle, certain localities were designated for *logements* and *étapes*, and specific houses within those localities. Their inhabitants had to have 'utensils', which comprised a bed, a pot with a bowl and glass, and provide a seat by the fire and near the candle; the soldier for his part had to pay for the food he was given for his 'subsistence'; provision was made for credits for these, named *subsistance* which rapidly became a supplement to the *taille*.

What actually happened was quite different. Nobles, ecclesiastics, royal officials, rich bourgeois, shrewd individuals of all types, and sometimes whole towns, were exempt from *logements* and *étapes*. Most of the burden fell on the country areas. All too often, as the administrators themselves complained to Colbert, the soldiers emptied hen-roosts and storehouses, rifled bins and cupboards, and made a nuisance of themselves to their hosts, particularly the women. For a long time the protests got nowhere. In times of war the frenzied troops would even cut down the trees and massacre the livestock (especially during the Fronde). The scourge was known among the king's entourage, and La Fontaine classified it under the lamentations of his 'poor woodcutter covered with green branches' hiding from 'the creditor and the *corvée*'. The only way to cope with the problem was by constructing barracks; Louvois introduced a plan to do this, and began putting it into practice, but the process was not completed for almost a century. Until then, the peasants had to demonstrate their disapproval in no uncertain terms on more than one occasion.

When it was announced that the soldiers were on their way, often preceded by scouts, the tocsin was sounded, work in the fields ceased, the tavern emptied, the beasts were led into shelter (in a fortified farm, or underground, or even in the church), and the peasants prepared barricades out of barrels, planks, bundles of thorn, and whatever else they could lay their hands on. If it was not possible to block the way, they took refuge inside the thick walls of the church, which was often fortified and had look-out posts in the form of battlemented platforms in the tower. Sometimes the soldiers gave up and went somewhere else. At other times they were met with musket fire or were ambushed from behind hedges, from the top of a ravine, or even among the vines. There are plenty of examples of peasant successes in Périgord, Bordeaux, and the mountains of Lavendan. Even the priest of Rocamadour gave thanks in 1653 (the last phase of the Fronde) that 'God himself' had 'withdrawn his blessing' from the soldiers, so that some perished and the rest decamped. In other periods, the vine-growing villages of the Côte, in Burgundy, were so often summoned by the tocsin that they formed a league so that they could pay the captains to take their men somewhere else, and if the soldiers returned a second time form a real peasant army to fight them off, wherever they came from. But that was at the time of Mayenne and Henry IV, somewhat before 1600. There were too many soldiers in Burgundy between 1636 and 1656 – with the movements of imperial and Spanish armies – for resistance to be any longer a possibility: the only course the peasants could take was to negotiate with the generals and resign themselves to paying over large sums of money; and even that did not always prevent them from being badly treated.

Under Louvois, *logements* and *étapes* became rarer, and certainly better regulated, and invasions became exceptional or very local-ised. Louvois, however, also made other arrangements which did not please the people in the countryside so much: from 1688 to 1697 and after 1701 he formed militias. Each village of any size had to provide one 'militia soldier', and at first these were chosen from among the young single men; but as this was followed (particularly in 1701–3) by a revealing epidemic of marriage, recruitment was extended to include young married men, and lots were drawn as almost nobody volunteered to go; young men went into hiding, and the richest peasants paid for others to go in place of their sons. This new form of extortion on the part of the military was strongly resented, and although it did not give rise to any movements of revolt (that did not happen until the Vendée) it provoked passive resistance on a grand scale. With the death of Louis XIV, the period of riots against *logements*, *étapes*, and the excesses of the 'men of war' was more or less over.

Against taxation

The death of Louis XIV did not, however, put a stop to the deeply rooted revolts against taxation – which we saw something of in the last chapter, and which occurred for the most part when the bailiffs and sergeants came to enforce collection – and against the clerks of the Farm.

When the peasants did not pay their *tailles*, the law stipulated that a demand should be sent by a bailiff, and that they could also proceed with distraint, supported by sergeants of the court, cavaliers of the *maréchaussée*, and sometimes 'fusiliers' (who were also detailed for the collection of *tailles* in recalcitrant parishes). When they arrived in a village to carry out their duty, they frequently met with a very cool reception, and it was not unusual to see a bailiff ride up on horseback, drop a scrawled summons and ride on without stopping, shouting out the name of the person involved. It was a more complicated matter trying to seize goods: the peasant refused to open the door, and his wife and children shouted to arouse the neighbours; insults and blows accompanied the removal of each animal and each piece of furniture. If the neighbours came running, the revenue authorities were in serious danger of being attacked, and there were cases of broken legs, cracked heads, and occasionally a death or two, hastily covered up. A simpler course of action was for the offender and his friends to let them proceed, and then recover the goods and livestock half a league further down the road at the corner of a sunken lane or where the road went through a wood. Sometimes, alerted as ever by the tocsin, whole villages rushed at the bailiffs, sergeants, constables, and soldiers, whose safety then depended on the speed of their horses. They would come back in force a few weeks later, though, and give the rebels harsh punishment.

The clerks of the *gabelle* and Excise Farm were even more detested, and more violently chased away, because of the king's practice of allowing his taxes to be collected by financiers who advanced the full amount to him and then got it back from the taxpayers, with the help of energetic and enthusiastic employees who had the right to requisition and to use armed force. The worst conflicts, which became pitched battles, took place, as we know, along the borders of the *gabelle* areas, at the gates of more favoured provinces like Cotentin, Aquitaine, and of course Brittany. There were also long guerilla campaigns where the king wanted to introduce the *gabelle* into recently annexed provinces such as Béarn and Roussillon.

Similar anger was turned on the clerks of the excise (or *aides*), who had to try to collect complex, large, and variable dues on the production, consumption, sale, and circulation of wines. These clerks (called 'cellar-rats') did not hesitate to go down into a vine-grower's cellar to check his declaration of his harvest, then to calculate how much he really drank with his family or with 'friends' whom they suspected of being customers. The deceit, the secret movement of wine, and the quarrels were endless. The worst period was the winter when the new wine was ready to drink and was distributed to the taverns and bars. Clerks and vine-growers lay in wait for each other, and traded insults and blows: it was a relation-ship which in some places did not improve until this century, particularly in the Midi, which later became the central wine-producing area.

In these contexts the name *gabeleur* or *maltôtier* (extortioner) became an insult that was often bracketed with others like fool, rogue, wretch, scoundrel, gallows-bird, and worse. The violence was frequent, and sometimes went as far as murder: they hanged *gabeleurs* and then dismembered the body and exposed pieces of it all round the locality, as happened in Saint-Benoist-sur-Mer in 1633, and in Gua in 1656, for example. More elaborately, the insurgents at Chalosse in 1664, the 'Invisibles', attacked the clerks, their offices, their documents, and their persons, declaring plainly 'Thieves and *gabeleurs*, we want your lives, and we want to exterminate your whole race so that the very memory of you is destroyed for ever.'

These massacres of tax collectors (collecting new, additional, or unusual taxes) several times passed through a sort of crisis, when they lasted longer than usual and were on a larger scale. There were the 'Tard-Avisés' in Limousin and the first Croquants in Périgord in 1593–5; there was generalised rioting from 1630 to 1650 with high points among the *communes* of Angoumois and Saintonge in 1636, the rising of the *communes* in Périgord again from 1637 to 1641, and the 'Nu-Pieds' in Normandy in 1639. In 1643 there were riots almost everywhere, when the people thought the death of the king was going to herald the end of the *gabelle* and all the so-called 'extraordinary' taxes. There was some overlap between peasant revolts and provincial *frondes* around 1650; the harsh revolt of the *sabotiers* in Sologne in 1658; the revolt of the Boulonnais in 1662; in the years from 1660 to 1670 there was almost permanent guerilla warfare waged by the *miquelets* of Roussillon both against the introduction of the *gabelle* and the Francisation of that part of Catalonia which had been unwillingly annexed; the revolt in Chalosse, Béarn, and Bigorre in 1664 ended, like all revolts against Louis XIV, in a blood bath; there was a revolt in the Vivarais in 1670 when the rumour gained currency that taxes were to be introduced on hats and births, and the musketeers, the king's Switzers, companies of guards, and several regiments were responsible for cutting to pieces several thousand men from the mountains of the Cévennes. Several hundred more were hanged or sent to penal servitude, and their chief, a former official, from Roure, was cut into five pieces and exposed on the gates of Aubenas. A similar scene was enacted in Guyenne in 1674, in Brittany the year after, in the Cévennes again in 1702 (the Camisards), and at Quercy in 1707. The same illusions resulted in the same process of military repression, executions, penal servitude, harsh *logements* of troops, and the whole steamroller of state unification which succeeded in obtaining relative silence for almost a century.

It would be pointless to describe all these movements one after another as they shared a great number of characteristics, apart from the Breton revolts which can be dealt with separately. It can be seen straight away for example that they almost always occurred in provinces which had recently been annexed and which believed they would continue to enjoy their traditional privileges for ever, and saw them becoming less clearly defined. We can also say that despite the attempts made by some of the rebels (in Normandy and in Picardy) there was never any liaison between one uprising and the next apart from the occasional contact between a province and its neighbour (in Aquitaine). No overall plan ever emerged. No leader of stature appeared, apart from some local members of the de-camped nobility (who were sometimes forced into it by their peasants), a few unimportant men of law, and a handful of over-enthusiastic or wrong-headed priests. But royalty, although some-times annoyed and embarrassed, was never in any danger from all these revolts.

This may have been because all these more or less short-lived and localised movements remained firmly turned towards a past which was more imaginary and illusory than rational or well-founded (and nobody then conceived of the future as bringing progress, or indeed of the notion of progress itself). There was nothing quite so unCartesian as this century, particularly, as one might expect, in the countryside.

All the rebels begged for or demanded a return to the past. Around 1600 they invoked the good days of King Louis XII, the father of his people; a little later the blessed reign of King Henry; later still, they harked back to the good old days before 1635 (when the wars began). Fundamentally the people, whose adoration of the king is visibly unanimous, nonetheless thought that he ought to live as he once did 'from his domain' like a seigneur or a large landowner. It seemed quite normal for him to ask for the traditional 'aid' from his people when he had to make war, or was in difficulties, and for him to levy contributions which were theoreti-cally seen as 'extraordinary'; but once the war or the difficulties were over, they thought the status quo should be restored – and this naturally seldom turned out to be possible. Above and beyond that, certain myths continued to exercise a powerful hold over the popular imagination: apart from the one mentioned above about taxes being reduced on the death of a king or at the declaration of peace, there were stories about cannibal *gabeleurs* which sometimes even involved ministers: some pamphlets of 1637 showed Richelieu bathing in the blood of the people; in 1652 Mazarin was shown at table being served with 'a ragout of villain, garnished with taxes'; and there is no knowing how many people really thought that all kinds of wolves and bloodsuckers sank their teeth into the taxpayers or physically drank their blood.

People nowadays may be more surprised by the myths about imaginary taxes. A province exempted or redeemed from the *gabelle* lived in the fear that it could reappear, and whenever unknown horsemen passed by, or men in black who looked like lawyers, or whenever a notice was pinned up which could only be partly read or understood, people immediately thought it meant the reintroduction of the *gabelle*, in which they included all the different kinds of new taxes and terrible extortions, and which before long came to be seen as apocalyptic monster, a stinking, spluttering beast to be hunted down, and not only in Brittany in 1675. Now and then rumours travelled around that taxes were going to be imposed on clothes, hats, ovens, eggs, and even on spring water and the water the housewives went to draw from the well. But the most frequently attested was the tax on births. The rumour crops up all over Aquitaine in 1627, and again in Quercy in 1707; it was partly responsible for the insurrection in the Vivarais in 1670, and the last Croquants' revolt. There is even a ghost of a rumour about taxes on marriages and deaths. The women, who are said to be more imaginative and more given to conversation than men, would have enthusiastically passed these stories on, with a surprising wealth of detail.

Around 1670 and in 1707 these latter rumours were actually a response to new legislation about parish registers which had not been properly understood. The main text dates from 1667, but in 1673 it was decided that all these documents should thereafter be drawn up on stamped paper, which had to be paid for by the parishioners, who of course became anxious and discontented. In 1707, posts of controllers of these registers were created, who in principle were the only people who could issue true certificates. And people saw this as devilry and extortion.

The issue of stamped paper, together with other taxes (on tin, which was very widely used, and on tobacco, which was beginning to be chewed and smoked in pipes in the Dutch manner) designed to palliate the financial difficulties caused by the unforeseen prolongation of the war with Holland, was at the origin of the worst and oddest of the major provincial revolts, the Breton insurrection which was first called the stamped-paper insurrection, and then the red-cap insurrection. It originated in the towns, with Rennes leading the way, and then linked the demand for provincial liberty with protests against the new taxes, particularly those on stamped paper. As often happened, some of the nobility, magistrates, and bourgeois supported the revolt, and at least did nothing to interfere with it.

It spread rapidly and brutally into the countryside, though it was mostly limited to the cantons in the west and the south of the province. 'Armorican liberty' was their slogan, stamped paper was denounced, and the *gabelle* execrated (and compared to a female monster accompanied by her children). But interestingly the peasants attacked châteaux as much as tax offices; they also attacked some of the wealthier religious establishments, and some towns (such as Carhaix and Châteaulin) whose bourgeois inhabitants were visibly unsympathetic. Manors were burned down, especially their archives, and nobles were beaten and driven out – a dozen or so were massacred – even rectors who took too much in tithes were given the same treatment as the officers of the revenue and beaten up, after first experiencing the shock of seeing some of their curates among the rioters. Once the first wave of anger had died down, the rebels decided to gather and discuss matters, under the influence of some eloquent speakers, village scribes, minor notaries, and rich householders. They ended by drawing up lists of complaints, thoroughgoing programmes, eight of which (probably the most moderate) have survived. The most famous of these is signed anonymously 'Torreben (break his . . . head) and its residents' and insists on the union of the communities of the parish, the liberty of the province, and the abolition of the new taxes; but, more interestingly, also called for the abolition of tithes (to be replaced by a pension for priests, which was something eventually introduced after the Revolution), and the abolition of champarts and *corvée* 'claimed by the gentlemen' and which they regarded as 'a violation of Armorican liberty'. In fact *corvées*, champarts, and rights of banality not only continued but had been increased in the course of the seventeenth century. The Breton seigneurie was particularly burdensome, but so also were those in Burgundy and Saintonge, and apart from a few incidents no serious traces of resistance have been discovered in those regions. West Brittany therefore remains the only place where there was a violent revolt against both the seigneurs and the nobility which was serious enough to provoke plans for reform.

However, nothing came of them. Shortly before the arrival of the soldiers, preachers like Maunoir and others took it upon themselves to promise that anybody who disobeyed the king or dared to revolt would find themselves in hell. The soldiers made the promise a reality. They tortured and hanged people (fourteen from one oak tree at Combrit), filled the prison at Brest, and the galleys, and quartered themselves on the countryside for the winter, all 20,000 of them 'as if they were still on the other side of the Rhine' as Mme de Sévigné wrote in December 1675. Even the governor responsible for the repression, the Duc de Chaulnes, made suitable protests about the events in Louvois in February 1676. The church-towers were stripped of their bells and the province was reduced to silence for over 100 years.

With the hangings in Brittany, the major peasant and popular revolts of the century were almost at an end (the final brutality was yet to take place in the Camisard region and Quercy). After that the conflicts only took place at ground level: a few trials, occasional outbreaks of violence, and solid passivity. Various historians have tried to explain the silence of the peasants during the greater part of the eighteenth century, and they have come up with a variety of explanations (such as harsh discipline, Christian resignation, and improved living conditions) which need not concern us here. It all broke out again under Louis XVI, when the peasants in Brittany and in a number of other places refused to pay the tithes, seigneurial dues, and royal taxes which they seemed to have become accustomed to. Thus the Revolution began as much in the fields as at Versailles and Paris: the most clear-sighted individuals anticipated it, but even they could not have foreseen the way in which huge numbers of peasants would suddenly burst into action.

17

Sundays and feast days

So much has been written about feast days and festivals over the last ten or twelve years – festivals and revolt, revolt and festivals, festive activities, and so on – that there is a danger of obscuring the facts of any specific period, in our case those of the seventeenth century.

Should we trust the spiritual recriminations of Jean de la Fontaine's Parisian cobbler?

> The only trouble is some plaguy Feast
> Is always cropping up to stop my stitches –
> Too much of a good thing, Sir! Why, the Priest
> Gives us a new Saint every time he preaches.
>   (trans. Edward Marsh, London, 1933)

And how relevant is it to remember the number of holidays of obligation imposed in the dioceses before the reaction at the end of the century? In Angers there were fifty-three, in Poitiers there were fifty, and in La Rochelle, forty-three. If one includes Sundays in this total it works out at one hundred days each year, or more, or practically one day of rest in three.

This represented a miscellaneous collection of set obligations, embattled traditions, and contrast between town and country which it is difficult to disentangle. What we do know is that country people (and towndwellers too) respected what Saints' days they chose to, that some degree of tradition was still operative, and that work in the fields, the vineyards, and the gardens took precedence over the various Saints' day activities, apart from a few that were still, in some way, sacred.

I want to look at festivals here as a time of rest, enjoyment, collective social contact, and some kind of 'liberation' or release, whatever its origin.

The sanctification of Sunday

Sunday, as its name in French, *dimanche*, suggests, is very simply the Lord's day, the day when God the Father, after having created the Heavens, the Earth, and everything else, rested. Basically, the more the century wears on, the more an increasingly serious-minded church wanted the faithful to do nothing on Sundays but practise piety; they wanted everybody to attend mass, vespers, and, where it existed, benediction. And with the exception of those who were ill, and a few strong-minded characters like the miller and the tavern-keeper, everybody did go to mass, to pray, probably to meet people and gossip as well. Every priest who wrote on the subject complained that vespers was deserted; and nobody mentions benediction.

From a few documents, originating with the church or the secular authorities, we can discover that two difficult battles were being fought at the same time. The first was against work in the fields; but it would have needed the army, at least, to stop peasants spending Sunday afternoons doing urgent tasks such as getting in hay when the rain threatened or other jobs made necessary by the approach of bad weather. Quite apart from the fact that behind thick hedges or high walls they could easily do some digging or pruning or weeding in the gardens. Both clergy and the law were well aware of this, as from time to time they made special arrangements to 'allow' this sort of work, which was equally out of the ordinary, at least in theory.

But the antidominical demons were not at work among these people. They flourished primarily in the tavern, mockingly sited next to the church, which opened officially the moment mass was over. So many religious and lay texts were continually denouncing their misdeeds that it is hard to believe that the tavern-keeper did not generally have the best of this unequal struggle. Besides, other judicial documents clearly specify the number of drunks on Sunday evenings. And after a week of hard labour, drinking foul water or sour *boisson*, they surely needed some human compensation.

The preachers and the pious bishops sent out by an administration which had recently become rigidly moralistic, on paper at least, were even more exercised about the after-dinner games on Sundays, especially the activities of the young people, the protection of whose virtue had become one of the major works of the catholic church. Walks in the woods, and dances (which were always ungodly) with fiddlers or a hurdy-gurdy man, gave rise to righteous anger and stern warnings. They do not seem to have had any substantial effect, though, as Paul-Louis Courier was pleading in Touraine at the beginning of the nineteenth century for the villagers to be prevented from dancing, so the activity must have continued. In fact it frequently took place in the square in front of the church, or in the cemetery.

What these puritans did perhaps manage to prevent was an activity that had been criticised since the end of the previous century, namely river-bathing, as any even half-naked body immediately instigated sin, or the likelihood of it. So the seventeenth century, in contrast to the middle ages, and even the sixteenth century, was the century when the body became indecent.

In the end, and all the catholico-royal legislation of the late seventeenth century was directed towards this end, Sunday had to be sanctified absolutely, and the traditional festivals kept to days which were not nominally devoted to the Lord. From that point of view it seems that the aim was not often achieved, except in a few melancholy, ultra-Jansenist parishes.

Traditions whose exact origins are unknown but do not appear to be recent in fact worked against this policy of repressive and pious goodness.

The old festivals

First of all there were a whole series of agrarian rituals which certainly seem to date back to Roman times. The Rogation Days, for example, were obviously agrarian fertility rites, as were others: St Mark's Day, 25 April, for one, and the three days before Ascension for another, when processions made their way across the fields carrying an altar (sometimes carrying drinks, too, which shocked the pious observers) reciting major and minor litanies, so that the green stalks of corn would ripen without being attacked by rust or beaten down by storms. May Day was possibly another, when they went out at night and selected a young tree from the wood, and replanted it, decorated, at a preselected site in the village. There were also those astonishing processions to springs or fertility statues, recorded in numerous provinces, even in the Paris region, on the slopes of Mont-Valérien or Créteil, which involved a great deal of walking and double or triple ferry-crossings of the Seine and the Marne, with rests at the ferryman's tavern.

Another aspect of the old rites was seasonal, or as they said calendrial, but these had been well-incorporated by the old christianity which was adept at absorbing paganism. The solstitial festivals, from the nativity to the fires of St John's Eve, included pagan elements: shepherds and lambs at one, torches and leaping the bonfire at the other, and evenings of feasting at both. The equinoxes were celebrated more in spring, when there were the three Easter festivals of Palm Sunday, Easter Sunday, and Low Sunday, and several feasts as well, than in autumn, when Michaelmas and St Remi (on 1 October) were marked by the renewal of leases and the opening of the meadows rather than any special festivities.

Nonetheless, certain christian celebrations had deteriorated into popular festivals against which the holy bishops fulminated continually; for example, Twelfth Night and Shrove Tuesday (or *Mardi gras*).

The christianised festival of the Wise Kings – Epiphany – seems to have originated in old pagan rejoicings that accompanied the choice of a 'king', and was signalled by collective libations. So much so that under the name of the 'festival of the drink-king' – a common theme in Flemish painting – the feast of Twelfth Night seems to have lost its christian connotation entirely, and was generally attacked by the ecclesiastical authorities.

As for Shrove Tuesday, just before Lent, and all the carnivals that preceded it, these seem to have been an essentially urban phenomenon, as most peasants (even at Romans, though there were exceptions in the suburban areas) had other things to do besides taking part in the processions, the follies, the 'inversions', and 'introversions' which may entertain modern folklorists and historians but which almost never took place in the countryside where at best they celebrated the 'fat days' in the richer households with a few pancakes or *galettes*, possibly washed down with some new wine. And the 'lean days' of Lent could not have troubled anybody, as it was what they normally had.

Patronal festivals and bachelleries

The real festival each year was the 'patronal' festival, on the parish Saint's day, and people often attended those in neighbouring localities. The festival included a fair and a market, and although it would be interesting to look in more detail at these aspects, we unfortunately cannot do so here.

The major anxiety of the post-Tridentine Church was that these festivals should not turn into orgies nor, if possible, take place on the Lord's day. Their fears were probably exaggerated, as there was little danger of that. Nor was there in the case of the markets and the big fair that was held in the local town, which almost always happened on a week-day, and attracted a crowd of people, some of whom came very early – on foot, or on horseback if they were rich – from several leagues around. It was there that sales and purchases and bargaining took place; at Michaelmas (29 September) or Martinmas (11 November) it was also the time for 'hiring' servants and domestics. Drinking sessions and dances often ended badly in brawls which were roughly dealt with by the *maréchaussée*, if there were enough of them. Whether these occasions acted as an annual or half-yearly safety-valve on lives governed by toil and privation, it is impossible to know for certain.

Frequently, especially in the provinces of Angoumois, Poitou, and the surrounding area, most of these festivals were organised by associations of young unmarried men known as *bachelleries*; these have a history which certainly goes back as far as the fifteenth century, and they crop up in other places under different names, but have been studied nowhere in such remarkable detail as in the central-western area of France, between the Loire, the mountains, and the Gironde.

These groups of young men, all of whom it seems were over the age of fifteen, were fully recognised in customary law and by what one might call seigneurial law, and the most firmly established among them even had close links with the seigneurie. They had rules, and they elected a 'king' (or in some places a 'prince' or an 'abbot'). Their main role was to organise a certain number of festivals in the locality, which might be a town and market town or a large village. (The last of these groups continued to do this at Melle until 1974). Although, inevitably, there were variations, the festivals fell into the following categories: patronal festivals, marriage rites, the 'calendrial' festivals of carnival (in the towns), Whitsun, St John's Eve, Christmas, and others. They took fairly diverse forms, but among them we can pick out the following.

A young people's banquet, with food and a lot of drink, which might take place in the tavern, or in fine weather in a meadow designated for the purpose.

It might also involve picking bouquets, which were often very carefully composed. These would be offered either to the seigneur or his wife, or to new 'bachelors', or most usually to newly married couples (who would have to 'pay' with offerings of drink).

More often, or more regularly, there would be the search for a 'may', which was sometimes a branch but more often a young tree, which they would solemnly plant after obtaining it in a raid on an uncultivated, tree-covered part of the village land; the 'raid' was not always authorised, and sometimes scandalised some observers by taking place at night.

The bachelors were also very often authorised to exact certain dues. These would come from newly-weds (especially in cases where the man came from a neighbouring parish, and removed an element of choice, in a sense, from the number of girls in the village), or from millers, who were a common target, or, more politely, from the seigneur, or his share-cropper. Also they often went out collecting particular foodstuffs or money at particular festivals – some of which traditional foods (such as Easter eggs) have survived – and eating them or distributing them in the meadow or the tavern. Nobody dared refuse these 'ransoms', as the young men's response could be rough, verbally and sometimes physically as well.

The high spots of the *bachelleries'* festivals were the contests which included fighting, throwing, and running.

For the fights it seems that one band of youths was matched against another, reflecting the conflicts between neighbouring villages, which often despised or hated each other for reasons whose origins are far from clear. Some of these fights, which might be barefisted or sometimes carried out on horseback, ended in serious injury, and even deaths were not unheard of.

More picturesque but less common were games like tilting at the ring and the quintain, both done on horseback, with the aim of threading the former, or breaking the basket stuck in the ground which usually served as the latter; more amusing to our eyes would probably have been the ritual of 'breaking the pots' (hung from trees or poles) by hitting them with sticks, blindfold. Berry seems to have been an area where people were particularly fond of that sort of spectacle.

We cannot leave these contests without a mention of the poetic bird hunt (the wren, particularly in the Vendée) to the accompaniment of the famous song, 'Alouette, gentille alouette'; nor without describing the ritual common in Poitou called 'smacking the sheep', in which the last girls to get married that spring had, on the last Saturday in April, to try to make the poor animal take some bread and wine, make it go three times round a barrel, after which the strongest lads lifted it onto their backs and spun it three times round their head, which naturally took a certain amount of strength.

Apart from these curious rituals, which seem to have no particular meaning, there were also races and games for young people which seem to contain the seeds of some much more recent sporting diversions. There was, for example, throwing the *soule*, a very large, heavy ball which had to go a certain distance; and games of *pelote* and *paume* from which tennis and its variants recognisably descend; and ninepins, bowls, and lacrosse, which was very like golf or hockey.

Although the *bachelleries* were so powerful in the central-west part of the country, and perhaps elsewhere, too, under less elegant or less familiar names, they did not provide all the occasions for festivals in the countryside.

The reformed priests of the latter years of the century were hostile to the 'patronal' festivals – which in theory celebrated the patron saint of the church – because the pagan element so quickly took over from the christian. All of these festivals had a pedlar, who was also something of an entertainer, and a tavern that spilled over on to the fields next to it, and a fiddler perched on a barrel, and – worst of all – dancing, the source of all sin. These festivals went by every name you can think of, a stock which bad christians tended to increase only too readily: *assemblées, ducasses, vogues, frairies, fêtes baladoires* (*balad* there being a dialect word for 'countryside').

It looks rather as if all the long and passionate condemnations which the bishops and clerics issued at the end of the seventeenth century were spent on traditions which outlived them, and lasted well into the twentieth century.

The nature of the human race means that nothing can be absolutely sanctified, even weddings which the priests wanted to turn into pure sacraments and nothing else.

If we trust the usual historical sources rather than just the discourse of these churchmen, one discourse among many, we see that marriage constituted the most important festivals in the life at least of an average peasant family (we do not know much about the poor). The ceremony was celebrated on a Monday or Tuesday, often after the slaughter of a pig, and was a unique opportunity for the family to stuff themselves; it could go on until the day after, and in the numerous parts which produced their own wine would be accompanied by the broaching of a barrel or two of the previous year's vintage, which would by then have completed its fermentation. There were doubtless pagan rites before, during, and after the exchange of promises which constituted the sacrament (such as nocturnal concerts, crude jokes, demands for drinks, which anticipate the later business of bouquets, garters, and hangovers the morning after).

This is all the more likely as it is difficult to see when, apart from at weddings (which were dreaded and denounced in advance by the pious authorities for their excesses), there was a comparable opportunity for celebration, certainly at the family level. Baptism, which took place on the day of birth or the next day, was not a suitable occasion; nor were funerals, as in the seventeenth century they seem to have been performed without much in the way of representation from the family or the village; and nor were betrothals, as the church in its role of guardian of virtue, had moved them forward to the eve of the wedding.

And of course it was only those who could manage them and pay for them who could have these feasts. That means that a good half of the population hardly had an opportunity to enjoy themselves, let alone have a blow-out, except for occasions such as weddings, the patronal festival, and 'May'. And certainly Flemish-style *kermesses*, or village fairs, remained the prerogative of the wealthy province of Flanders, or else a good, undemanding subject for apprentice painters to depict.

The majority of French peasants had nothing but slightly better soup than usual to offer their friends on feast days, except at Twelfth Night, Easter, and Christmas; it was a century when there was a great deal more fasting than feasting.

18

Death and the peasant

Never before had so much writing, meditation, and discussion been devoted to Death. It ranged from flippancy to the severest gravity, but the subject in all cases was Death with a capital letter rather than death, the anonymous, everyday event. People in the seventeenth century discussed 'attitudes' towards Death, not the naked and unpalatable fact of death itself. There were more people bed-ridden, dying and dead of starvation than ever before, and the only excuse for this cowardly evasion of the facts is that they were in some way occupied by a *fin-de-siècle* atmosphere.

Death: the great unknown

The task facing us now is to describe the death of the seventeenth-century peasant 'with its circumstances and appurtenances', as they used to say about land. But in all honesty it must be admitted that we know very little about it. Yet there have been plenty of studies on the subject: they have relied on literary texts, on variously edifying ecclesiastical texts, on accounts of funeral 'ceremonials', on a few record books, on the remains or records of memorials, on hundreds and thousands of wills, and on the inexhaustible, unanswerable (and recent) material produced by folklorists, who started to appear in the nineteenth century and show no signs of becoming extinct. At the risk of appearing pretentious and ruthless, historians determined to describe, in as much accurate detail as possible, the lives of the country people of an inadequately charted century – the seventeenth – simply cannot accept most of this heteroclite material.

For example, describing the 'popular' custom of covering mirrors when people 'passed on', the average folklorist will cite the place where he collected it, and occasionally the social context; but he blithely asserts that it dates from the 'old' days of 'traditional civilisation', whereas the nit-picking historian, with no poetry in his soul, knows that in the seventeenth century no peasant ever possessed a mirror.

People who gather information from wills usually work in towns (where literacy was more widespread and the task is easier), prefer the eighteenth century – when the writing was fuller and more legible – and are prepared to admit, if pressed, that the wills of poor peasants very seldom turn up. Likewise there are very few record books, at least for the humbler peasants; we know of only a very small number of examples, like the one from Vareddes, near Meaux, which contains an incomplete genealogy, a list of the times when the weather was bad, and the harvests. None of the seventeenth-century peasants except the richest had anything to write or say or dictate about their death: inheritance was governed by well-established local custom, although allowance was made for any special provisions set out in the marriage contract (that being its principal purpose).

As for funeral furnishings and particularly memorials, apart from lower Brittany, which has been excellently studied by Alain Croix, they have either not survived, or they never existed, the second of which hypotheses seems the less unlikely.

The surviving religious documents, such as treatises, instructional books, the themes of sermons, and church painting and sculpture depicting death and the after-life, are certainly much more deserving of attention. The only question is whether they really reflect peasant ways of thought or the new, purified impression which the church wanted to create after its reorganisation in the wake of the decrees of the Council of Trent in the previous century, in which case their testimony is valuable but indirect.

Whatever the case, it will never be possible to discover all the secrets of those dead souls, even supposing they had any. More than anywhere, perhaps, the historian here is a researcher, and with few illusions that he will find the answers he is looking for. However there are one or two things we do know.

The most reliable information comes from the inexhaustible parish registers, which do not just provide useful material for demographers and genealogists. Priests had long been supposed to record burials, but their instructions on the subject were neither exact nor clear; some bishops nonetheless insisted on it, and for the period after 1667 it was covered by royal legislation. In fact they tended to do as they felt like. And there were really two sorts of deaths: those which merited a mention in the parish register, and those which did not.

The first category consisted of adults, or sometimes 'communicants' (which normally meant those over the age of twelve); less commonly children of five and over were included. But these only warranted a line or two. Even adult burial certificates (except for those of notables) were usually less than four lines long, three or four lines shorter than a baptismal certificate, and five or six times shorter than a certificate of marriage. As the eighteenth century draws nearer, with its more rigorous and earnest approach to such matters, all the entries double in length and accuracy, with even more detail given in the case of marriages between powerful farming families, attended by a crowd of friends and relatives who all signed the register with varying degrees of literacy. Entries of death, which are not always easy to identify, had to include an indication of whether they had duly received 'the sacraments of the Holy Church'. In the case of young children, this was not necessary, and there was therefore no need to go to the trouble of writing a couple of lines in the register.

The death of children

All the same, these anonymous deaths of young children give rise to some thought. Not so much about the unpleasant circumstances that often surrounded them, which have often been described – terrible labours, torn bodies, foetuses taken out piece by piece – but for the form of baptism practised by the midwife, which was often her only real skill. Nor so much about the familiar numbers of these 'little bodies' (as they were generally called) which were wrapped in their dozens – at the rate of one neonate in four – in cheap cloth and buried on their own, often without even the father present, but about the fact that these burials took place in consecrated ground because at least the appearance of baptism had taken place, and the 'little soul' had gone to join the angels and intercede for his parents in Paradise. If baptism had not taken place, the 'little body' was condemned to wander indefinitely in the undefined spaces of 'limbo', and his earthly remains would not be allowed to rest in sanctified ground, which would have been a severe blow to his family, if they thought about it clearly or for any length of time.

This brings us to the heart of the problem, which is what the peasants themselves felt and thought about this great massacre of the innocents. For the richer, educated people who kept an account book or a family bible (which usually contained one line of family records to a page of gossip and ten pages of accounts) the answer is clear enough. They hardly bothered to note the appearance and disappearance of a new-born child, whose name sometimes does not figure at all: when a child of a few years died they sometimes included a few words of emotion or regret, but nothing else.

In the depths of the country, therefore, where people were illiterate, stupefied with work and superstition (or what we now regard as superstition), frequently malnourished, cold, and sunk in dirt and fever, we tend to think of them (although there is no actual proof of this) as resigned or even indifferent. The only exception might be the mother herself, despite the rather weak recent argument that there was no maternal love, who perhaps comforted herself with visions of her 'little angel' baptised in time and now praying for her in heaven, as well as with the thought that there was one less mouth to feed. As La Fontaine's wood-cutter said, children could indeed be a heavy burden; and after all it is only in the last fifty years that large families have received any help from the state. Even more likely is that the death of young children was seen as a natural phenomenon, governed by God or destiny, like the succession of day and night, or the waxing and waning of the moon, or the rhythm of the seasons marked by the pagan–christian festivals, or the pattern of good and bad years, or the 'ages of man' (each of seven years), and the cycles of epidemics and scarcity. These probabilities and possibilities show how difficult it is to fathom people's souls (rather than their pockets), and how far removed the seventeenth-century countryside is from western life in the well-fed and cared-for twentieth century, where the death of a small child is felt as something dreadful, unjust, and heart-rending (so long as we are personally involved in it).

The death of adults and the law of inequality

As time goes on, the records of adult deaths improve. The priest no longer forgets to specify both the baptismal name and the surname of the deceased, he often indicates the marital status, and sometimes the profession or *estat*, particularly in the case of important people or artisans. Sometimes he notes the age, or an approximation to it. And he always records the sacraments that were administered, the names of at least two witnesses (often the priest and the 'sacristan–gravedigger'), and the place of burial. As usual, the northern Loire provides the most detailed and reliable testimony.

On the basis of this more reliable information, and other data, the first 'arithmeticians' were encouraged by Colbert and Vauban to begin to draw up tables of the 'state of population' (which the tax-farmers, particularly those of the *gabelle*, knew at least as well) so as to give an idea of the age-pyramid.

In this connection we may recall some noteworthy facts which we have already encountered. There were very few old people, for instance, despite the admiring notes recorded by priests as they proudly buried some supposed centenarian. In reality, those over the age of sixty accounted for no more than 7 per cent of the population during Louis XIV's reign (today the figure is more than twice that), and of these women outnumbered men, perhaps by as much as three to one. Octogenarians (1 or 2 per cent of the population?) were sufficiently unusual to become curiosities in their cantons, and to have all kinds of powers attributed to them. On the other hand, it is known that more women than men died in their twenties, in their first childbirth. Male vulnerability struck later, and the 'male menopause' cut down large numbers of men in their forties, who were often worn out by then anyway as a result of hard, unremitting toil. This is why so many widows, difficult to 'rehouse' at that age, burdened the villages and the tax-rolls.

Another interesting factor, which became less pronounced after the death of Louis XIV (although the two events were not actually connected) was the extraordinary unevenness with which deaths were distributed. We know that more children died in the summer, and more old people in the winter; and in the marshy areas, of which there were then a good many, the greatest number of deaths in all age groups occurred during the mosquito season, as malaria was still endemic. But apart from these seasonal patterns, there were also huge differences between one year and another. There were some years when by good luck – apart from the usual contingent of 'little bodies' – practically no members of the parish went to join the heavenly hosts, and others when the gravedigger hardly had time to stop digging, until he succumbed himself. That was when the region was struck by 'contagions' or 'mortalities', plagues and pestiferous illnesses, whose dreadful ravages have been recorded by historians. They came like hurricanes, and descended for several months at a time in an unpredictable course, or covered whole provinces, but apart from those of bubonic plague, the symptoms are so imprecisely described that it is often not possible to identify them. They included 'pernicious' fevers, profuse sweating, rashes, 'bad chests', 'stupors', and most often of all attacks of chronic and sometimes contagious diarrhoea. It is occasionally tempting to diagnose some of these devastating illnesses as typhus, or influenza, or scarlatina. But it is more remarkable to picture the conditions that gave rise to these deaths: the excrement, the contamination, the putrescence, the promiscuousness, and the powerful smell of the death-bed on a massive scale. That is one image of the seventeenth century, although in good years, especially later in the century, there were more attractive scenes. And yet however bad the year was, the endless fecundity of the countryside managed to soften the effect of all those deaths, and maintain a small overall growth in population.

People often wonder what our ancestors' 'attitude' was to death. And we can answer this question fairly well as it affects the rich and those who lived in the towns. But as far as the people in the countryside are concerned, all I know is that I hardly know anything. We may, however, make some guesses.

Ignore everything that has been written about custom and customs, about death-beds, vigils, and funeral rituals. It is always hard to find an exact source for these tales, but the oldest of them cannot date from earlier than the end of the eighteenth century, and many of them are more recent. Anyway, they can be found in plenty of other books.

What we do know is that in the century we are looking at, the poor deceased, after being given 'all the sacraments of Our Mother the Holy Church', was placed – naked and usually washed – in a piece of material which may originally have been linen, hence the word *linceul* (shroud) which in Picardy meant simply linen cloth or *lincheu*. A kind of wooden box (there were two in each parish, a large one and a small one) was used to place the body in the ground, after which the box was recovered to be used again: the shroud was doubtless left. The gravedigger – or in the first instance a relative – covered it all up with a few shovelfuls of earth, probably after a blessing. Only the rich had individual, closed, coffins, and that was originally an urban custom. Both canon and civil law required at least two witnesses. Few other people seem to have been present, and it is not always certain that even the immediate family bothered to attend. Long processions, elaborate ceremonies, and even the funeral baked meats themselves seem to have been later imitations of urban practices, apart from in certain provinces which were in some way enamoured of death, like the Breton-speaking areas of Brittany.

It also seems that at one time (probably not in the seventeenth century) people were buried almost anywhere – at the roadside, on their own land, under a large tree – but very soon (the exact date is uncertain, but in most places by the mid-century) all burials, except those of protestants, took place either in the church or the parish cemetery or both.

We have inherited a clear image of the churchyard, which may to some extent be an accurate one. It consisted of an enclosed area containing the church, the cemetery, and sometimes an ossuary; and it was at the heart of the community of souls that made up the parish, bringing together the living and the dead. For both alike the most sought-after position for burial was always the one closest to the altar. All the ecclesiastical and lay dignitaries were buried there, in real coffins, underneath real tombstones, and pride of place often went to the seigneur (as in the *enfeus* or recessed tombs of Brittany). At successive distances from the altar came the notables and the rich. As everybody could not be fitted into the limited space available, tombs were opened up from time to time, and new bodies put in. This sometimes created an extremely unpleasant smell which upset the faithful during the offices – but it was usually in towns that this happened.

The great majority of peasants were buried in the cemetery, without a coffin. The corpses were scantily covered, tombstones were very uncommon, and the cemetery itself was often only rudimentarily enclosed, if that. There are a surprising number of records of this. People and carts cross the cemetery, beasts graze in it, as the grass is abundant (and free), children play in it, lovers meet there, itinerant stallholders set up there on feast days, and pigs and dogs scratch and burrow in the earth. At the insistence of both the ecclesiastical and the civil authorities some progress was probably made in changing this state of affairs, but it was not until 1776 that a royal statement required all cemeteries to be moved out of the centre of the villages (and towns), and it took another fifty years for the ruling to be fully implemented.

A seventeenth-century cemetery could not, therefore, have been less like a modern one, or even like a late nineteenth-century one. Our distant rural forebears could not be shocked by anything which they believed, perhaps wrongly, always to have existed; and this close relationship at the heart of the parish and the community between the living and the dead must have stemmed from customs which we can no longer understand, so that we cannot even say whether they signified human warmth or mere indifference.

One corner of the cemetery, it should be added, was often reserved for children who had died without either formal or informal baptism, the still-births, most of whom were probably premature. This unsanctified ground was also used for burying suicides (little was said about these, as suicide was felt to be profoundly shocking and unnatural) and for burying those few vagabonds or unknown strangers who carried no sign of christianity about them. The protestants always had separate cemeteries where, by order of Louis XIV, burials had to take place at night, when the corpses would not be vilified. Much further away from the houses, the plague victims had been buried, together, since at least the fourteenth century, often in a common grave, sometimes after the corpses had been covered with quicklime, which suggests that people were aware of the danger of contagion.

This still leaves the perplexing problem of attitudes of mind, which is largely insoluble in the case of the seventeenth-century countryside, as we cannot really rely on any discourses or edifying books about a 'good death' or figurative representations, because they did not emanate from the peasants, and so may not have been chosen by them, and could only indirectly have been meant for them.

Nonetheless, there are a few guiding principles which can be put forward, some of them with a degree of confidence. It seems certain, for example, that the one great, widespread aspiration (except perhaps for one or two perverse or weak-minded individuals) was to enter Paradise, to be near God, among the angels, the saints, and the blessed, and to avoid the pains of hell with its fires (or its sloughs, the 'infernal marshcs') and the monstrous creatures that tore you to pieces. Thousands of sermons, thousands of images, and hundreds of booklets built up these hopes and fears in the people of France, and the process intensified after the reform of the church, when the fearful aspects received greater stress than the consolations, except during the last moments of life. This was probably why the death of a child could be borne more easily if he had been properly baptised, as there could be no doubt about his heavenly fate, and the beneficial consequences of this for his earthly family. And from the moment the dying adult received the sacraments, his survivors could be sure of the same thing. It may also explain why widows and more especially widowers did not long remain in a state of widowhood. Of course they needed somebody to look after the house and the children, and to maintain the crops; but some men married again within a month, and some women, despite the understandable obligation to respect at least ten months of solitude, often waited a much shorter period, almost certainly because the community (and the priest, who may well have been given some reassuring information) had recognised that they were 'not bearing any fruit'.

Was death, then, a familiar companion, the gateway to heaven, and not something to be afraid of? The peasants usually had other fears to occupy their minds, such as lightning, will o' the wisps, evil creatures, strange noises, demons, ghosts, phantoms, 'Egyptians' (as they called gypsies), soldiers, and wandering beggars. But their greatest fear was of sudden or accidental death, when there would be no time for the priest to be called, and although pious subterfuges might be proposed, such as a sort of *post mortem* blessing during which the corpse was meant to be able to give a fleeting sign of resurrection, miracles such as that were hardly part of everyday life.

We cannot share the deepest and most private thoughts these peasants had about death, when their remains would be buried in the earth they trod all their lives and from which they made their living. Their thoughts must have been manifold and confused, influenced by tradition and local opinion and the priest's sermons – if he could command attention: they may have been commonplace, or they may have been very complex. But, faced with impenetrability, the historian can only remain silent.

Bibliography and Acknowledgements

By its very nature, a book of this sort cannot include a detailed bibliography, as it would be far too extensive. Interested readers may wish to consult those in the recent four-volume *Histoire de la France rurale*, ed. G. Duby and A. Wallon (Paris, 1975–6).

Although most of this book is the product of my own research, writing, direction, and lectures, I have incurred considerable debts in at least three chapters, which I would like to take this opportunity to acknowledge.

Chapter 10, on vine-growers, could not have been written without the work of Georges Durand, *Vin, vignes et vignerons: en Lyonnais et Beaujolais, XVIe–XVIIIe siècle* (Paris, 1979), and Marcel Lachiver's *La Vigne et les vignerons à l'ouest de Paris du XVIIe–XIXe siècle* (1982).

Chapter 16, on the revolts, owes much to the two-volume work of Yves-Marie Bercé. The first is *Histoire des Croquants: étude des soulèvements populaires au 17e siècle dans le sud-ouest de la France* (Geneva, 1974), and the second is in the series 'Archives', under the title *Croquants et Nu-pieds, les soulèvements paysans en France du XVIe au XIXe siècle* (Geneva, 1974).

For the penultimate chapter, on festivals, I am also indebted to Bercé on a number of points (see *Fête et révolte: des mentalités populaires du XVIe au XVIIIe siècle* (Paris, 1976), and at least as much to Nicole Pellegrin's thesis, 'Les Bachelleries, organisations et fêtes de la jeunesse dans le Centre-Ouest du XVe au XVIIIe siècle' (1982).

Finally my friends, and sometimes former students, will have recognised themselves in various parts of the book: Alain Croix (Brittany), Jean Jacquart (Ile-de-France), François Lebrun (Anjou and elsewhere), Nicole Lemaître (Ussel, Quercy, and Rouergue), Jean-Claude Peyronnet (La Courtine), Gérard Sabatier (Emblavès), Roland Warion (Ubaye), Anne Zink (Azereix and Gascony), as well as others, and those whom I can only thank posthumously, Louis Merle (Gâtine in Poitou), Pierre de Saint-Jacob (northern Burgundy), and, for all aspects of the seventeenth century, my teacher, Jean Meuvret.

Supplementary bibliography

Compiled by P. M. Jones, University of Birmingham

Bercé, Y.-M., *Histoire des Croquants: étude des soulèvements populaires au 17e siècle dans le sud-ouest de la France* (2 vols., Geneva, 1974)
Fête et révolte: des mentalités populaires du XVIe au XVIIIe siècle (Paris, 1976)
Bloch, M., *French Rural History: An Essay on Its Basic Characteristics* (London, 1966)
Braudel, F., and Labrousse, E., eds., *Histoire économique et sociale de la France* (vols. 1 and 2, Paris, 1970–7)
Briggs, R., *Early Modern France* (Oxford, 1977)
Cabourdin, G., *Terres et hommes en Lorraine, 1550–1635* (2 vols., Nancy, 1977)
Croix, A., *La Bretagne aux XVIe et XVIIe siècles: la vie, la mort, la foi* (2 vols., Paris, 1981)
Davis, N. Z., *Society and Culture in Early Modern France* (London, 1975)
The Return of Martin Guerre (London, 1983)
Duby, G., and Wallon, A., eds., *Histoire de la France rurale* (vol. 2, Paris, 1975)
Dupâquier, J., *La Population française aux XVIIe et XVIIIe siècles* (Paris, 1979)
La Population rurale du bassin parisien à l'époque de Louis XIV (Paris, 1979)
Durand, G., *Vin, vignes et vignerons: en Lyonnais et Beaujolais, XVIe–XVIIIe siècle* (Paris, 1979)
Flandrin, J.-L., *Families in Former Times: Kinship, Household and Sexuality* (Cambridge, 1979)
Goubert, P., *Cent mille provinciaux au XVIIe siècle: Beauvais et le Beauvaisis de 1600 à 1730* (Paris, 1968)
Louis XIV and Twenty Million Frenchmen (London, 1970)
The Ancien Régime: French Society, 1600–1750 (London, 1973)

Gutton, J.-P., *La Société et les pauvres: l'example de la généralité de Lyon, 1534–1789* (Paris, 1970)

La Sociabilité villageoise dans l'ancienne France: solidarités et voisinages du XVIe au XVIIIe siècle (Paris, 1979)

Jacquart, J., *La Crise rurale en Ile-de-France, 1550–1670* (Paris, 1974)

Lebrun, F., *Les Hommes et la mort en Anjou aux XVIIe et XVIIIe siècles* (Paris, 1971)

Le Roy Ladurie, E., *The Peasants of Languedoc* (London, 1974)

Mandrou, R., *Introduction to Modern France, 1500–1640* (London, 1975)

Merle, L., *La Métairie et l'évolution agraire de la Gâtine poitevine de la fin du moyen âge à la révolution* (Paris, 1958)

Meuvret, J., *Etudes d'histoire économique* (Paris, 1971)

Mousnier, R., *Peasant Uprisings in 17th Century France, Russia and China* (London, 1971)

Pillorget, R., *Les Mouvements insurrectionnels de Provence entre 1596 et 1715* (Paris, 1975)

Porshnev, B. F., *Les Soulèvements populaires en France de 1623 à 1648* (Paris, 1963)

Segalen, M., *Love and Power in the Peasant Family: Rural France in the Nineteenth Century* (Oxford, 1983)

Zink, A., *Azereix: la vie d'une communauté rurale à la fin du XVIIIe siècle* (Paris, 1969)

Index